D1603586

WHY WOMEN AND POWER DON'T MIX

WHY
WOMEN
AND
POWER
DON'T MIX

The Perils of Feminism

J. P. McDermott

PATRIARCHIC PUBLISHING COMPANY

First Edition
ISBN 0–9654987–0–0
Library of Congress catalog number 96–92884
Printed in the United States of America
© 1996, Patriarchic Publishing Company
(888) 757–2665

Contents

Foreword

The most powerful weapon we have—indeed the most powerful weapon that any people can have—is truth. If we ever find ourselves in a position where we cannot tell the truth, or where we feel that the telling will injure us, we will have sacrificed that most powerful weapon.

— Dwight Eisenhower

Prior to this generation, in every society ever known, the power of women has been strictly limited, which is why societies have prospered. If or when a society failed to do this adequately, it simply ceased to exist. This is only one reason, though, why it is possible to make a moral case for limiting the power women possess. It will be shown that women as a group are no longer fulfilling their natural and essential roles adequately—a predictable consequence of the power and influence women have obtained and utilized via feminism. The negative impact this has had on male behavior is rarely discussed. Generally the discussion ends with the negative behavior. By uncovering the true causes of the degenerative social trends in America, this book will demonstrate that feminism is, in fact, our greatest peril.

It is a tribute to the powerful manipulations of feminists that although nothing is advocated in this book that wasn't a universal norm only thirty years ago, even the concept of this type of book is now looked upon by most Americans with disdain or disbelief. Efforts have already been made to censor it. These realities do not alleviate the need to tell the truth. However distasteful it may be to some, truth is exactly what is needed in response to feminist efforts to censor criticism. Censorship is one reason society is in the degenerative state it is today. The wisdom of the entire combined population has shrunk as result of a lack of spoken truth. Wisdom has been replaced with feminist illogic.

Contrary to the recent opinions of some, feminism shows no real indications of declining. We may see and hear a great many women dissociating themselves from the words "feminism" and "feminist," but few are truly divorcing themselves from the philosophy, or from the "tolerant" points of view that enable and ensure its continued success.

There are, of course, all different types of feminists. Not all are women, not all are strident. Not all are atheists. Some are even priests. Because of this, no attempt is made here to group all feminists together as though they are the same. Sometimes the discussion pertains or refers to strident feminist activists, sometimes to more passivist feminist supporters, and sometimes to those who lend support only through their tolerance of feminism.

Because this book constitutes a critique of modern feminists and their movement, no attempt is made to present an equal amount of time to the already over-expressed feminist points of view.

As history has shown (notes historian Arnold J. Toynbee), civilizations more often die by committing suicide than by being murdered. Feminism is a form of societal suicide because it is in direct conflict with human nature and with most fundamental human values. As the logical Judge Lawrence Yetka said when making a ruling, "before abandoning fundamental values, we must pause and take stock of our present social order." Hopefully, this book will encourage its readers to pause, take stock, and take action, because that is what is needed.

J. P. McDermott
October, 1996

Acknowledgments

To those who had the most immediately direct impact on the manuscript, the greatest thanks go to Max Gordon, my nomination for the world's greatest editor. Dealing with difficulties that cannot be described, he dealt patiently with a fired-up author and one of the most jumbled up—albeit complex—manuscripts an editor has ever been handed. In doing this, Max showed a combination of positive talents and traits I cannot adequately describe. What I can say is that they included bountiful amounts of doggedness and wisdom.

To my beloved mother and father, I thank them for showing me what a loving marriage can be, and for giving me the most wonderful of childhoods.

To my sweet and loving wife, Kim, thank you for your love and strong support, especially the times you've heard me criticized for holding the views that I do.

To the customers, associates and employees of my small business. Without them, I could not have afforded to see the manuscript to its completion. I truly appreciate the loyalty.

And finally, I thank the rest of my family and friends who have supported me throughout.

PART ONE

CHAPTER ONE

The Big Lie

The first part of this book is devoted primarily to describing feminism. This is important because without a description of it, it would be impossible to understand or believe it to be perilous.

It is essential to recognize the influential power of feminism, and that feminism is a contrived movement. Doing so encourages us to begin using a new type of vocabulary that helps us better describe and understand feminism, as well as feminists themselves. This better understanding heightens our awareness of both its methods and its perils.

Identifying feminism as "contrived" means that the common, popularly held understanding of feminism is inaccurate, despite what many feminists themselves believe and wish us to believe. It is not simply an instinctive movement, spontaneously occurring among a group of victims. On the contrary, the recent course of feminist history has been the result of a tremendous amount of conscious effort and planning.

Even though it is a loosely organized movement with no official leadership, multifaceted, constantly mutating, and generally lacking complete consensus among its followers, there are goals (and methodologies) common to many groups and individuals. This set of goals is posed here as the feminist agenda. The fact that the feminist agenda is so methodically becoming reality makes it crucial that we become more aware of the type of future feminists have planned for us.

Just as assuredly as feminists have an agenda, they also have a variety of very real, conscious, and successful methods for getting what they want, a modus operandi. An example of one of these methods is evident in the words of Beverly Byron, a Maryland Democrat of the

House Armed Services Committee. While discussing her argument for the lifting of the exemption of female pilots from combat, she stated that the lifting is "what America perceives as the next step; totally consistent with the reasonable, acceptable, incremental process that I have found so successful over the years." Implicit in Byron's words is her intention to champion the assignment of female troops to every combat role. The fact that Byron has found this process "successful over the years" speaks to the consciousness of her efforts on behalf of feminism and her willingness to implement her long-range plans in a very careful-not-to-offend manner, always mindful of public relations. What is surprising here is not the insidiousness of the plan, but the fact that she has made such an open admission of its existence and of her long-term commitment to it. While a confession of this type is extremely rare, such plans are widespread in the feminist community, and serve to warn us of our need to increase our respect for, and awareness of the clever and manipulative strategies of influential, powerful feminists.

In the early 1960s, Chief Justice Warren Burger informed Congress what would be required of civil rights legislation in order that it pass into law. Ironically, while describing what discriminatory barriers the legislation must prohibit, he used a list of words—"artificial," "arbitrary," "unnecessary," "invidious," and "impermissible"—that very accurately describe what feminist-initiated laws and programs have in fact brought about.

Unfortunately, feminism's modus operandi is like feminism itself in that, though it is identifiable, it is not easy to grasp. The feminist modus operandi consists of four principal tactics, as well as many lesser ones. And though each tactic fulfills individual purposes for feminists, they are to varying degrees reliant upon one another, their effects interrelated. All four have been essential in spreading feminism's influence.

The first tactic is the misrepresentation of reality, which began with what we will refer to as The Big Lie. The Big Lie is the one with which past and present feminists have endeavored to convince us all that the life of every woman prior to the modern feminist movement was hellish. This ongoing deception is a cornerstone of the movement's foundation and has been a model for other feminist misrepresentations.

Of all the pro-feminist books that have portrayed the post-WWII era negatively, there is one book that stands out from the rest. A key reason 1963 is frequently acknowledged as the beginning of the modern feminist movement is because that is the year in which Betty Friedan published her incredibly influential book, *The Feminine Mystique*. It is frequently, and with substantial justification, called the impetus for the modern feminist movement. In it, Friedan literally claims to speak for all American women, speculating not about the happiness and contentment of any group of women, or even of women as a whole, but about the happiness and contentment of "each" American woman.[1]

In stark contrast to the avalanche of books that would follow, this book is at least realistic in that it doesn't attempt to paint all men as being immoral. The gist of this book is that all American women were bored, unrespected, unchallenged, and unfulfilled, living meaningless lives of solitary desperation.

Since Friedan's publication, the flood of books, articles, and teachings falsely depicting the post-WWII era as a nightmare for women has been overwhelming. Thousands of examples are available in any library, under the headings "women's studies" and "women's issues." Dozens of magazines have sprung up to target primarily a female readership with just such material. Daily newspapers have been full of negative images of women's lives. Incredibly, though, some of the most radical of feminist propaganda is now taught in colleges and universities across the country, under the guise of women's studies programs.

At the elementary school level, after 30 years of feminist influence, pictures of women even appearing to be content in any type of traditional role have been removed from textbooks in accordance with feminist wishes. In today's school books, you are unlikely to find a picture of a woman in a nurse's uniform—let alone a picture of a contented woman in an apron, smiling, holding a child, *or* kissing her husband good-bye as he leaves for work. Feminists, and their supporting institutions (the mass media and the educational systems), refuse to acknowledge such a woman ever existed. In line with today's

---

[1] The reader may well have noted that her pattern of speaking on behalf of all women is a pattern that has since been continued by other feminists, regardless of topic.

education, if you were to ask 18-year-old high-school girls about the lives of women in the post-WWII era, most would likely not have a single positive thing to say about them.

What the feminists have done in portraying this era is eerily Orwellian: they have repainted the past. Thirty years have passed and it is now unheard of for a pre-1960s–1970s woman to be described as either happy or content, by feminists, unless that woman happened to be an early feminist. In George Orwell's book, *1984*, he wrote about Big Brother's similar distortions in regard to the past, and what became of them:

> Everything faded into mist. The past was erased, the erasure was forgotten, the lie became the truth. . . . Within twenty years at the most . . . the huge and simple question, 'was life better before the revolution than it is now?' would have ceased once and for all to be answerable. But in effect it was unanswerable even now . . . when memory failed and written records were falsified—when that happened, the claim of the Party to have improved the conditions of human life had got to be accepted, because there did not exist, and never again could exist, any standard against which it could be tested.

Friedan was one of the first to bluntly claim that a woman "could not" attain happiness and contentment by filling traditional roles.[2] Her primary hypothesis was that all women of this era were destitute because, whether filling primary roles and responsibilities as wives, mothers, and homemakers, or working in traditionally feminine jobs outside the home, they did not have the opportunity to face and overcome challenges of enough difficulty and importance to develop the respect of others, self-respect, or healthy self-esteem. Friedan theorized that because women weren't given the opportunity to compete and achieve on the same playing fields as men, status, sense of accomplishment, and self-esteem were unattainable for them—all because they worked only among their own sex, or under the supervision of men.

In the opinions of Friedan and other strident feminists soon to follow her, there simply were no happy wives, grandmothers, moth-

---

[2] Friedan has since recanted this opinion. In the June 17, 1991 issue of *U.S. News and World Report*, she is quoted as saying, "It's time now to change the rhetoric and admit that many women want nothing more than to stay home with their children."

ers, or daughters at all. Gradually, their relentless and diverse efforts to brainwash the public with this untruthful viewpoint succeeded in large part. Today, this feminist premise has been adopted by large numbers of women, both those who are too young to have been alive at that time and those who are old enough but whose lives were, for whatever reasons, less than perfect.

In regard to her claims about the feelings of "each" American housewife, it is difficult to understand how Friedan came to conclusions of such unanimity. It certainly cannot be from having interviewed the same housewives, farmers' wives, daughters, mothers, grandmothers, and great-grandmothers of that era that this author has known. The majority of mature women interviewed for this book— those who lived through that era, and particularly those who remained married—say they "wouldn't" trade places with today's women. They give a variety of reasons for feeling this way, but the most frequent are that they feel their relationships with their husbands—while not necessarily perfect—were loving and secure, and that they would not want to raise their children the way so many of today's women do, "or fail to do." Several of these women mentioned that they felt their happiness was more closely related to the happiness and success of their husband, children, and family, than with today's women.

In the years just prior to 1963, the great majority of women hoped and expected to marry young, have children, and become homemakers. The median age for first time marriages in 1960 was 20.3 for women and 22.8 for men.

The responsibilities of the homemaker normally included providing the bulk of care for the children, complete maintenance of the interior of the household, cooking meals, cleaning and maintaining the family's clothing, the budgeting of household finances, and providing love and understanding, not only to children, but to husband as well. These are responsibilities requiring understanding, wisdom, resourcefulness, and the selflessness and commitment that have characterized mothers through the ages. Mothers often had some type of involvement in children's outside activities (Cub Scouts, Girl Scouts, Indian Guides, P.T.A.), or took part in civic or church programs.[3]

---

[3] Involvement of this kind is invaluable in providing structured activities outside the school environment, and in setting the example of good citizenship through participa-

Mothers with school children frequently took part-time jobs, rarely full-time careers.

Due to feminist pressures stigmatizing women in the home, little has been written about the positive aspects of homemaking. Helen Lopata's book, *Occupation Housewife*, is one of comparatively few books written on the subject that doesn't undermine the importance or challenges of the role; she instead describes a wide range of opportunities for a housewife to challenge herself, obtain personal fulfillment and, in turn, derive self-esteem from homemaking. She doesn't regard the role as being in any way less important, less fulfilling, less exciting, or less challenging than the roles men fulfill as primary breadwinners, regardless of their occupations. Lopata points out that most of the jobs men held were far from glamorous, that more men were assemblers, tree climbers, garbage collectors, accountants, bricklayers, painters, and ground combat soldiers, than were rocket scientists or Nobel prize winners.

The 1950s and 1960s were prosperous times. In fact, they are considered the two most prosperous decades, back-to-back, in U.S. history. The gross national product almost doubled in the decade of the 1960s alone. Though the American family had, by far, the highest standard of living in the world, and one that was rapidly improving, the leaders of the feminist movement were to deem this meaningless. Despite the high standard of living, despite husbands who most often religiously performed their roles as providers, despite being the managers of home life, despite—as mothers—being given possibly the best overall environment in the world in which to raise their children, American women were told that the role could not, and would not, bring fulfillment.

Generally, women in the work force hadn't yet been married, were married but childless, or were middle-aged women who had completed the task of raising their children. During this era, it was commonly assumed by businesses that young women would get married, have children, and leave the work force. This was most often the case, though some women did forego marriage and family for a career.

Women in the work force of the 1950s and '60s found positions

tion in community programs. The constructive use of time and the caring necessary to promote healthy communities are lessons not nearly enough of today's children learn.

as nurses, teachers, secretaries, telephone operators, light assembly workers, in food service, etc. At that time these jobs were deemed, by both men and women alike, to be women's work. That women pursued certain occupations voluntarily, or were channeled toward them by social expectations, is hardly surprising. Nursing and teaching, for example, are easily seen to be suited to people with strong nurturing personalities. While men may be capable of performing the tasks required by either of these professions, there is little argument that women, as a group, have always been acknowledged as being the more nurturing of the two sexes.

The best-paying, most difficult, most dangerous, and "highest status" occupations—within the realm of competitive work spheres—were generally reserved for men. Regarding the importance and status of positions reserved for men, such divisions have existed in all societies, for a variety of reasons that will be discussed throughout this book. One reason for pay differences in 1963, though, was that the law that a man must provide support for his wife and family was taken very seriously. It was generally accepted that men needed more money because they were usually the sole support for their families, and were always expected to be the "primary" support, by people at all levels of society. In that era, it was standard practice for many employers to give male employees pay raises when they married or became fathers, to help support their wives and families. This was in addition to the truly significant tax advantages that were provided to male heads of family. Abandonment and failure to provide (or to attempt to provide) adequate familial support, were rare and penalties harsh. Imprisonment was a possibility for men who abandoned their wives without paying support and, in cases of divorce, the woman virtually always got title to the house and custody of the children. Complaints by single men against married men because of pay or tax discrimination, however, were almost nonexistent.

Another factor of sex discrimination in the workplace was that, during that era, there were fewer of the technological advancements being utilized today that effectively serve to alleviate the need for physical strength. Men were more capable at many of the jobs they chose to fill because of the strength factor alone. Minds made for problem solving and engineering enabled men to design and construct such projects as the Golden Gate Bridge, without the need for

assistance. In tune with biology and with every other society that has
ever existed, the socialization of boys took into account their naturally
greater drive to compete and achieve. While on the surface such a
system might seem unfairly discriminatory, it was a successful system,
in tune with nature—meaning that it both recognized and accounted
for sexual differences. This was as opposed to the present system (currently under construction by feminists), which attempts to deny that
sex differences exist.

It certainly cannot be argued that all men of that era had glamorous or prestigious positions.[4] Millions of American men died fighting twentieth-century wars to protect our country, freedom, their
mates, their offspring, "mom and apple pie," their honor, and themselves—probably in that order. That the men of this country took the
protection of women seriously in the past is proven by the deaths of
those individuals and by the fact that, at one time, rape was a crime
punishable by castration.

Any stories telling of good, masculine men, or of people content
within traditional families—which generally included masculine men
—are now depicted as being nothing more than fairy tales. Television sitcoms picturing families to any degree typical of that day are
now ridiculed by feminists. They not only laugh at the concepts but,
for the benefit of our unknowing children, feminists now deny that
there ever was even one family remotely resembling those portrayed,
whether it be the Cleavers of *Leave It to Beaver*, the Cramdens of *The
Honeymooners*, or the Bunkers of *All In the Family*. True, such shows
were idealistic exaggerations of family life and personal behavior, but
they were successful shows. Without the aid of the titillation most
of today's sitcoms seem to require, they entertained and made people
laugh—precisely because audiences could relate to nuclear families,
with a man at the head and a wife who could somehow get her way
almost any time she felt it important.

While preparing the manuscript, this author had a conversation
with a woman in her sixties, on the bus from Duluth, Minnesota,
to Minneapolis. The discussion involved various aspects of this very

---

[4] Many assemblers and police officers routinely worked two jobs, while many farmers
and coal miners worked 12–16 hour days at hard labor and in dangerous environments,
to provide for families. (The fact that men had a significantly shorter life expectancy
than women is also worth noting.)

subject. She had been talking about how men of the post-war era were overly and unfairly dominant. She happened to be divorced, her children living at various corners of the country far from her. She talked incessantly about what scoundrels men were, back then, and how glad she was that both of her unmarried, 30-year-old daughters had college educations. Soon the subject turned to birth control, abortion, and the evils of Catholicism. She said that, in those days, she had a girlfriend who was married to a man named Harry. The couple had a few children and the woman decided she didn't want to have any more. In line with church policy, though, she didn't want to use birth control. So, she simply told her husband that there was going to be no more sex, and that was that. The lady on the bus told that story, chuckling and saying, "Poor Harry." It is not within the scope of our purposes to offer an opinion on church policy here, but Harry couldn't have been too "overly dominant" to have put up with that. Anyone who lived through that period will recognize that situations such as Harry's were not infrequent.

The fact of the matter is that all women of the post-WWII era, whether they were homemakers or part of the work force, did not endure a living hell, and all men were not overly dominant, abusive, or scoundrels. Feminists would seemingly have us believe that half of all men ran off with their secretaries, which is simply not true, and is certainly belied by the low divorce rates of the period.

Individual women derived different levels of happiness and contentment from their lives as wives, mothers, homemakers and occupational workers, as did men with their occupations and their own domestic roles. Was it pure misery for women? Far from it. There were unarguably many happy, contented women in the post-WWII era, so why the attempt to make us believe there weren't? Why the Big Lie? Motivations, justifications, and rationalizations.

The Big Lie originally functioned as an impetus and motivator for the earliest group of feminists. Suddenly, any woman with any regrets about the way her life had gone was offered a very tempting excuse. She could now shirk any responsibility for her own unhappiness, simply by adopting the guise of the oppressed "victim" of "a man's world." Younger women were offered excuses, as well, for all sorts of future failures.

From that early time in the movement, feminists of all ages have come to rely upon this distortion of history to rationalize any number of their own and their followers' amoral, destructive, and aberrant behaviors. At the same time, this distortion of history has helped them justify their promotion of a growing number of illogical and historically unprecedented theories on how we should socialize ourselves.

The Big Lie has provided the main source of rationalization for what has amounted to an attempt by feminists to convince the entire population that virtually every pre-movement social concept, every tradition, and every social institution regardless of its universal nature —including marriage and the nuclear family—was unfair, dysfunctional, or unnecessary, and should either be altered radically or discarded completely.

It has served as a rationalization in yet another way, by justifying the endless run of general repercussions brought about by feminist-produced turmoil. In the minds of feminists, "Life was hell before we came along, and if it isn't perfect yet, it's because of the lingering effects of patriarchy. Just give us a little more time to make things perfect."

The Big Lie and all of the lies in support of the Big Lie have helped feminists and their recruits to form, on both conscious and subconscious levels, the mindset that not only is any type of change acceptable (because life was, or is, hell for women), but that lying to promote any part of the feminist agenda is also acceptable because, under these conditions, the end justifies the means. This belief is now common, regardless of the fact that feminists have no concept of what the end will be, even should all of their present wishes come true.

1963. Of course things needed to change. Things can always change for the better. Women's lives had the potential to improve, as did those of men. The fact of the matter is that this was happening, gradually, without the help of feminism. Only 40 short years before, women had been *granted* the right to vote. The labor of women's domestic chores was being made easier by new technologies developed specifically for them, brought home by husbands trying to make life easier for their wives. Every year more women were going to college and women's roles in the work force were expanding. American women didn't have it bad, by the standards in any other country, and things were changing for the better until Betty Friedan and feminism came on the scene and so many women accepted the illogic of feminist arguments. Sadly, men not only allowed this to happen; many men encouraged it. And now, individually and socially, we must suffer. The fact that some things needed to change doesn't mean we needed to throw out all past means of socializing ourselves, means that made the U.S. a role model and a dream destination for people around the world.

Things weren't perfect in the years leading up to 1963; not for any-one, men or women; nor will they ever be perfect. There will never be a utopia. A world with no jealousy (sexual or otherwise), greed, anger, or resentment would be a dull world, impossible even if de-sired. A world without authority or responsibility would be anarchic. We wouldn't wish for the first to exist, in perpetuity; and the second couldn't exist, in perpetuity. If we were ever able to solve all of our problems, we would have become dehumanized robots in doing so. In any event, utopia and being human are incompatible.[5] If we choose to make an effort to become as close to utopian as possible, the first thing we must do is recognize our humanity or human-ness which, ipso facto, means we must recognize the differences in the sexes.

How can happiness be measured? Can today's family be measured with yesterday's? Will today's women feel as contented with their lives when they become senior citizens as women who lived the prime years of their lives in the 1940s, '50s, and '60s? Do today's senior women feel jealous of today's younger women? Or do they feel sorry for them? Will the majority of today's children, increasingly step-parented or fatherless because of divorce and illegitimacy, receive the love, at-tention, care, and education that yesterday's children received? Will today's children, increasingly value-starved because they are latch-key kids with only a television as a moral guide for hours each day, receive the love, attention, care, and education that yesterday's children re-ceived? Will today's children, increasingly abandoned to daycare (with supervisors who are often too busy to instill any moral judgment and, so, find themselves being raised by their peer groups instead of by adults), receive the love, attention, care, and education that yesterday's children received? Or has that no bearing? And even if the major-

---

[5] As is the case with each and every ideal humankind conceptualizes, utopia is un-obtainable because each individual has his or her own unique concept of it. What is "perfect" for one is imperfect for *all* others.

ity do receive what they need, will they have to reach adulthood in
a society where an increasingly large minority—those whose needs
were not met—have become violent, amoral people with no respect
for anyone but themselves?

What is clear is that the era prior to the initiation of the feminist
movement was, in many ways, our country's most prosperous. Men
were generally content. Children generally had good environments in
which to grow up, and were a priority for most parents. The change
is obvious in the care children are given now, as opposed to then.
It shows in the increased numbers of prisons, rehabilitation centers,
abortion clinics, and psychiatric offices. It shows in our growing illegitimacy rates, violence and suicide statistics. It shows in the divorce
records, the welfare rolls, and the general decline of morals. It shows
in the classrooms, where, in the 1950s, teachers worried about gum in
the classroom, instead of guns in the classroom. It shows in the level
of our self-esteem, both male and female. It shows in the divisiveness
that permeates all areas of society.

In effect, America was strong; as opposed to today, it was admired
by the rest of the world, its citizens envied; it was an ascendant nation.
Even if Friedan's claims are true, and the majority of women were
truly discontent and unhappy, history is showing that too many of
them have taken the wrong, and overly selfish, paths toward correcting the situation. This is due to feminism's influence.

Betty Friedan was a dreamer. Unfortunately, her dreams fail to take
into account factors such as history and human nature, as if the sexes
have no differences, as if there is no need for sex-based roles, and
as if women must do the same things in life as men to obtain self-
esteem. The truth is that there *are* differences between the sexes,
there is a need for sex-based roles, and women do *not* need to do
the same things in life that men do in order to obtain self-esteem.
Farm wives certainly fill different roles on farms than their husbands,
and it would be difficult to argue that farm wives have, or ever had,
problems maintaining self-esteem and a sense of self-worth.

The media, which was controlled prior to the 1960s by traditional
males, may have been guilty of portraying the "ideal," or "most attractive," women as narrowly feminine—the Donna Reed stereotype
—but the media is not responsible for originating sex-differentiated
roles or feminine behavior. Both of these were present in all soci-

eties—as they still are in primitive cultures today—long before there was any such thing as a mass media. In short, our media stereotypes, though exaggerated, have been in tune with our nature all along. In just this way, the post-WWII era was in tune with most of the major, universal social principles.

The fact of the matter is that the originators and leaders of the feminist movement have ridiculed, degraded, and devalued the domestic roles of women in "urban" settings more than men have. A person's self-esteem is determined, in large part, by their perception of how others perceive them (especially their peers). It is no wonder, then, that the self-esteem of many homemakers dropped between 1963 and the present, a period during which they were repeatedly told by the most vocal of their peers—who happened to be feminists—that their job was degrading, undemanding, stunting, and meaningless. Hillary Clinton's recent sarcastic reference to "cookie bakers" is only one example of a feminist deriding women who are fulfilled and happy in their roles as wives, homemakers, and mothers. Sadly, it is women like Mrs. Clinton who command the voice of the media in this country. But even beyond belittling homemakers, feminists can frequently be seen to hold the same type of contempt for women working in traditional female occupations.

After 1963, women were told by feminist leaders that mother, homemaker, and wife are not roles producing challenges with their own rewards, that these roles cannot lead to healthy self-esteem, and that bearing and raising children, in conjunction with bringing happiness to a spouse, cannot be considered primary reasons to exist. If bearing children, and caring for them properly, and watching them grow cannot be considered reasons to exist, what can?

Women did not begin the fight to work in all fields out of economic necessity, or for freedom from oppressive husbands. The primary reason women grew to feel the need to work as if they were men was a problem with self-esteem that can be demonstrably linked to the inception of the modern feminist movement, and which has been greatly compounded by feminism's growth in influence.

CHAPTER TWO

The Amity-Enmity Principle

The Big Lie. It began by being synonymous with discontent, but it grew to become synonymous with mistrust and enmity.

It is obvious that hate and mistrust between the sexes have proliferated in conjunction with the growth in influence of the feminist movement. Given the nature of feminism's goals, and its methods for achieving them, this was both predictable and inevitable. Beyond the promotion of discontent among women, the movement and its spokespeople have intentionally promoted hate and distrust towards men as the second integral tactic of their modus operandi. The welcomed results have been their followers' anger, resentment, and vengefulness toward men, and an ever-stronger desire for change.

Ardent feminists, aided by the media and by academia, have labored tirelessly to convince the American public that all unemasculated men are abusers of one sort or another. If men are not portrayed as abusive to their wives, they are child abusers or pedophiles. If not those, they are rapists or deadbeats or adulterers or guilty of harassment in the workplace. At the very best, unemasculated men are depicted as insensitive, beer-guzzling louts.

The reasons for this are manifold: First, characterizations such as these unite women, motivating them to believe in and fight for the feminist movement, and for change in general. Second, they cultivate guilt feelings among men in regard to women, leading first to tolerance of the movement, and then to affirmation. Third, by combining the first two, they have given birth to the body of societal taboos known as "political correctness." This provides feminists with immunity from dissent and opposition by silencing those who would otherwise be critical of feminism.

The women who originally understood the potential benefits of promoting hate and distrust of men, and who practiced and developed this tactic, became the early leaders of the feminist movement. They were, and still are, extremely open in their contempt for men. They are also very vocal and unquestioning in their support for the movement's ever-mutating agenda, while having either no understanding of, or an absolute disregard for, the inevitably harmful future consequences of the events brought about by their actions.

Observers accessing the American mass media of the present day, and seriously contemplating the content of what they see, will realize that it is almost impossible to find a positive word about American men, collectively or individually. Negative messages about them, however, are everywhere. The exact opposite is true of media coverage of American women. And even in those few instances where a woman receives negative coverage, it is almost inevitable that some man, or men, will be found guilty of having somehow been the cause.

Feminists have targeted their indoctrination so that it would seem acceptable to, or enticing enough to influence, the widest range of different types of women. For the benefit of the most narrow-minded type of feminist, one leading feminist author went so far as to say that all sex is rape and that, therefore, all men are rapists.[1] For the benefit of the less ardent feminist, or the non-feminist, arguments are put forth more subtly, in ways that sound rational. But whether the arguments seem rational or irrational, they have a cumulative, propagandizing, even brainwashing effect on the mind of anyone exposed to them so frequently.

Beyond uniting women, and motivating them to fight for the feminist philosophy, feminists use the mistrust and hatred of men that they themselves have created as a means of promoting their agenda for change. When feminists use misleading or false statistics, or withhold certain types of information, in their efforts to convince women that they are surrounded by misogynists and that all men are villainous (implicating all men equally, and implying that men are united

---

[1] Not surprisingly, more than one campus rape crisis center has adopted that attitude and has gone so far as to claim that up to 75 percent of women will be raped at some point in their life. Those feminists who classify all heterosexual coitus as rape are insensitive to the niceties of distinguishing between consensual intercourse and forcible rape. In their eyes, no woman in her right mind would ever involve herself physically with a man.

in some kind of conspiracy against women), the goal is a destructive one.[2] To accomplish that goal it is not enough to simply foster discontent among women, they must build fear, mistrust, and hatred toward all men.

Most of us going to college, or reading newspapers and magazines, or watching television, are familiar with the word "misogynist." (It was even used in the movie *Mrs. Doubtfire*). It is in constant use by feminists as a means of building the hate and mistrust referred to above. But how many people are familiar with its counterpart, the word that refers to one who hates men? The fact that this word, "misandrist," is not in common usage cannot be due to the fact that there aren't a significant number of women who hate men—not after 30 years of feminist dogma being disseminated as the right thing to think. The reason is simply that it does not serve the purposes of feminists to openly admit that many of them are motivated to do the things they do because they hate men. Better to be perceived, by all concerned, as the victims rather than as the aggressors.[3]

This method is well-documented throughout history and is still in common use today; it is recognized to be a very effective motivator. It is referred to as the "Amity-Enmity Principle." The United States government used the Amity-Enmity Principle in World War II against both the Germans and the Japanese by printing posters depicting people of these nationalities committing sabotage, or killing American women and children. Saddam Hussein used it against the United States during the Persian Gulf war in his diatribes to his soldiers and his country's citizens.

Feminists utilize this principle not only to breed discontent towards men, but to attack and portray as valueless or detrimental to women virtually anything possessing any type of tradition in which men have

---

[2] For instance, feminists do not try to pinpoint what types of men rape, or what types of men abuse wives or children in an effort to prevent rape or stop abuse by those men. Rather, they seek to agitate and motivate women, exaggerating problem areas in an effort to mislead women and promote the dissolution of the family as an institution. Their agenda does not call for improving families, but instead for disbanding them.

[3] Note that no one has been telling men to hate or mistrust women. If a growing number of men *are* feeling these emotions, it is not because there has been a men's movement encouraging them. Perhaps it is time to look for the deeper sources of male anger.

had an involvement.[4] Feminists know that not only do anger and discontent motivate, but that these emotions are especially motivational
to people inundated with alternatives to the real, or imagined, causes
of their discontent. Quite simply, and perhaps above all, feminists
know that *contentment* does not motivate. This is why they literally
breed discontent at every opportunity.

An article about ethnic wars was published by the *San Jose Mercury
News* on January 3, 1993. It was written to help us better understand
the troubles in Serbia and Bosnia. Much of the material about the
psychology in wars of these types applies to the behavior of a great
many feminists, and to feminism itself. The article, written by H.D.S.
Greenway of the *Boston Globe*, was titled "Making a demon of the enemy." The following is excerpted:

> A Serbian militia member in Bosnia, hitchhiking to Sarajevo, tells a
> reporter in all earnestness that the Muslims are feeding Serbian chil-
> dren to the animals in the zoo. The story is nonsense. There aren't any
> animals left alive in the Sarajevo zoo. But the man is convinced and can
> recall all the wrongs that Muslims may or may not have perpetrated
> during their 500 years in Bosnia-Herzegovina.
>
> Many of these ethnic conflicts have characteristics in common. Both
> sides in an ethnic conflict will demonize and dehumanize the other
> side, just as warring nations do. Dehumanization is necessary not only
> to strengthen the sense of self, but also to make it possible to kill the
> adversary without guilt.

These two paragraphs bring to mind feminist referrals to sacrificial
rituals involving virgins (in cultures that ceased to exist 500 years ago),
and feminist claims that up to 75 percent of women in this country
have been raped. These are attempts to demonize and dehumanize
men, as well as to instill in women the feeling of victimization. The
article continues:

> The degree to which dehumanization is achieved determines the
> amount of savagery each side is psychologically able to impose on
> the other—the zoo story being a case in point.

---

[4] It is obvious that feminists want change of every sort, and they know that discontent (whether based on reality or on implanted beliefs) is an additional way in which
to effectively motivate women to support their causes for change or, at the least, to
accept them.

Another characteristic is what (Harvard psychiatrist) [John] Mack calls the egoism of victimization. "Among traumatized national groups," writes Mack, there is a tendency "analogous to the narcissism or self-centeredness of individuals, who see themselves as having been so hurt or deprived in the past that they can attend only to their own needs, feeling little or no empathy for the hurt they inflict upon others."

This brings to mind feminists' selfish lack of regard for the needs of children and their failure to either comprehend—or to care about —the needs of men, emotional and otherwise. And:

As the late Jeanne Knutson, founder of the International Society of Political Psychology, wrote: "One never erases the identity of a victim," even if the foe loses power and the credible threat is removed.

Ethicist Sissela Bok calls this the "pathology of partisanship." In times of intense conflict and community stress, "partisanship goes beyond the emphasis on loyalty and cohesion . . . and leads people to become obsessive and heedless of their group's long-range self-interest, even survival." Communities, like living organisms, can succumb to stress, internal weakness or contagion.

She quotes Thucydides writing about the wars in the fifth century B.C. between Athens and Sparta. "Each side viewed the other with distrust. . . . No guarantee could be given that could be trusted, no oath sworn that people would fear to break; everyone had come to the conclusion that it was hopeless to expect a permanent settlement and so, instead of being able to feel confident in others, they devoted their energies to providing against being injured themselves."

The first paragraph sounds like a discussion of the slender chances of lifelong relationships, the divorce rate, and reasons for distrust. This inability to divest oneself of the identity of victim ensures that long into our nation's future, many women will regard men as "the enemy."[5] This, in turn, leads to emotions, viewpoints, arguments, and the belief that each woman in society must therefore, above all else, be self-sufficient.

By continually depicting men in the villainous ways that feminists have done for the past 30 years, and simultaneously depicting all women as being poor and suffering in the ways that they have, fem-

---

[5] It also brings to mind a quote from Steven Goldberg: "Back in the Sixties, many ridiculed the idea of lifelong marriage because they saw it as inherently undesirable. Today the idea is ridiculed because it seems virtually impossible."

inists not only justify their arguments for change but they have also succeeded, to varying degrees, in causing men to feel guilty. These feelings have, in turn, prompted the types of emotions that have made men all too frequently question themselves—many to the point that they began succumbing to the arguments of feminists for no other reason.

The guilt that arose within men (even if subconscious and largely unnecessary) also helped to create the atmosphere in which the political correctness syndrome surfaced and flourished. Without some guilt in men, political correctness would never have become as pervasive as it has. A person made to feel guilt, even unwarranted guilt, is generally reluctant to speak out against those over whom he feels guilty. The greater the feelings of guilt, the greater the reluctance. Such reluctance leads first to tolerance, then to affirmation, and finally to support of the aims and goals of those supposed victims.

In time, with massive support from the media and academia, feminists had instilled in enough women enough negative emotions toward men—including hatred, jealousy, distrust, resentment, spite, anger, and disrespect—and had brought about enough guilt and self-questioning in men while indoctrinating these women in the virtues of feminism—that all of this turmoil between sexes brought about a social climate in which it became literally taboo to question feminist principles or to discuss (in public or in the presence of a feminist supporter) the principles of feminism in a negative light.

Though this became known as "political correctness," it precisely meets Webster's definition of the word taboo. A taboo is: 1) something that is banned on grounds of morality or taste; 2) banned as constituting a risk; 3) a prohibition imposed as a protective measure. Speaking out against feminism, or any aspect of it, came to fill each of those requirements in nearly every social situation, and most certainly in mixed company.

As to the first definition, opposition to feminism was banned because it came to be considered a sign of bad taste, if not outright immorality. As to the second, dissension against feminism was banned because feminists themselves considered open discussion a risk or threat on the grounds that opinion would be expressed on both sides of the issue, pro and con. As to the third definition, banning open discussion of feminism has obviously acted as a protective measure for feminists and their cause. Unfortunately, it has had the opposite effect on society as a whole.

If people did speak out, or even attempted to speak out against feminism, in the wrong company, they would literally be treated as if they had broken a taboo. The punishment isn't jail, though. It is difficult to over-emphasize the ridicule and anger anyone suffers for speaking out against feminism today, a time in which feminists have become increasingly intolerant, vindictive, self-righteous, and easily inflamed. Depending on the company, the punishment is likely to be a response containing cruel indignation, an attack on personality, or even ostracism. Feminists have succeeded in silencing their critics because most people (often due to bitter experience) have chosen to avoid conflict with feminists, rather than suffer these consequences. This is what political correctness has accomplished.

Though the above appears to refer to very strident feminists, to lesser degrees the same rules apply among men and women who don't even regard themselves as feminists. The indoctrination has been that effective. Many of this author's female relatives and acquaintances have shown that though they may recognize and abhor what is happening to our society due to the influence of feminism, they are loathe to discuss any actions that may serve as remedies.

Dinesh D'Souza has written an entire book regarding the phenomenon known as political correctness. The book, entitled *Illiberal Education*, offers a lengthy list of examples of how political correctness flourishes in the academic environment (of which more will be discussed later). D'Souza quotes Donald Kagan, Dean of Arts and Sciences at Yale, who discussed what it means to express viewpoints that conflict with politically correct opinions. Kagan states:

> These are questions that are not really open to argument. It takes real courage to oppose the campus orthodoxy. To tell you the truth, I was a student during the days of McCarthy, and there is less freedom now than there was then.

Thomas Fleming, editor of *Chronicles*, has written:

> Europeans lie about politics all the time, but occasionally in the course of the day, you can hear someone speaking his mind, telling the truth. In America, if a politician or journalist tells the truth for a change, it is called a gaffe. Everyone is talking about the problem of political

correctness, even the leftist thought police, but the PC terror goes far deeper than we are willing to admit. Nearly all of us are PC nowadays on both left and right, and the national symbol is no longer the coiled rattlesnake but the Three Chinese Monkeys: Hear no evil, See no evil, Speak no evil—the evil in question being any truth that might make someone uncomfortable.

Fleming's comments say a great deal about the state of freedom of speech in contemporary America, but he has not quite hit the mark. The recognizable truth is that whatever group is perceived by the public as a "minority" can indulge in politically incorrect rhetoric at the expense of non-minority status groups without suffering the same kinds of consequences as would be suffered by individuals within the non-minority status group. The type of statements that women are excused for making about men would never be allowed in the reverse direction. An excellent example is provided by Ohio State Senator Linda Furman, who was quoted in a feminist convention newspaper, "The Getting It Gazette," as saying, "If it has tires or testicles, you're going to have trouble with it." If the word "ovaries" were substituted for "testicles," a male elected official would have either had to make a public apology, or would have been run out of office for exhibiting prejudice. After all, nearly half of the voters the Senator was elected to represent fall into the category she so forthrightly maligned. But, because she is a woman, and because feminists have succeeded in obtaining for women the status of a minority (despite the fact that they outnumber men), she could openly display such prejudice without suffering consequences that—according to the rules of political correctness—should attend such a display.

The reason for the phenomenon of political correctness has been the needs of feminists. They have never been able to justify their goals in open and fair debate so, instead of attempting to compete in the open marketplace of ideas, they attempt to silence competition. They are so insecure in their own beliefs that they are unable to deal with alternative viewpoints. But too many have too much invested to retreat.

CHAPTER THREE

The Capture of the American Mass Media

Though the spreading of the Big Lie and successful implementation of the Amity-Enmity Principle have been crucial tactics in the feminist movement's modus operandi, the third tactic has perhaps been the most crucial of all. This is the capture of the American mass media.[1] This "capture" is not the sort that occurs when armed combatants occupy a building, or a hill, or a town, but it is essentially a capture, nonetheless. It is a capture in the sense that when either side in a dispute has gained control of something valuable, so as to be able to use it for its own ends, that side can be said to have captured that thing. In just such a way, feminists can be said to have captured the mainstream American mass media.

Basically, this was accomplished by effectively silencing all those who aren't feminists by making dissent a taboo, and by filling the media ranks with a high percentage of feminists. Nowhere is dissension against the tenets of feminism more a taboo than in public discourse. Since feminists connected with, infiltrated, captured, and learned to manipulate it, the media has literally served as feminism's representative, its repetitive loudspeaker, its indoctrinator, while still being perceived as credible and unbiased by the American public. The importance of this is overwhelming when we recognize the enormous influence of the media.[2]

---

[1] The mass media is here defined as including radio (music, news, and talk shows); TV (including sitcoms, movies, documentaries, news programs, etc.); movies; newspapers and magazines; and all forms of advertising associated with any of them.

[2] In regard to influence, and as it affects feminism and society as a whole, the time has long since passed that our mass media system can be classified as a reactive institution.

From the very beginning of contemplating and studying feminism, in preparation to write this manuscript, it was obvious to this author that the mainstream mass media was going to provide virtually no sources of conservative information or thought, supporting any type of traditional belief. At first, this caused self-doubt, but soon it became apparent that the information disseminated by the media is heavily biased. It can be easily observed that the media do not offer rational viewpoints of people on both sides of the issues. Though often infuriating, the media have provided this author with both the motivation to present opposing arguments and an endless amount of easily discreditable material.

Just how influential and powerful has our mass media become? With the exception of feminism itself, today's collective mass media system could be classified as our society's most influential institution. It influences how we think, what we believe in, how we lead our lives, and what our future will be. It is our preeminent source of seeds for thought, and our number one means of guidance—unfortunately, feminism has been *its* source of guidance. In other words, feminists are truly our leaders.

If it is not true that the media is the "number one means" of direct influence over individuals, it is certainly true in the sense that the media wields tremendous influence over the four other institutions that would vie with it for influence, and also undermines their influence. The four institutions referred to are family, religion, school, and government.

How can it be that our media has become so powerful in comparison to those other institutions? First, technological advancements assisting in distribution, publication, and transmission have increased the number of mass media outlets from which we are bombarded on a daily basis. Seven thousand years ago, we didn't have even the written word. We had no schools, and certainly no media. But we did have influence from families, from some type of religion and from some type of government. Five thousand years ago, we began to write. Only

---

Whereas, in the past the media—particularly the news media—viewed its function as "reactive," distributing and presenting information that might otherwise escape the public's notice, today's "proactive" media often seeks first to create the information it then disseminates.

90 years ago did we get radio; 80 years ago, silent movies; 40 years ago, television; 25 years ago, color television; 15 years ago, VCRs.

Prior to the past century, we were influenced almost exclusively by family, religion, and government. Whatever media and educational systems existed were primarily reactive institutions, most often reflecting the morals and the cultures of the population they served, and almost never presuming to supersede the importance of the first three. This is no longer the case.

Today, people are "taking in," by far, more types of media-created informational material than ever before. We read more newspapers, magazines, and books than ever before, and it is increasingly difficult to know when the material we read is true or false, educational or editorial. Magazines regularly featuring, or focusing exclusively on, social issues have become abundant. Newspapers increasingly editorialize—where they purport that they do not—and go on at greater length with editorial commentary in those cases where they admit to printing it at all. But newspapers and magazines and books are only the tip of the print-media iceberg. There are newsletters and circulars, pamphlets and petitions, junk mail and signs and billboards. It is nearly impossible in America to pass through a grocery store checkout line, or drive to work, or take the dog for a walk, without absorbing hundreds or thousands of pieces of information seeking to change our minds about something. Often, the messages simply ask us to buy something, but even then, what we are asked to buy is something that may very well influence what we think or the way we live our lives. A billboard solicits our subscription to a specific newspaper, for instance, or the sign on the side of a transit bus suggests we attend a new movie.

We watch more television and see more movies (either big screen, or rental movies) than ever before in our history. The movies and television, in their roles as entertainment, might seem innocuous, but they are not. Increasingly, these forms of entertainment focus on the political and social issues of today, albeit in often subtle and nearly undetected ways.

Television and radio have, in many cases, thrown over their role as providers of light entertainment, in favor of becoming media for the exchange of "news" and opinion. In the not-too-distant past, we had three major television networks, each of which featured the 6 P.M.

and the 11 P.M. broadcasts of half-hour news programs. Now, we have several cable channels entirely devoted to broadcasts of news 24 hours per day. The three networks have responded by allotting ever larger portions of the broadcast day to news, gossip (tabloid), commentary, and opinion (talk shows).

It has been said that Americans live in the most information-rich environment in the world. But the truth is that Americans live in the most information-polluted environment in the world, and that, during most Americans' waking hours, someone is making a conscious effort to manipulate their thoughts and actions.

Second, in addition to the technological advances assisting in media distribution, the capabilities of the media's personnel to be more influential have grown rapidly, as well. Writers, news broadcasters, and advertisers for every section of the mass media have all (through more intense and scientific education) increased their psychological understanding of the public's mind. Coinciding with the massive changes in the media that have increased its abilities to reach and influence us, our vulnerability to the media's influence has been exacerbated by changes in our schools, our religious beliefs, and our faith in government, and by changes in the state of our families.

The historical influence of the family upon the individual has been severely diminished. More than 25 percent of pregnancies are aborted, 28 percent of children in this country are born illegitimately, 50 percent of marriages end in divorce, and 10–15 percent of the population will never marry. These facts indicate such instability, such lack of respect for family among the American people, that it is indisputable that the individual is not influenced by the family as much as in times past. Even when families remain physically intact, their influence is lessened for a variety of reasons also primarily related to the growth of feminist and media influence. More children every week are put in daycare for 9–12 hours per day, or become latchkey children while their mothers work. How can these children receive significant influence from their families when they see them only a few minutes each day? And, if the family does attempt to instill a given set of values in its children, the other influential institutions (most particularly schools and the media) often undermine those values by instilling counteracting values. This is nowhere more evident than in America, a society so inherently diverse in thought and opinion as to guarantee considerable difficulty in forming a consensus about proper values.

When individuals do not belong to intact nuclear families, they are, by default, going to be influenced to greater degrees by more outside factors than those who belong to nuclear families. The boy without his father present as a teacher and role model to influence him (whether the influence would have been good or bad) will have that void of influence filled, in one way or another.

Today's elementary school systems, in line with feminist policy, increasingly teach students "values clarification." Students are taught—by teachers belonging to feminist-dominated teacher's unions across the country—that there are no fixed values to adopt. William Bennett's book, *The De-Valuing Of America*, gives a clear picture of how true this is:

> In 1985 *The New York Times* published an article quoting New York area educators, in slavish devotion to this new view, proclaiming that "they deliberately avoid trying to tell students what is ethically right and wrong." The article told of one counseling session involving fifteen high school juniors and seniors. In the course of that session a student concluded that a fellow student had been foolish to return one thousand dollars she found in a purse at school. According to the article, when the youngsters asked the counselor's opinion, "He told them he believed the girl had done the right thing, but that, of course, he would not try to force his values on them. 'If I come from the position of what is right and what is wrong,' he explained, 'then I'm not their counselor.'"
>
> Once upon a time, a counselor offered counsel, and he knew that an adult does not form character in the young by taking a stance of neutrality toward questions of right and wrong or by merely offering "choices" or "options."

Society-wide, the lessening in the influential role of religion can be seen and has been widely acknowledged. (General feminist policy is to deny or subvert belief in the need for any type of religious principles. And even in those occasional cases of alliance between the feminist movement and the leadership of individual churches, for whatever common cause might bring them temporarily together, the churches supported are generally those whose ministers are very much caught up in liberal social activism.)

The changes in the messages the media itself gives us are obvious enough. Those messages do not advise that we listen to our family or to our religion, but instead discredits them. Rather, they seem to say, "Listen to us (the media), be pluralistic, be individualistic, be tolerant of anything, be anything you want. Cut loose the anchor, relax and drift where you may, just as long as your way doesn't conflict with the future we have in store for you. If it does, not only will you have no hope of using us to tell your story, but we will condemn you because we already have our own agenda. So trust us, let us, the winds of the media and feminism, carry you."

The government does have influence in determining the ways in which we live, but increasingly little influence on the ways in which we think. Most of us see our government and its actions only through the veil of media description. We rarely have the chance to fully observe what George Bush or Bill Clinton say and do. Instead, what we get are sound-bites and brief newspaper accounts; we get words and actions taken out of context in such a way as to virtually prevent our true understanding of what was said or done.

Because of the media's incredible ability to influence everyone, regardless of social or economic stature, it can be said that the media plays a more important role in determining the future of this country than any other major institution of influence, perhaps more than all of them combined.

Not only does it influence each of us as individuals, it also directly influences each of the four other major institutions of influence. Starting with the family (assuming, for the moment, that the reader is a parent), what influences you and your children? In comparison to the morals and values you received from your parents and they from their parents, to what degree will your children adopt your morals and values? To what degree will they "take after," learn from, and generally emulate, the ways in which you, your spouse, and your extended family think and try to lead your lives? If the influence your family has on its youthful members has been lessened significantly, in comparison to past generations, is it predominantly because of changes in the outside influences of religion, the schools, the government, or is it because of the influence of what they read, hear on the radio, and see in the movies and on the television—in other words, the media? And if there has been a major change in your thinking and attitudes, what are the sources of input in your life that have brought them about?

What type of value system does your school system teach? Does your child's school teach values that you believe in? Does it teach any type of religious values, any type of traditional values at all? Or does your child's school teach values more in line with those preached by the media? If the answer to that last question is yes, then that school is teaching your child a combination of feminist values and situational ethics, which means making up your own values as you go along.

Do you and your children go to church? If you do, does your church or religion respond to what appears in the media? Or does the media respond to your religion? Does the media respond to decisions made by your church by criticizing them, by praising them, or simply by ignoring them? Is it likely that the media will either ignore or criticize your church's decisions, but very unlikely the media will praise any decision your church makes, unless it follows feminist philosophies? If your church were to accept women in the priesthood as righteous, if it were to accept homosexuality as being a lifestyle morally equal to heterosexuality, or to accept unbridled promiscuity as equally righteous to sexual relationships within the bounds of marriage, if it were to deem abortion or birth control as morally acceptable, or to accept divorce as virtually expected and not to be discouraged, these things would most certainly be considered newsworthy and would draw not only the attention of the media, but its validation as well. If your church were to oppose or even advise against any of these subjects, and decide to retain its traditional policy regarding them, this might also be considered newsworthy, but the coverage would take on an entirely different flavor—that of condemnation.

Does the media respond to our government, or does our government respond to the media? We do have the vote, but what is our primary source of information about much of what matters in an election—candidates, economics, environmental and social issues—between elections, when we are developing our philosophies? Who edits the dialogue and the information we are given on specific candidates and the specific issues they address when it is election time? Who increasingly attempts to tell the government what we think and what we want? Who tells us what they think we need to know about the government? The media.

From an entirely different perspective, what is the single greatest influence in determining, or creating, our role models? Remember the important part role models play in determining what goals we set, how we think, and how we lead our lives. Do we choose these role models with the help of our increasingly unstable relationships, marriages, and fragmentable families; our increasingly "value neutral" school systems; our churches, with their shrinking congregations and their policies of conciliation toward what the media presents as "public opinion"; our government; or do we choose them with the help of the media? We choose them with the help of the media. As these other institutions of influence have declined under the effects of the mass media, the media has in turn filled the vacuum of influence it has helped to create. The only reason our mass media isn't this country's preeminent influence over thought and action is because feminism is. Feminists own the media.

Some people might question whether members of the various forms of the mass media really do attempt to influence us. (Remember, here, that the media includes more than just those who write for newspapers and magazines, and those who write books. It also includes people in every aspect of radio, television, and movie production.) Without a doubt, they do attempt to influence us. There's really no form of communication between humans without a cause or reason. When we communicate, our most basic goal is to transfer an idea to the person we are communicating with. At this time, we either ask a question, make a request, give an order, or we attempt to inform someone of something. When we attempt to do the latter, we usually attempt to make that person believe that the information we are giving them is true. It may be mundane, it may be common knowledge, or seem obvious. It may even be open to debate. (This book is an attempt to influence your way of thinking. When you talk to someone about it, you will try to influence them, hopefully by convincing them that the views expressed here are right.) Though the motives are endless, simply put, when humans communicate, it is just human nature to want to influence the other's thoughts, in one way or another.

Who are the mass media? They are a collection of individuals who are, by and large, educated from a liberal viewpoint, usually feminist-indoctrinated, and almost certainly politically correct, a collection of humans who can be assumed to have a greater desire to communicate, and hence to influence, than the average person. If this weren't true, they wouldn't have chosen to enter such a profession. Each of these people has his or her own set of visions, beliefs, and goals. Each of them has special training. Each knows that he is in a special position to communicate with the public and forward his thoughts. These people aren't pursuing media careers only to make money; they assuredly have other types of personal goals, as well. For example: the producers of the television series *Murphy Brown*, *Roseanne*, and *The Simpsons* are aware of the positions of influence their respective successes have created for them, and all of these people have their own, unique, social agendas to promote, whatever they might be.

Even theoretically objective members of the news media, making an "honest" effort to write, edit, and report only facts, can't avoid attempting to influence and persuade, to some small degree (though it may well be done subconsciously). Because most people are well-intentioned, they usually want to tell the truth. Writers and reporters will want to report what they believe to be the truth, whether they know the entire truth or not. If there is no absolute truth (and there rarely is) to what they're reporting, they will assume, hypothesize, and editorialize in the attempt to have others share their understanding in a situation. When they are wrong, or even when their reports are incomplete, we have been told something other than the truth. If we have believed them, we have accepted and been influenced by falsehood.

The ability to influence others, combined with the opportunity to do so, gives media personnel a great deal of power. Few individuals can refuse the opportunity to exert some degree of power, when it offers itself. It would not be unreasonable to assume that many people in such positions would look upon it as an opportunity to act "altruistically," and thus to add meaning to the communication. To media professionals, this would also mean increasing the importance of their work. "If I can influence people to follow my line of thinking, it will benefit society," would not seem an unlikely thought, or an infrequent one. Such a thought need not even be conscious.

Even though the people with access to our attention may not be consciously attempting to influence us, it is increasingly obvious (when contemplating the news they give us) that editorialization has become standard operating procedure. More and more often they can't resist telling us how to interpret what we hear—"I think what the President meant by that is. . . ." More and more often they can't resist telling us what to think—"Obviously, so and so has won the debate. . . ." Increasingly they openly claim to speak for us—moving from "The American people mourn the loss of . . ." to "The American people are angry . . ."; "The American people are ready for change . . ."; "The American people are confused. . . ." The effect of this is that the media have begun to be perceived as the voice of the American people, whether that voice is reverberating upward to our governmental leaders, or downward to the little people, us.

When it became clear that Bill Clinton would be the 1992 Democratic candidate for the Presidency, did anyone else notice that that was when the media's praise for him began and the serious questioning and criticism of him slowed to a crawl? Such a thing should come as no surprise, considering the political make-up of the group of journalists whose job it was to cover the election. Joseph Sobran, writing for the *Conservative Chronicle* phrased it this way:

> Funny how the paranoid fantasy over time becomes settled fact. A recent poll of journalists in Washington found that 89 percent of them had voted for Bill Clinton in 1992, only 7 percent for George Bush; that 50 percent are Democrats, only 4 percent Republicans; and so on, every question eliciting ratios that would startle even the paranoid.
> Journalist James Glassman of *The Washington Post*:
>
> > "Journalists no longer deny that they're liberals. Instead, they argue that they don't let their political leanings affect their work."
>
> Mr. Glassman, himself a recovering liberal, is skeptical of this claim.

One need not give it much thought to realize that the media attempts to influence us; it's obvious to any conscious observer. The Fall 1992, issue of *Time*, for example, was completely devoted to telling its readers, "What to expect in the new millennium." Readers of that issue might well believe, as a result of the prestige of the publication and the certainty with which the predictions were written, that the scenarios presented are as good as fact. In effect, we are not charting our own course of history naturally, one day at a time; the editors of *Time* are at least attempting to chart it for us in advance.

Another example of the bias that creeps into news media reports can be seen in the *San Jose Mercury News* newspaper. Soon after Bill Clinton won the Presidential election with 5 percent more of the popular vote than George Bush (43 percent for Clinton, versus 38 percent for Bush) this paper claimed that the voters had given him a "mandate." Clinton did not in fact win by a landslide, and the voters did not give Clinton any mandate. It was the newspaper attempting to give him a mandate, not us. Had Bush won by the same margin, the paper would most likely have claimed that Ross Perot's entrance into the contest cost Clinton the election, and would very likely have called it a narrow victory proving how unhappy people were with Bush.

Even taking all of the above factors into account, there might not be too much of a problem of undue influence if the balance of media viewpoints didn't get overly lopsided toward liberalism, conservatism, or any other general set of beliefs. If, for every media source implying we should accept the feminist agenda, there was another source validating traditional virtues, they would tend to counteract one another and we could live with the influences. We have problems when the influence of the media gets as far out of balance as it is now.

Academia is one reason our media personnel have become so liberal. As academia has become increasingly liberal in its teachings, so have the individuals that now make up the majority of our media personnel. Media personnel, taught in an increasingly liberal educational system and attuned to its substantially liberal beliefs, serve to further promote women's issues. In this sense, though, the media and academia have fed off each other.

With its tremendous power, the media's responsibility to promote an objective climate, and to report objectively, has never been more important. Unfortunately, this has been lacking in recent history, because the mass media has come to be dominated by feminists. Up to this point, as the media goes, so goes the nation.

In January 1988, during the first day of actual research for this book, the main library in San Jose, California, provided a look at the entire past year's *San Jose Mercury News* newspapers. It showed that articles promoting change, building enmity, bashing men, or simply strongly pro-movement, had been present on a daily basis in the newspaper's "Living" section, for the entire year.[3] Most daily readers probably

---

[3] A complete and thorough analysis of the newspaper articles of the previous year revealed just how many heavily biased articles there could be, directly promoting fem-

never realized, much less paused to contemplate, exactly what they were taking in.

A retrospective of 15 years of having read that same newspaper could not bring to mind one single article focusing on the merits of the traditional family household, or a happy, traditional type of family, in which the father was the primary breadwinner. The front page of the "Living" section once featured a large (6 by 9 inches), full-color picture, showing two lesbians cheek-to-cheek in an affectionate embrace. Their recent marriage was described, in bold print, as "a traditional, lesbian marriage." Throughout the article, their lives were depicted as nothing less than perfect.

It should be recognized that the influence of the newspaper media alone has been incredible. Not only are newspapers read in every part of the country every day but, in this regard, it can be seen that across the country they have tended to carry very similar types of information. The point is that the feminist-forwarding type of articles printed in the *Mercury News* are prevalent across the country, and not confined to a minority of papers.

But it isn't just the newspaper media at play. The combined media sources of this country now form an environment that makes it almost impossible for Americans to dodge feminism's daily influence.

The periodicals section at the San Jose main library lists over 4,500 articles under the heading "women's issues." In one month, November 1979, during the height of the battle over the ERA (Equal Rights Amendment), 36 women's magazines, with a combined circulation of 60 million, ran articles supporting the ERA. They included magazines such as *Ladies' Home Journal, Cosmopolitan, Ms.,* and *Vogue*.

The feminist movement (including its entire agenda) has been "our" media's single most written about, talked about, and promoted subject for over twenty years, with very little written in the way of

---

inism, frequently using the formula that follows: a headline to inflame women readers; a few scientific facts; a small amount of legitimate, scientific opinion (easily—and generally—manipulated); a large number of biased, quasi-scientific and professional opinions; and mountains of anecdotal evidence, typically based on "he-done-me-wrong" stories and lay opinions. Most of these articles were put forth under the guise of objective journalism. Generally, these articles could be easily discredited and they would not have been allowed in print if their focus had been different. But whether these articles had any truth to them or not, there are still two sides to every controversy, and only one side has been, or is being, presented.

balance. Feminists, of course, would reply that the media is only made up of people and that it therefore fairly represents the peoples' thinking and will.

Wrong. Sanity doesn't get press. Harmony doesn't get press. Traditionalism doesn't get press. Conservatism doesn't get press. Stability doesn't get press. These things do not make the news. Either there is nothing to sensationalize about them, or they don't aid feminism's cause. It is easy to find examples of life not being utopian, easy to find the causes in traditional things, and easy to forget—or forget to be thankful for—the rewards that certain traditional lifestyles have given us.

Change is news. To promote change is a challenge. The hope of promoting positive change can be even more of an incentive to take up that challenge. These are the thoughts that have been going through the heads of all the people in our media who do want to influence us, many for altruistic reasons. Promotion of the status quo brings them no reward. For them, it is the promotion of change that brings personal reward.

No other society has ever been subjected to the same duration and volume of overt and subliminal mass media support as has American society over the issues and agendas of the feminist movement. Even attempts at Communist indoctrination in countries behind the Iron Curtain failed to produce the same degree of changes in the thinking of the multitudes that the media-supported feminist movement has achieved. (A smaller percentage of those people suffered the delusion that they were being given objective information.) The amount of information taken in by individuals is also important in that the audience of any new debate will already have been well informed of feminism's general contentions and will have a foundation for believing the points pro-feminist debaters make in subsequent debates. The case is similar to that of a prejudiced juror.

This long-term subjection to a virtually unidirectional flow of information has not only had varying degrees of brainwashing effect upon a large majority of the public, but it has also been an important factor in bringing about acceptance by academicians, their subsequent promotion of the movement's manifesto, and changes in traditional teaching practices and subject matter, research focuses, and objectivity. As already stated, the media and academia, with direction from feminists, have aided feminism in its successful efforts to produce certain social pressures that create a climate where public dissension against feminist ideology cannot occur—the politically correct environment.

Though thousands of books could be filled with examples of the media giving full support to virtually every one of the movement's needs and visions, the following is an attempt to convey an adequate picture with only a few examples.

Example: The April 1991 issue of *Life* decided to help redefine the word "family" for the general population and, in so doing, demonstrated how the media follows and promotes the movement's agenda, often as if it were the movement's paid advertisers. Starting in April 1991 (right in line with movement policy), *Life* began observing and discussing a number of so-called "families." The lead article explained to the reader:

> The people you will meet—a young couple awaiting the birth of their first child, a mother who kidnapped her son from her ex-husband, two gay men, a divorced couple whose children sleep every other night in a different parent's home—have little in common except that all are striving, with varying degrees of success, to make their families work.

Who gives the media, or this author, the right to alter, however slightly, the definition of a word? Who decides that two homosexual men constitute a family? That is exactly what is happening when articles like the one above are written. The author of this article is knowingly attempting to support what he believes, trying to convince, persuade, or even dictate to us that this definition of family should be accepted. Consciously or not, this writer (or *Life* magazine) is also actually attempting to have an influence on public policy, intending to get this definition of family accepted by the public, and then by law- and policy-makers, so that these groups gain the same privileges as traditional families.

Example: *Time* devoted its entire Fall 1990 publication to women's issues, entitling it, "Women: The Road Ahead." In this issue, they quoted Charlotte Whitton, former mayor of Ottawa, in large print: "Whatever women do, they must do twice as well as men, to be thought half as good. Luckily this is not difficult." Novelist Erica Jong was also quoted: "Beware the man who praises women's liberation; he is about to quit his job." Both of these highly sexist statements were repeated with impunity in a national publication. Obviously, a mainstream national publication wouldn't print such inflammatory remarks—if they were reversed and stated by men—unless, perhaps, the writer were somehow using such quotes to promote a negative view of men. Such statements would not be allowed from men because they haven't been politically correct for over 20 years. If it were said, in regard to sexually integrated trucking companies, that "the most physically grueling trucking and delivery jobs are, by necessity, always given to men," (which, by the way, is virtually true) the speaker would be heavily criticized for making a sexist statement and be informed that he had no right to make such a generalization. For certain, that statement would never see the light of day in the mass media (it would be censored prior to publication) unless it were used as an example of male chauvinism, expressly to inflame women readers. This issue of *Time* is only one of many examples of the movement's access to the media, its unquestioned right to free speech without fear of reprimand or censorship—demonstrating the influential power the movement possesses, that no form of opposition has.

Example: The animated Disney Studios version of *Beauty and the Beast* typifies the role models feminists wish our children to have. Watch it and notice that the only male character possessing any masculine traits in the entire story possesses only masculine traits of a stereotypic, negative variety. He is insecure, vain, overly aggressive, violent, stupid, sneaky, sinister, jealous, and insensitive. The heroine is beautiful (in a carefully scripted, *au naturel* [without even any need for makeup] sort of way), strong, independent, self-assured, secure, intelligent, well-read, and loved by everyone. And what type of Prince Charming does the noticeably insecure, wimpy Beast turn into. He becomes almost as beautiful as the Beauty and just as sensitive, if not more so, but in far different ways than in the original tale. The Beauty remains true to her character throughout the movie; only the Beast (the male) needs transformation, to exemplify the new idealized male. The perspectives, pictures, and storyline are becoming the norm for children's shows. The message is clear: "Whatever you do, boys, don't ever be strong or aggressive; girls don't like those things. And whatever you do, girls, don't ever be weak or passive; boys will take advantage of those things."

The mass media promotes feminism at the expense of journalistic integrity in many ways beyond the simple misuse of facts—to promote, for example, such things as androgyny and enmity. It is no longer safe to believe any information from mainstream media, because those who earn their living from it don't simply twist the truth, they unquestioningly repeat out-and-out lies.

Mona Charen, a journalist for the *Conservative Chronicle*, recently wrote an article about Christina Hoff Sommers' book, *Who Stole Feminism?* While discussing feminism's relationship with the media, Charen came up with a few typical examples of the media promoting the lies of feminists. The following is from her article of May 26, 1994:

> Two best-selling authors, Gloria Steinem and Naomi Wolf, note in their books that 150,000 females die of anorexia nervosa per year. Wolf is particularly outraged. "How," she writes in *The Beauty Myth*, "would America react to the mass self-immolation by hunger of its favorite sons?"
>
> It's an arresting statistic. And Wolf would perhaps be justified in her outrage if it were true. But in her new book . . . Professor Christina Hoff Sommers of Clark University demonstrates that it is not.
>
> The National Center for Health Statistics reports that the annual death toll from anorexia is fewer than 100 per year—usually 50 or 60, with 101 in 1983. . . . Wolf has promised to correct the error in future editions of her book, but the statistic was so useful—from a certain point of view—that it has been repeated again and again. The Anorexia "holocaust" has already shown up in newspaper columns and college textbooks.
>
> On Nov. 4, 1992, Sommers recounts, Deborah Louis, president of the National Women's Studies Association, sent a message to the Women's Studies Electronic Bulletin Board saying, "According to the last March of Dimes report, domestic violence (vs. pregnant women) is now responsible for more birth defects than all other causes combined."
>
> Horrifying, right? But false. Sommers called the March of Dimes and spoke with members of its public relations department. They said the rumor of a March of Dimes "report" was spinning out of control. They had been deluged with calls from governors' offices, state health departments and Washington politicians. The press had picked it up as well, with references to the pseudo-fact about violence against pregnant women causing birth defects making it into *Time* magazine,

the *Boston Globe*, the *Dallas Morning News*, the *Chicago Tribune* and the *Arizona Republic*.

Time had relied on information provided by an advocacy group called the San Francisco Family Violence Prevention Fund. Sommers traced the "datum" back farther, to discover that the giant canard had begun with an introduction of a speaker at a nurses' conference. The master of ceremonies referred to a March of Dimes report, which said that more women are screened for birth defects than are screened for domestic violence. She said nothing about a causal link.

"Why was everyone so credulous?" asks Sommers. "Battery responsible for more defects than all other causes combined? More than genetic disorders . . . more than Down's syndrome . . . more than alcohol, crack or AIDS?"

The pattern of false "facts" being circulated easily in the press was repeated most spectacularly last year when another bogus "report"— this one claiming that more women are victims of domestic violence on Super Bowl Sunday than any other day—was given wide coverage. Ken Ringle of the *Washington Post* was the only journalist who bothered to check it out, and he discovered that the claim was totally false.

In another report on Hoff Sommers' book, Alyson Todd addressed these same concerns in the May/June 1994 issue of *Heterodoxy*:

> But what if these statistics and sound-bites are false? Moreover, what if these "facts" are the product of politically motivated advocacy research? Christina Hoff Sommers' new book, *Who Stole Feminism?*, proves just that. A professor of philosophy at Clark College, Sommers carefully reviews the numerous popular "studies" done by women's advocacy groups on domestic violence, female self-esteem, depression, and gender bias, and finds that *not even one* is based upon credible evidence. (Emphasis added.)

Tom Goff recently brought to light another totally erroneous, but well-publicized statistic bandied about by feminists. This one regards the economic consequences of divorce. Accepted wisdom has it that women's standard of living decreases by 73 percent after divorce, while the men's goes up by 43 percent. Goff, writing in *The Argus* newspaper, points out that this so-called fact:

> . . . has altered public perceptions of divorce. It has been cited, but never questioned, repeatedly in news stories and scholarly studies. It was cited by President Clinton in his budget proposal attack on deadbeat dads. This year. And it's 10 years old!

Not only that, it's wrong.

The 73/43 figures came from Lenore Weitzman's 1985 book, "The Divorce Revolution." Weitzman got the number by sampling all of 228 people in one place—Los Angeles. Amazingly, it wasn't until last June that anybody seriously looked at Weitzman's methodology. A researcher duplicated Weitzman's study and concluded her figures were the result of computer transcription errors. After correcting the errors, the new researcher arrived at a 27 percent decrease for women, and a 10 percent increase for men.

But . . . even these figures are out of step with later studies, not to mention the experiences of divorced men. . . .

By the way, here's a statistic from the U.S. Department of Health and Human Services: 46 percent of non-custodial mothers default on (child) support. The figures for fathers is 26.9 percent.

Haven't heard that before, have you? Probably not.

It does not conform to the current orthodoxy. You know—women are always the victims; men are always the cause.

In an extremely rare article, written by Armin Brott and published in the *San Jose Mercury News* on July 3, 1994, the less well-known, but equally ugly, side of the domestic violence problem was revealed:

. . . the National Family Violence Survey, one of the largest and most respected studies of family violence ever done (and the source of the "every 15 seconds . . . [a woman is beaten by a man]" statistic) found that:

Each year more men than women are victimized by their intimates.

While violence by men against women is decreasing, violence by women against men is increasing.

In 1991, to avoid accusations of gender bias, one of the authors of the survey recomputed the rates based solely on the responses of the women surveyed. The new results found that even according to women, men are the ones more likely to be assaulted by their female partners.

Many women's rights advocates—if they acknowledge the problem at all—suggest that female violence against men is purely a self-defense response to male violence. However, a 1990 article in *American Psychologist* found that among couples reporting violence, the violence was unilateral by the woman in 24 percent of the cases and unilateral by the man in 27 percent of the cases. The rest of the time, the violence was "mutual." Other critics say that since women are physically weaker and can do less damage, only "severe assaults" should be compared. But research has shown that whether the analysis is based on all assaults, or is focused exclusively on dangerous ones, domestic violence is still a two-way street.

If violence against men is so widespread, why haven't we heard about it before? First, several studies have shown that men minimize their abuse and, like many abused women, remain in violent relationships for economic reasons or out of fear that the violence would be directed against their children if they left their abuser. This is particularly important, give [sic] the fact that over 60 percent of all child abuse is committed by women. In addition, men in general, are extremely reluctant to report that they've been the victims of assault. (Overall, men report all types of violent victimization 32 percent less frequently than women.)

Thanks to the Simpson case, much has been made of law enforcement's reluctance to get involved in "family matters" and arrest violent men. But when it comes to dealing with violent women, the police are even less likely to react appropriately.

Moreover, a study published in the *Journal of Interpersonal Violence* found that "physical violence of any kind was perceived less negatively when the female in the arguing couple was the aggressor." This double standard apparently extends as far as murder; a recent Department of Justice survey found that people rated a husband's stabbing his wife to death 40 percent worse than a wife's stabbing her husband to death. Women's violence, it seems, is somehow less "real" (and therefore more acceptable) than men's.

Perhaps the most powerful reason we haven't heard more about battered men is that the women's movement has been in complete denial about women's capacity for violence. According to sociologists Susan Morrow and Donna Hawxhurst, acknowledging women's violence "would endanger a feminist gender-specific analysis . . . that views battering as a consequence of male privilege." And if women are serious about their demands for gender equality, they're going to have to start taking responsibility for their behavior and for their contributions to the cycle of violence.

None of this, of course, is intended to excuse the actions of . . . any . . . man who beats his wife or girlfriend. But using O.J. and Nicole Simpson, as we have, to somehow "prove" that all men are violent and that all women are victims, and insisting that spousal violence is solely a women's issue is not only wrong—it's also counterproductive. Domestic violence is neither a male or a female issue—it's simply a human issue.

The truly unfortunate part of the spread of such lies as those exposed by Christina Hoff Sommers is that by the time they are discovered to be lies, they have already influenced the thinking of millions of readers. And even when they are discovered to be false, those media sources that printed them either print retractions in so small a space as to be unnoticeable, or fail to print any retraction at all because it would mean admitting to slipshod journalism. In a better world, the fact that *Time*, and other prestigious publications, had printed erroneous information would be newsworthy enough to become a feature story in *Newsweek*. But, as is the case with Congress, the media is eager to investigate the doings of others but reluctant to investigate itself too closely. As Carl Bernstein so appropriately warns:

> We need to start asking the same fundamental questions about the press that we do of the other powerful institutions in this society— about who is served, about standards, about self-interest and its eclipse of the public interest and the interest of truth. For the reality is that the media are probably the most powerful of all our institutions today, and they are squandering their power and ignoring their obligation. They—or more precisely, we—have abdicated our responsibility, and the consequence of our abdication is the spectacle, and the triumph of the idiot culture.

Does the media express thoughts and philosophies that you relate to and agree with? Does it offer commentary on lives like your own? Does it have more influence on you than your religion, or perhaps even more than your parents? When does our government receive praise for decisions regarding social problems? Haphazardly, or only when those decisions fall in line with feminist philosophy?

Throughout our evolutionary history, societies were shaped by alpha males: conquering generals, kings-by-birth, elected officials, clergymen, academics, and dictators, as well. We have always been led by men acknowledged as leaders. Today, we are led by the mass media. The biggest differences are that our former leaders were recognized as such, and they were men. The media's true leaders (those who set the tone) are women who are feminists, and who are using this network of influence—which presently wields more power in determining the ways we think, lead our lives, and shape the future of this society than our families, churches, schools, or government—to infiltrate those other institutions and to gain influence and authority in them, as well as to gain psychological power over the masses of unwary private citizens who fall prey to their influence.

This is a key to why the feminist agenda is rapidly becoming reality, and why it is so important to develop a better understanding of what feminism is and where it is leading us. It is also important to recognize that the media, in and of itself, can't be blamed for all our ills, as some people are now attempting to do. The media might, almost, be to blame for the social changes it promotes if it weren't for the fact that feminism is the primary philosophical guide for the media.

CHAPTER FOUR

Academic Support

The fourth tactic in the feminist modus operandi was learning to manipulate the nation's academic environment. This was accomplished by using typical feminist tactics, though the manipulation of academia may be more complete than feminism's manipulation of any other of our influential institutions.

What is going on at today's institutions of higher education is another frightening example of how feminism's influence has grown and is growing, and why its agenda is rapidly taking hold. It is also further evidence that the feminist movement isn't just a spontaneous "peoples' movement."

Incredibly, most of this country's academic institutions have become nothing less, and sometimes little more, than feminist ideology brainwashing clinics. What is being taught in today's social science departments is mind-boggling. The great majority of academicians who teach in these departments haven't simply let themselves be intimidated by rabid feminists; they have become hard-core believers of almost everything that feminism represents. Without doubt, political correctness has played a significant part in encouraging academics to fall into line with feminists. But political correctness doesn't just affect certain departments—politically correct rules, drawn up primarily by feminists, are everywhere on campuses across the country.

All anyone has to do is read *Illiberal Education*, by Dinesh D'Souza, to find out how serious the situation really is. His book is well-written, and gives such a good explanation of so many important points, it is recommended for everyone capable of reading.

Literally, the situation is so out-of-hand that most degrees received in the past few years in the social sciences—psychology, sociology, etc.—are worthless. (Degrees granted by Women's Studies programs have been worthless since the inception of those programs.) Why? Because, as stated previously, social science courses have been little more than courses in feminist ideology. Based on conversations and relationships with those who have been unfortunate enough to enroll in them, the conclusion is inescapable that these courses are, to some degree, detrimental to student sanity. Classes within these fields are generally run by individuals who could more appropriately be called radical social engineers than professors of education—puppets on the strings of feminism.

It is shocking that there are now over 500 universities in the U.S that have either Women's Studies programs or complete departments. What do these departments teach? *Illiberal Education* discusses the case of Pete Schaub:

> When Pete Schaub, a business major at the University of Washington, at Seattle, enrolled in a Women's Studies class in early 1988, he expected to learn about "the history of women and the contributions they have made." Schaub said his mother was a 1960's rebel who divorced his father and moved to rural Washington state to live "close to the land."
>
> Introduction to Women's Studies, taught by Donna Langston and Dana-Michele Brown, was not what Schaub had expected. On the first day of class Brown asserted that "the traditional American family represents a dysfunctional family unit." Students who protested that their families were functional were shouted down by teaching assistants hired by Langston and Brown. "Denial, denial," they yelled in unison. A few days later Langston brought guest speakers to talk about masturbation. "They said you don't need a man," Schaub said. "They proceeded to show how to masturbate with a feather duster, and they had dildos right there."
>
> When Professor Brown claimed that U.S. statistics showed that lesbians could raise children better than married couples, Schaub asked for the source. "I asked after class," Schaub said. "I wasn't challenging her." But the teacher "wouldn't hear of it. She said: 'Why are you challenging me? Get away from me. Just leave me alone.'" A member of Brown's undergraduate circle called Schaub a "chauvinist goddamn bastard." The next day, Schaub was banned from class.

In the initial phase of preparation for the writing of this book, the author approached Dr. Ira Reiss, a leading sociologist at the University of Minnesota, at Minneapolis, in hopes that he might provide direction for the research by providing the names of anyone who had done recent studies of universal or instinctive behavioral differences between men and women. After inquiring about the need for this type of information, Dr. Reiss promptly and flippantly dismissed the project, saying that consideration of biological differences between sexes was a thing of the past when theorizing about ways in which to socialize humans. Dr. Reiss' reaction was, unfortunately, representative of the majority of people who occupy positions in academia.

It is important to realize that what is being taught today in this country's institutions of higher learning is primarily a response to, and a result of, the influence of feminists and their number one mouth-piece, the mass media! This body of teaching (the "social sciences") is another important reason the feminist movement has gained the influence it has, and why it has had such an impact on our society.

In an article appearing in the September 1994, issue of *Heterodoxy*, Steven Goldberg (a sociologist and author of *Why Men Rule* and *The Inevitability of Patriarchy*—and predictably, the subject of much feminist criticism) described the situation in these terms:

> The intrusion of ideology into the social sciences is so extensive that one who simply describes it sounds paranoid. The logical and evidential inadequacy of most feminist works is so great that anyone who has not read these works would think that I must be misrepresenting them. While the hard sciences are to a great extent immunized against this sort of sloppy thought, sociology has deteriorated into something not much more than rationalization for what people want to believe. Truth is declared to be nothing more than opinion invoked for political purposes and is assessed in terms of its imagined social consequences and its ability to soothe anxiety.

Frank Salter, writing for the *National Review*, made similar observations regarding the feminist views that dominate *The Concise Oxford Dictionary of Sociology*:

> On account of its vast biological ignorance the practice of sociology today is often as fanciful as the alchemy of the Middle Ages. . . .
> The *Dictionary's* omission of the intellectual provenance of sociobiology undoubtedly has political roots. (A sociobiologist's) understanding of innate human behavioral tendencies revives and refines the concept of human nature for our times. The academic Left, however, detests the concept of human nature because it is a barrier to their

utopian schemes for transforming man by changing society. Therefore the strong support for a biologically based concept of human nature in evolutionary theory—by any account one of the most important scientific discoveries of the millennium—must be suppressed. Most sociologists would ridicule Biblical creationists, but to sustain their politics they must remain creationists themselves—only with society rather than God as man's creator.

On "childhood," Salter goes on to note:

Most people understand that childhood is a state of progression from infancy to adulthood that is a natural fact of the physical world. But listen to the *Dictionary*:

"[C]hildhood is constructed on the inabilities of children as political, intellectual, sexual, or economic beings despite empirical evidence to the contrary, . . . [T]his serves the needs of capitalist states."

. . . The entry pays no heed to the voluminous scientific evidence on cross-cultural universals in the states of a child's development from infancy to adulthood and in parent-child interaction and play. Only willful ignorance of the most elemental facts of biology could lead the *Dictionary* to describe the child's dependent state as constructed by exploiting capitalists. . . .

Of the Dictionary's entry on "marriage," Salter reports:

Incredibly, the reproductive function of marriage is not mentioned. The question, "Why do people marry?" does not even raise the possibility that providing a secure base for child-rearing is a prime function or concern.

And of its treatment of "maternal deprivation":

The *Dictionary* offers a cautious definition:
"[T]he absence of maternal care *considered* necessary for later mental health" (emphasis added). . . . "Feminists denounce the idea for its ideological role in subordinating women to motherhood."

It was the early feminists who long ago won control of the media; it was feminists—with the support of the media they controlled —who long ago gained influential control of academia—relentlessly coercing, persuading, and encouraging academicians (administrators, teachers, and students alike) to adopt its principles and to do research on its behalf. As a result of this influence, and that of political correctness, there have been mountains of biased, undebated, uncritiqued, and faulty material produced by academia (much of it contributed to by students who are only 18–22 years old)—to further justify and rationalize feminism. This faulty material has been sent directly to feminism's mouthpiece, the media, where it has been treated as though it were legitimate research and, hence, hugely important. The support this has lent to feminism's legitimacy and promotion is indescribable.

Academic studies on the values of conservative thought, in public institutions, have been few, and have even more rarely been referenced by any arm of the mass media. From discussions with a number of professors, it's apparent that they frequently perceive themselves as the brilliant and brave leaders of a foresighted leftist rebellion, but fail to realize that they exist only as pawns in the pockets of feminists. They are so naive that they are incapable of understanding that leftist thought and speech no longer require intellectual bravery and that the reverse is now true.

This author is not the first to notice that professors have frequently been vulnerable to intimidation. As author and professor Thomas Sowell—who is familiar with the academic environment—commented in the *Conservative Chronicle*:

> Anyone who has not lived in an academic community may not appreciate how much intimidation there is in this apparently genteel setting —or how little backbone there is to stand up to it. When the fate of certain programs at Berkeley was up for a faculty vote a few years ago, a ferocious battle raged as to whether that vote would be secret or open. Both sides realized that this could well determine the outcome.

Aside from feminist pressures, academicians, particularly those in social science areas, whose careers are often advanced on the basis of theories, feel personally less rewarded when promoting the virtues of traditional thought (as do media personnel), as these are not perceived as innovative, nor do they provide a significant means of exerting influence. This has been another factor helpful in generating the tremendous amount of research data available on the merits of new reasoning and change in regard to the feminist movement.

Examples of how academia has been influenced are easily recognized. Al Maleson, publisher of "The Diatribe," on the University of Minnesota Extension catalog:

On one page, they're writing about how they offer absolutely equal educational opportunities for everyone, regardless of sex. And then, a few pages later, they start this whole big section of "Continuing Education for Women"! Can you imagine what would happen if they were to offer a program of "Continuing Education for Men"? There'd be hell to pay.

Imagine, over 500 universities across this country have Women's Studies programs or departments. The inherently biased, unscientific, and rarely questioned classes within them teach feminist ideology to our youthful and undeniably impressionable students, as though it were based on rational truth. The depth, redundancy, and lack of alternative viewpoints in today's academic environment serves to create something of a brainwashing environment. In this arena, feminist visions aren't just being taught as though they are unequivocally righteous, but also usually as though they are inevitable.

By adopting feminist principles, and by challenging traditionally patriarchic ideals, today's students are made to feel by their teachers (academically institutionalized feminists) that they are questioning authority. They are told that they are fighting for freedom. They are told that this country restricts their freedoms in many ways, including its oppressive insistence on a completely capitalistic system. What they don't realize, after all is said and done, is that it is the socialistic type of system feminists envision that restricts freedom. It is the socialist system that has grown like a cancer in every society and nation where it has appeared. It is the socialist system that indoctrinates its citizens.

It is important to note how many students seem so willing to rebel against government and authority and then espouse the virtues of feminism, which ensures that both government and authoritarianism will inevitably increase, as though this new authority will somehow be better than the old.

While this manuscript was in preparation at the University of Minnesota, a research aide was needed and an advertisement was placed on the Psychology department bulletin board, which made clear the intentions of the book.

Only two students responded to the ad, both female. Asked about her ability to remain objective and dedicated, given the purpose of the book, the first student replied, "Oh, it won't really concern me, I rated very highly masculine on the Bem Sex-Role Inventory test."

The Bem Sex-Role Inventory is a test created to determine through a series of questions to what degree individuals possess opposite-sex characteristics.

This student had developed a terrible case of tunnel vision. All she could see was feminism. She was truly unable to answer even the simplest questions put to her, when she felt that they contradicted feminist principles. It was very obvious that she had received such a one-dimensional education it was, in effect, worthless. Unfortunately this seems to be the case with the great majority of the current generation of students educated in the social sciences.

It was naive to hope to find a student to do research, who could remain unbiased on behalf of the noble cause of academic objectivity (which should lead to free thinking), and who might, thereby, provide a measure of objective research. It was naive to hope that there would be one single shred of objective material about this subject in the entire library, and that one of those students would be able to find it if there were. The academic system simply does not allow for the questioning of the ideologies it promotes. The media and the rules of political correctness dictate to teachers what they are to convince the students to believe, then dictate that they, or the students, go and find information and develop theories to back it up. The professors are so politically correct that they can't put forth an anti-feminist viewpoint, let alone ask the students to support one by their research.

In another part of the research effort, additional information was needed on ways in which the mass media has furthered the causes of the feminist movement. The Mass Communications Department at the University of Minnesota, at Minneapolis, seemed a good place to look. The Mass Communications Department at U.M.M. is huge. They take pride in having done thousands upon thousands of studies on "almost every facet of the media," including hundreds or even thousands of studies on "almost every way in which the mass media has promoted sex-roles and sex-stereotypes." One might assume that there have been many studies examining the mass media's role in supporting the feminist movement. Three different professors, each of whom said he was the one to talk to, had never heard of a study being done on the positive support the mass media has given to the feminist movement. Are they blind? Are they too intimidated to suggest that one or two such studies might be called for? Whatever their reasons, by not recommending a study on this very subject, they are lending their tacit support to the feminist movement and to the media's support of it.

The following is a typical example of the one-two punch of academia and the media. We have read or heard of hundreds of studies completed by academia—and announced by the mass media—on the fact that women make less money than men. What we never hear, even if some of those studies may have investigated the "causes," are some of the logical and fair reasons why women don't earn as much as men; and there are many legitimate reasons.

Men still have, on the average, much greater seniority in their professions and with their companies than women. This translates to higher pay across sexual lines. Among the population at large, men still hold more college degrees than women. This also translates to higher pay. Men still possess a higher percentage of the degrees that are more difficult to earn or require more years of study (engineering being one example of this type of degree). Again, this translates to higher pay.

There still exist highly physical jobs, which most women either can't perform at all, or which they find beyond their abilities if in performing them they must compete with male counterparts on an equal footing. Such jobs can provide men not only with good pay, but can provide men of lesser mental capabilities the opportunity to earn a good income. This avenue is generally unavailable to women of comparable intellect. Some highly physical jobs (particularly those within what are commonly referred to as "the trades") help men gain experience that can lead to contractor status. Here again, higher pay. Women don't often become cement contractors, or even laborers with good incomes, for obvious reasons.

Men are more driven by the need to achieve—at work, in athletics, in life in general—than are women. There are more than a few people out there working 100 hours per week. Who are they? They are men. Statistically, men still work considerably longer hours, at non-salaried jobs, consistently earning far more overtime pay than women. Men don't take time out to have babies (some women do still work with the intention of quitting, or taking extended absence when they start a family; this alters career desires and ambition). Few women work with the intention or hope of becoming the primary supporter of an entire family, as many men still do. Married men earn almost double what their single counterparts earn—proving that the role of breadwinner does provide motivation. Superior male aptitudes (such as math and reasoning) that pertain to engineering skills are proven to exist—most mathematical geniuses are male—and do lead to opportunities to earn more. Most musical composers are male, as are leading singers and musicians, due not to prejudice but to some combination of ability, drive, and popular demand. The best, and most highly paid, professional athletes are male, for obvious reasons, and by public demand. Women are still statistically less willing than men to relocate for higher pay, or during times of unemployment in their home area. The list goes on and on.

Because of all the factors above, men have more money to invest in money-making opportunities and make money from their investments. But regardless of what justification there might be, academia and the media continue to throw the one-two punch of studies and publicity to promote the belief that women's lower pay levels are due exclusively to discriminatory factors.

The attempt to place the blame only on discriminatory factors is only one example of thousands of the unfair, untrue biases academia and the media intentionally promote. It would be difficult, if not impossible, to prove that this highly encouraged misconception has been promoted consciously. It would be equally difficult to prove it has *not* been put forth with the conscious effort of many. Realistically, no author or researcher who produces such material can lay claim to objectivity on this subject without being morally and intellectually negligent.

Academia is an important pro-feminist supporter. It creates feminists. It creates new feminist theories. It conducts studies to support and rationalize feminist theories. It pays feminists good money, while they work to advance feminist causes. It is almost as if sociologists in academic settings don't believe that there has ever been a society which developed in response to the basic principles of human nature, either common to both sexes, or identifiable as belonging to one sex or the other. It is as if they believe that easily recognizable, universal, behavioral differences between men and women are nothing more than a series of coincidences. Today's social scientists are best described as feminists. They believe society can be designed so as to successfully sidestep human nature, so as to erase human nature, or they believe that there is no such thing as human nature to begin with. George Gilder, in his 1986 book, *Men and Marriage*, gives good insight into the ways modern sociologists think:

> In *Society*, Francoeur (a scientist-theologian and university professor) writes: "Hopefully ten, twenty, or perhaps more years from now Americans will be comfortable enough with our sexuality that we will not need to use explicit sexual behavior films" in the classroom. But until then, he makes clear in his article, students in his course at Farleigh Dickinson University will be required to attend a weekend workshop that he terms a "sexarama."
>
> It begins with soft-core openers—"a little lighthearted campy film on nudity,". . . . Then our liberated theologian gets down to business: nine full hours of movies on "the varieties of sex, with male and female masturbation; male and female homosexuality, and a couple of paraphilias films—sado-masochism, beastiality [sic], and the like."
>
> . . . There seems to be something about the great leveler, sex, that transforms the most somberly learned social scientists, editing the most highfalutin magazines, into prophets of a fatuous sociology of wet dreams. . . .
>
> What is interesting about these kinds of books and articles is the strange spectacle they afford, of high-ranking professors at prestigious state universities palling around with pimps and prostitutes, poring over pornography, sampling sessions of sexual therapy, investigating behavior at homosexual bars, attending orgies at Esalen—all, ultimately, at the expense of the American taxpayer, who supports what are humorously termed our institutions of higher learning.

Will there ever be a pendulum swing? As long as students and teachers continue to indoctrinate each other in the principles of feminism and lend support to the media, there will be no swing. Feminism will continue to grow as the dominating social force.

CHAPTER FIVE

A Rigged Debate and
A Lack of Logic

The feminist movement doesn't owe its success to only those previously mentioned contrived aspects of its modus operandi. There is far more to it than that. However, after recognizing those factors, we can begin to realize something else. In debate, with the exception of a very special few, those putting forth anti-feminist arguments have usually wound up being humiliated. If we look for reasons why this is so, we can come up with a long list.

Using talk shows as only a single example (though any arena of debate could be used as well), it becomes apparent that the pro-feminist representatives usually appear to be expert debaters, as compared to their opponents. They come across as having great knowledge of their subject, whether they actually do or not. In many ways, the reasons feminists have been winning individual debates is a small-scale illustration of why feminism is becoming reality.

Why have antifeminists fared so poorly in debates? First of all, it has never made sense for conservative-thinking men to even enter the fracas, other than for purely altruistic reasons. Because it so directly opposes prevailing thought, there is little to be gained by it personally. It has certainly not been a way to make a great deal of money, and why get involved in something (the debate) that has almost no chance to bring monetary profit and less chance to bring pleasure? And, due to the politically correct atmosphere, any male conservative who has entered the fracas has been made to look like the devil himself by feminist debaters who have acquired expertise at this.

In this instance, the debate process itself creates a significant amount of stress for men. In these brief, highly emotional, seemingly diplomatic, seemingly fair debates, men are routinely put down, condemned, and generally mistreated in ways at which the feminine sex excels. In arguments between men, even arguments that occur in public places, there always exists the potential for the eruption of physical violence. Because men are aware of this potential, in most cases, they will avoid making certain remarks to one another. Few men, unless they are absolutely convinced that they can physically triumph over an opponent, are willing to push the wrong buttons. The dance that men dance regarding these types of arguments, with so much possibility for pain and humiliation, is relatively unknown to women. In arguments with women, particularly arguments that occur in public, physically striking out at an opponent who has gone too far is not an option for most men. Feminists realize this and take advantage of the situation—frequently with glee. The stress on the male debater becomes incredible during this process, because the man must restrain himself from using physical force as a response to verbal abuse—even though he theoretically has it as an option. The arena of the debate (one of mixed company) also rules out undiplomatic verbal responses. Never having had to deal with disrespect at the level they do today, and never having had to deal with taking orders from women, men have not developed any mechanisms that would allow them to do so without experiencing a great deal of stress. The stress in these situations is such that it is another significant reason for male avoidance of this debate. There are many more men who are conservative in their thinking about relationships between the sexes than anyone realizes, yet few are willing to speak their views in public. As George Gilder has observed:

> In the entire world there is no job—so far as I know—so thankless as criticizing feminism. In general, feminists rarely read or fondle anything whatsoever except other feminists. Faced with a male anti-feminist, even conservatives cringe and curl their lips, thinking him somehow sullied by the contagion of his subject. . . .

Men cannot gain status in any kind of direct competition against women—on the basketball court, on the tennis court, in the work force, in debate, or any place else—even if they win. Status can only be lost. This, combined with all the other negative factors, and in the absence of any significant reward, has been sufficient reason for most men to stay clear of the debate. Men simply haven't become involved in the debate process on a full-time basis, as feminists have. The few men who are involved are feminists themselves—men like Phil Donahue and Alan Alda. Note, though, that these men stood to profit greatly from their efforts on behalf of the feminist cause. The popularity resulting from their publicly adopted positions has directly translated into financial reward. For the most part, however, through the entire developmental stages of feminism, the public debate has been for the most part exclusively between women.

This is not intended to suggest that men cannot win debates, but simply that, in regard to this subject, and in this era, the above reasons are why men haven't made the concerted effort that would be necessary to win them.

Conservative American women have also been outmatched in debates with rabid feminists. Although there are myriad reasons for this, only nine are listed below.

First, the great majority of the good, traditional-minded women of this country have different priorities than do feminists. They've been busy at what they believe to be important in life: being good wives to their husbands, and good mothers to their children—which includes ensuring that their children have a father to grow up with, if at all possible. These women are positive, contributing members of society, with little time to involve themselves in public matters that would take them away from what they know to be most important in life.

Second, feminist debaters have had, on average, far more education than the women who have devoted themselves to their families. This has been almost assured, because if a young woman did go off to college with high morals, as a thoughtful conservative, to become "educated," she would be unlikely to leave any college in this country, four years later, feeling the need to debate *against* the logic of feminism. On the contrary, after having listened to four years of feminist dogma, both in and out of the classroom, she would be more apt to repudiate every value her parents ever tried to instill in her.[1]

Third, full-time careers (of the type in which learning is an ongoing requirement) can be had from supporting feminism. There has

---

[1] She certainly wouldn't have had her choice of over 500 universities across the country wherein she might reinforce her values of social conservatism!

been an abundance of both media positions and teaching positions open to feminists. Career opportunities such as these aren't available to those supporting traditional thought. Women in these "careers" have naturally become experts on pro-feminist arguments, it being their business.[2]

Fourth, feminists have had "quasi-facts" and pro-feminist theories supplied to them, by both academia and the mass media across this entire country, on a daily basis.[3] Conservative journalists, who might support traditional views, haven't been allowed a voice in mainstream newspapers for thirty years.

Fifth, conservative women have been faced in debates by women who aren't simply pro-feminism, but, because of their positions, are usually strident feminists—women very powerfully motivated to act and speak out on behalf of feminism—women motivated by the tactics the movement uses to generate strong feelings of discontent, mistrust, and hatred of men.

Sixth, feminist thinkers have mastered euphemism and spin control. They have made a science of twisting and turning words and phrases to put important issues in a strongly positive or negative light. Feminists don't believe in abortion, but only in "choice." That certainly sounds harmless enough. Feminists don't want to deprive men of the historical and universal freedom to hire and work side by side with other men, they only want "equal rights." According to feminists, however, the other side of the coin is not so innocent: men don't want the right to work shoulder to shoulder with other men, or to hire discriminately; instead, men want to do that heinous thing —"discriminate." As quoted in the *Atlantic Monthly*: "'We put sex-discrimination provisions into everything.' Representative Bella Abzug once recalled about the 1971–1972 congressional session. 'There was no opposition. Who'd be against equal rights for women? So we just kept passing women's-rights legislation.'"

When a sexually promiscuous girl gets pregnant in early pube-

---

[2] This factor not only provides feminists an advantage in expertise, but also in the number of expert debaters to pool from. As the number of people in any competition increases, the number of "high caliber" competitors will generally increase, as well.

[3] On the other hand, anyone looking for recent articles supporting "traditional thought" in regard to social issues, has generally been constrained to look in the letters-to-the-editor sections of local newspapers.

scence, because of personal irresponsibility or irresponsible parenting, we don't hear any argument from feminists that mothers would be well-advised to spend a little more time with their daughters, perhaps teaching them about the facts of life; or that mothers might be wise to retain a little more authority over their 15-year-old girls; or even about the fact that unbridled promiscuity might not be a good thing, and that some degree of chastity wouldn't necessarily be harmful. What do we hear from feminists beyond women having choices? Only more requests for pity and compassion: "Think of the poor child and her child-to-be . . . "; and easy sounding solutions, such as, "once our school systems are effectively teaching every known form of birth control, all problems related to our sexuality will be solved." In listening to feminist debates, you would think their wants to be incredibly few, and that life will be nothing but hellish without them.

Seventh, pro-feminist debaters (whether female or male) aren't faced with the severe pressures that result from going against the flow in our politically correct atmosphere, nor do anti-feminist debaters get the "sisterly" support that comes from activist organizations like N.O.W., The Gay and Lesbian Task Force, and Planned Parenthood.

Eighth, feminists have had the benefit of historical hindsight while debating against traditional lifestyles and traditional societies, as opposed to the ones they envision. As discussed, feminists have long done their best to paint pre-movement history in the worst light possible to help their debate, at the same time claiming that once their philosophies come to dominate, the world will be perfect.[4]

Ninth, whether or not they are cognizant of it, media personnel from Oprah Winfrey to Phil Donahue to Dan Rather, having been taught in a liberal educational system and being in tune with its substantially pro-feminist beliefs, assist feminists in televised debates and in encounters described as "discussions," which really are debates.

For a combination of these and other reasons, the women who have debated against feminism have usually expressed *extremely* conservative viewpoints. For many of these women, it has been the fact that

---

[4] The anti-feminist, though, has relatively little past history to critique, save the societal degeneration since feminism's inception, and feminists promptly claim this to be left over from patriarchy and from society's (in particular, the male portion of society) failure to have yet adapted.

feminism contradicts an extremely strong belief in strict adherence to the principles of Christianity that has motivated them to speak out in the face of the feminist onslaught. Their arguments for conservatism, regardless of the merits they possess, are extremely difficult to communicate fully in the brief time usually allotted. This is in comparison to the "scientifically developed," seemingly simple, righteous-sounding arguments feminists have practiced and learned to rely upon. Many conservative arguments, based as they are on the principles of Christianity, have been disallowed, ignored, or treated as though they are meaningless simply because of their relationship to religion.

Short debates, verbal or otherwise, are not the place to argue against feminism. Its arguments are simply too easily put forth, too often easily rehearsed. The pro-feminist debater, having heard the litany of feminist dogma a million times via the media, will have a repertoire of claims, counter-claims, accusations, and defenses at easy reach and is, thus, very difficult to debate.

Nevertheless, feminism can be debated. On his own, anti-feminist radio personality Rush Limbaugh has had a great impact on how millions of listeners now think about feminism. But he has had the rare luxury of a daily forum to do this. And he has faced tremendous ridicule for expressing his viewpoints. Tellingly, in the past 20 years, he is one of only a handful of individuals even given the opportunity in the media (or, one could say, "allowed to exercise his *right*") to speak out on a daily basis against feminism.

Because of the fact that the argument over feminism has been as twisted and lopsided as our media and academic institutions' promotion of it, results from the debate should neither be accepted as right, nor treated lightly. The ways in which the debate over feminism has unfolded have been as contrived and illogical as feminism itself.

Virtually the entire feminist movement is based on illogic. Though a man's abilities to think, rationalize, and act logically may be impacted by his needs to achieve, a woman's abilities to think and act rationally are impacted by the very essence of her nature. Women have never been stereotyped as being the logical sex anywhere, and because of this, it shouldn't be surprising that a movement led by women is illogical. In an attempt to explain this, it has been said that men use logic to form conclusions and that women form conclusions based on their feelings, then use logic—after the fact—to try to justify those con-clusions. In other words men base their conclusions on logic, women base theirs on emotions. This probably comes close to explaining why, when the emotion is taken out of the pro-feminist debate, all that is left is the illogic of feminism. As with the above statement, the following is not a truism regarding all women, of course, but in developing an understanding of the irrationality of feminism, there is unarguably substantive truth to it, and it is unarguably a serious factor that deserves discussion. As business woman Edith Melvin wrote in *A Business Women's View of Suffrage*: "The instability of the female mind is beyond the comprehension of the majority of men. . ." A serious factor the more we realize to what degree feminists are guiding us into the future. Life is not a basketball game, it is more important, but an analogy including the game of basketball can be made. When deciding whose logic will lead us into the future, we need the best team on the court, and the best team is not women, any more than the women's olympic team is superior to the men's.

The illogic of feminism, in fact, results from attempts to justify or rationalize feelings or the emotional component of feminism's agenda. The primary example of this, and a key to the majority of feminism's most basic arguments, is the assertion by feminists (spoken or not) that there are no "truly significant," inherent differences between the sexes.[5] The feminist denial that differences exist is necessitated by their perpetual arguments that because men do something, women should do it also, or because women don't do something, men shouldn't do it either. In short, it forms the basis of the argument that there are no inherent reasons men have universally felt the need to male bond, discriminate, achieve and be patriarchal. Or, in other words, felt the need to be men. This denial also provides justification for the sub-sequent argument that since there are no significant, inherent differ-ences, there are then no reasons boys and girls should be brought up in any way different from one another, or live in any way different

---

[5] Feminists claim that any recognizable drives and emotions possessed primarily by one sex or the other are solely the results of our socialization processes. They make the Lockean claim that men and women are born with equally "blank slates," and are virtually endlessly malleable—they will, however, admit that there are exceptions to this, and any rule for that matter, when doing so serves to assist in furthering a goal.

from one another as children or adults. In the end, feminism both builds and rests its entire case on this illogical assumption.

Recent history has shown that feminists will go to any length to find ways to justify their ambitions. Among other things, feminists have argued that there is no need for marriage, or for fathers in families, because the nuclear family is a dysfunctional social unit anyway; they argue that there is no level of promiscuity that can be considered harmful; and they argue that women should be allowed to perform any combat role, as a right. The following example epitomizes the astounding lengths to which feminists may go with feminist illogic to rationalize their desires, or what they perceive as their needs. It is also an appropriate example of the type of feminist arguments we are continually faced with.

Shortly after the Persian Gulf War, despite attempts to scuttle it, the story came out in the press about Major Rhonda Cornum being sexually violated while held captive by the Iraqis. Under the circumstances, her being violated was bad enough, but her statements about it afterwards revealed a serious assault on her *psyche* that presumably preceded the physical assault.

> Everyone's made such a big deal about this indecent assault. But the only thing that makes it indecent is that it was non-consensual. I asked myself, "Is it going to prevent me from getting out of here? Is there a risk of death attached to it? Is it permanently disabling? Is it permanently disfiguring? Lastly, is it excruciating?" If it doesn't fit one of those five categories, then it isn't important.

In this case, feminist Major Cornum used feminist logic in an attempt to ease her concerns that women won't be allowed in combat for fear that those who become prisoners will be raped, and will suffer the normal, negative consequences of being raped. In other words, for the right to fight in combat alongside men, she is willing to deny that being raped is either excruciating or even important!

Rape is a serious crime, and should continue to be considered so. It should be punished severely because rape is one of the most traumatic events anyone (male or female) can experience. Most of us wouldn't want to live in a society where rape was classified only as "indecent," as Major Cornum would have us believe, rather than as important or excruciating. Such a society would dehumanize all of us, and would further de-feminize women. Neither of these things is desirable, regardless of the fact there is no absolute proof that rape need inherently be emotionally traumatizing to women, as Cornum has pointed out. From Major Cornum's point of view, forcing sex upon unwilling women could be looked upon as being of no more discomfort to those women—after proper training—than doing 50 sit-ups.

Feminists use illogic to turn around such "old fashioned" concepts as the propriety of people feeling some sort of guilt when making the choice to be promiscuous. Instead, they attempt to make anyone confirming the virtues of chastity feel the guilt. Feminists disbelieve that high levels of promiscuity may be harmful in some way to individuals, to long-term relationships, or to society.

A pertinent example of the illogic of feminism appeared, in the form of a review, in the "Books" section of the *San Jose Mercury News*, on June 26, 1994. The review is written by Frances K. Conley, a professor of neurosurgery at Stanford University School of Medicine, and "the first woman finisher in the 1971 Bay-to-Breakers footrace across San Francisco." The book reviewed is a feminist attack against professional football entitled, *The Stronger Women Get, The More Men Love Football*. Interestingly, the book is written by Mariah Burton Nelson, a "former Stanford University and professional basketball player" who "continues to coach girls basketball." Without personally reading the book, directly commenting upon it would be unfair, but the review itself raises enough questions about feminist illogic that it will suffice:

> The dominant emotion that shrieks from the pages of Mariah Burton Nelson's latest book is anger, and if one can absorb this rage to the extent of looking beyond it, one finds a well-written, anecdote-rich study of sport and its impact on society, gender relationships and education programs in the United States.

As can be seen from this direct quote, the first thing the reader is asked to do is "absorb this rage" (the emotion), so as to look beyond it. In other words, reader, take this anger toward men, consider it normal and justified, and make it a part of yourself. The review goes on:

> Body shape, size and power are a determinant of success in athletics and, as such, serve to maintain gender difference. Once women "intrude" in a sport, it no longer serves as a yardstick for masculinity.

Ice skating, swimming, gymnastics, distance running and increasingly tennis, volleyball and even soccer are sports where participation by women has blurred gender variability. As Burton Nelson's title indicates, football is the last bastion where men can be men; a spectator sport where men identify strongly with their hero(es), vicariously enjoying men destroying other men, on a stage where women are objectified as the ultimate sex object in flimsy costumes and without a voice.

The first part of the first sentence here is a statement of the obvious. The second part, about "serving to maintain gender difference," is surprising only in that it admits that gender differences do exist —something the reviewer and the author evidently wish they could change. The business about women's intrusion into a sport blurring "gender variability" seems to be wishful thinking. The reviewer's by-line is graphic proof that gender variability is not blurred by women's participation—she was the "first *woman* finisher" in that footrace (emphasis added). Without doubt, she finished the race ahead of any number of men who were less fit than she, and slower than she, but she also presumably finished the race behind a number of men who fit neither description. There are almost no professional sporting events where men and women compete head to head against each other, with the exception of mixed doubles tennis events where each team consists of one man and one woman.

As to football's being the "last bastion where men can be men; a spectator sport where men identify strongly with their hero(es), vicariously enjoying men destroying other men," again this is patently false. We could point to World Cup soccer and note that there are no women players. We could point to Davis Cup tennis and note the absence of women on the courts. We could point to professional boxing and note the lack of female contenders. But regardless of which of these sports we chose to examine, the one place we wouldn't find a lack of women would be in the audience. Perhaps female fans don't "identify strongly" with the male athletes they watch and admire, but they seem happy nevertheless to watch and admire the skill, the grace, the strength, and the courage of the athletes. But our reviewer, Conley, is far from finished:

And, while the majority of men don't have the physique or talent to play big-time football, it is a ritualistic sport all have been exposed to. That exposure has taught and continues to teach men about the superiority of men vis-a-vis women.

How does it hate women? Let us count the ways: The ultimate insult to a male athlete is to be called woman, in degrading, demeaning terminology. Young men learn to debase women, learn how to conquer, to "score," to "penetrate". . . . Women are objects to be used and trashed.

As to football's being "a ritualistic sport all [men] have been exposed to," one that teaches men "about the superiority of men vis-a-vis women," there is, perhaps, finally, a grain of truth to what Conley says. Perhaps men are bigger, faster, and stronger, in general, than are women. And, if football is a sport that draws on size and speed and strength to the extent that women cannot compete, so be it.

Whether the "ultimate insult to a male athlete is to be called woman, in degrading, demeaning terminology" or not, it certainly is an insult to the great majority of men. In just the same way, most women would be insulted if they were called "man," in degrading, demeaning terminology. Few individuals, of either sex, enjoy being degraded or demeaned. There are, of course, those women who would consider being perceived as manly the ultimate compliment, just as there are some men who would consider being perceived as feminine the ultimate compliment. As a percentage of the entire population, neither of these groups occurs in particularly large numbers. And none of that has much of anything to do with teaching men to "hate" women. O.J. Simpson's situation notwithstanding, there are any number of professional football players whose domestic lives are unlikely to end up in the headlines. The fact that some few of these players do have a difficulty that brings notoriety is no more a logical reason to cast aspersions on all of them than is the misbehavior of one woman athlete (Tonya Harding, for example) a logical reason to call for the cancellation of all women's athletic programs. The review goes on:

> The sport (football) teaches homophobia along with misogyny. The author contends that viewing the male body is far more exciting to men than it is to most women. "Football is narcissism; a male love affair with the male gender." Because it is sport, body admiration, touching, patting and hugging are practiced and condoned by, and to, men in ways that would not be accepted in other environments. Women

who excel in the more "manly" athletics (not skating or gymnastics) often are called what is considered the ultimate insult—to be labeled lesbians or dykes.

There can be no doubt that football and other strenuous athletic sports teach those who play them to admire and respect strength over weakness. The author, or the reviewer, translates this to mean that these sports teach homophobia and misogyny. Logical? No. If this were the case, then women's basketball, women's soccer, and any other strenuous women's sports are equally guilty. Those are activities that glorify speed, strength, physical stamina, and mental toughness, in exactly the same way that football does.

The author's contention that football is "a male love affair with the male gender" could be made with equal validity for any women's sport. But, to do so is to rely on the same sort of illogic that the author and the reviewer do. On the one hand, they claim that football teaches homophobia, and on the other hand they claim the opposite—that it encourages homosexual delight among both players and viewers. What is more likely is that players who form a part of a team engaged in strenuous physical effort, whether male or female, encourage and congratulate each other through physical contact. Does that translate directly into homosexual desire? Perhaps in some cases it does, but most assuredly those cases form the minority. Professional football (and most other professional sports as well) is no doubt a "love affair"—the public loves its successful athletes—but it is physical prowess that the public (both men and women) loves.

As to the "women who excel in the more 'manly' athletics" being "labeled lesbians or dykes" there are certainly a fair number of female athletes who have succeeded above the norm who have claimed to have homosexual preferences. In the face of the lack of scientific or statistical evidence, it would be foolhardy to suggest to what degree, or for what reasons, these women succeed in their chosen sports, but it would not be difficult to compile a list of names familiar to the public who admit to practicing such a lifestyle.

For those who may not be aware of the history of the sport of football, it was not always the media circus it is today. Football arrived in the United States in the early nineteenth century, as rugby, and from there evolved into a sport that, on the whole, is much safer and less bloody than its parent game. The point is that when football was increasing its popularity—during the late nineteenth and early twentieth centuries—no one, male or female, was inclined to think that it taught homophobia or misogyny, nor would they necessarily have thought that a game which taught homophobia was a negative game. Granted that times have changed in this regard; there are now greater numbers of homosexuals in our population (at least greater numbers of avowed homosexuals), but this seems irrelevant to the point.

With all the illogical claims made by Burton Nelson and her reviewer, Conley, we might be well advised to inquire why Harcourt Brace would opt to publish this book. What we would undoubtedly find is that it is at this very point that the "illogic" comes to a dead stop. The folks at Harcourt Brace are familiar enough with the demographics of their customer base to know that more than 70 percent of the book-buying public in the U.S. is comprised of women. This, then, is the sort of book that Harcourt Brace perceives will be well-received. They may very likely make a great deal of money by releasing it and promoting it. The fact that they can so easily have such a book reviewed by someone as sympathetic to its claims as Frances K. Conley and, just as easily, have it promoted free of charge in the mainstream mass media is simply icing on the cake.

Other evidence of the illogic of feminism is the inability of its philosophies to withstand the test of time. The philosophies of many other systems of belief have withstood that test. For example, over 2,000 years ago, Confucius had the wisdom to state, "The strength of a nation derives from the integrity of the home." Two thousand years from now, feminists will have no such quotes. In fact, the beliefs of feminists change with alarming frequency. In the 1970s, most feminist dogma included ridicule of male competitions, claiming they were detrimental to society. Today's feminists talk about the wonderful opportunities young "ladies" will have to show off their abilities to bench-press (a weightlifting event) and to play ice hockey at future Olympics, even to wrestle against highschool boys. (Note that there is a U.S. women's wrestling team).

In his book, *Inevitability of Patriarchy*, Steven Goldberg notes the consistency of sexist wisdom between cultures:

It might be worth noting . . . how seldom the aphorisms and proverbs concerning masculine and feminine qualities contradict one another no matter how disparate the societies that produced them. Could this not be because such aphorisms and proverbs have long since penetrated to the core of our nature to find the truths whose physical correlates we are only now discovering? It would hardly be the first time that wisdom preceded knowledge.

This is why old sayings about men and women (pointing to differences) are still around—they're true.

Feminine logic, or lack thereof, may be one of the most precise reasons there has never been anything other than patriarchic societies: once feminine logic began to be the dominant logic of a society, the shortcomings of that same logic doomed it.

CHAPTER SIX

Truly Different

Feminist illogic aside, the first reality about the two sexes is that they are drastically different from one another in some very important ways that need to be recognized.

Normally, the first thing people notice about a new person they are meeting is whether that person is a man or a woman, a boy or a girl. This information is important to each of us as individuals, because it provides a partial basis for the expectations we develop within the first few moments of the encounter, and the ways in which we are likely to behave toward the newcomer from that point onward. If the new person is male, a male will expect particular things and begin the interaction in one manner; if the new person is female, he will expect different things and proceed differently. Conversely, if the new person is a male, a female will expect particular things and begin the interaction in one manner; if the new person is a female, she will expect different things and proceed differently.

We develop these expectations (and the behaviors that follow from them) on our understanding of whether the new person is the same as we are, or different from us. Much the same sort of process occurs as we identify whether the new person shares our ethnic background, our age group, our language, our national heritage, our religious beliefs, our political philosophy, etc.

Of all the characteristics we note about the new person, however, the most fundamental is sex. In terms of sex, a new person can only be either the same as us, or the opposite of us. And sexual difference automatically guarantees experiential differences. For "feminist logic" aside, the first reality about the two sexes is that they are dramatically different from one another in ways that are insurmountable. Science is increasingly proving what every society has recognized: Men and women have significant neurological, hormonal, and behavioral differences. Observation and study tell us that in line with these differences, the two sexes have had (and still do have) different roles and behaviors in all societies.

One of the biggest lies that feminists seek to perpetuate—in terms of both dimension and significance—is that the sexes are not universally, inherently, or significantly different. In fact, that argument is the keystone which supports the entire construct of feminist hypotheses. Basically, feminist ideology maintains that we should socialize and educate boys and girls exactly alike, so that women will be prepared to think, work, and achieve, to compete, lead, and exert authority, on an equal basis with men. In essence, feminism is the belief that women's fulfilling traditionally masculine roles is preferable to their fulfilling universal, traditionally feminine roles. A doctrinal feminist would only admit that there are differences between the sexes when the admission would serve to elevate women, denigrate men, or to somehow advance the feminist agenda.

As has been the case whenever humankind chose to disregard natural law, the attempt to socialize boys and girls as if they were the same has the potential for disastrous long-term consequences, which we are incapable of predicting completely.

To ignore or deny our differences, when contemplating or suggesting ways in which to socialize ourselves, is more than just an attempt to ignore nature, it is actually an attempt to rule nature. George Gilder put it this way in his book *Men and Marriage*:

> the differences between the sexes are the single most important fact of human society . . . the drive to deny them—in the name of women's liberation, marital openness, sexual equality, erotic consumption, or homosexual romanticism—must be one of the most quixotic crusades in the history of the species.

Anne Moir, a Ph.D. in genetics, and David Jessel are authors of *Brain Sex*, a 1989 scientific study on our sex-based differences. They write:

> Men are different from women. They are equal only in their common membership of the same species, humankind. To maintain that they are the same in aptitude, skill or behaviour is to build a society based on a biological and scientific lie.

The truth is that for virtually our entire tenancy of the planet, we have been a sexist species. Our biology assigned separate functions to the male and female of *Homo sapiens*. Our evolution strengthened and refined those differences. Our civilisation reflected them. Our religion and our education reinforced them.

Many feminists deny the universality of patriarchy, but the truth is that there has never been a society that wasn't patriarchal. The history of patriarchy is as old as the history of humankind. In fact, patriarchy (along with male dominance in interpersonal relationships) is one of the defining characteristics pointing to the differences between the sexes.[1]

Steven Goldberg, who makes this subject the focus of his studies, writes:

> Patriarchy is any system of organization (political, economic, religious, or social) that associates authority and leadership primarily with males and in which males fill the vast majority of authority and leadership positions. . . . Patriarchy is universal. For all the variety different societies have demonstrated in developing different types of political, economic, religious, and social systems, there has never been a society that has failed to associate authority and leadership in these areas with men. No anthropologist contests the fact that patriarchy is universal. Indeed, of all social institutions there is probably none whose universality is so totally agreed upon. While I think it fair to say that most anthropologists consider the family, marriage, and the incest taboo universal—and believe that, while it is easy to imagine societies without one or more of these institutions, no real society could survive without them—with each of these institutions anthropologists debate problems of definition and borderline cases. There is not, nor has there ever been, any society that even remotely failed to associate authority and leadership in suprafamilial areas with the male. . . . I have consulted the original ethnographic materials on every society I have ever seen associated with matriarchy, female dominance, or the association of high-status roles with women. I have been unable to find one which represents any of these.

Even Gerda Lerner, famed historian and feminist, and author of *The Creation of Patriarchy*—though seemingly reluctant to do so—admits in her book that there has never been a matriarchal society:

---

[1] It would be impossible to conclude that the universally patriarchal structure of the more than 5,000 cultures studied by anthropologists could be the result of coincidence.

Those who define matriarchy as a society where women dominate over men, a sort of inversion of patriarchy, cannot cite anthropological, ethnological, or historic evidence. They rest their case on evidence from myth and religion. . . . It may be noted that I am defining matriarchy as the mirror image of patriarchy. Using that definition, I would conclude that no matriarchal society has ever existed.

There have been, and still are, goddesses or female deities to worship, but these have been allowed by men. And none of them has been associated with high authority over culture; instead, each has been associated with motherhood, creation, etc.

Given the era in which we exist, it is not surprising that there are very few current books available which discuss either the nature of patriarchy's existence, or the fact of its universality. It is also not surprising that books which make the invalid claim for the past existence of successful matriarchies are comparatively plentiful.

The individual "nuclear family" mirrors the patriarchal structure of society. The majority of all families are patriarchal, or male dominant in structure. Steven Goldberg confirms this:

Male dominance refers to the feeling acknowledged by the emotions of both men and women that the woman's will is somehow subordinate to the male's and that general authority . . . ultimately resides in the male. . . . As was the case with patriarchy, male dominance is universal: no society has ever failed to conform its expectations of men and women, and the social roles relevant to these expectations of men and women that it is the male who "takes the lead." Every society accepts the existence of these feelings, and conforms to their existence by socializing children accordingly, because every society must. . . ."

In the human species, male dominance is the natural and instinctively programmed existence. Though it doesn't make sense to compare humans with less-evolved animals—especially the non-primates—feminists do it anyway. They argue that because there are animal species which are organized in matriarchal systems, we cannot legitimately make the assumption that humans are naturally patriarchal. Hamsters and hyenas are the two primary mammalian examples feminists offer up for comparison. While it may be true that these animals have matriarchal social systems, they have virtually nothing in common with humans, including the fact that in both species, the females are characteristically considerably larger than the males.

If we are going to compare humans to less-evolved animals, the only logical choice would be to compare ourselves to primates. In all primate species (regardless of whether or not there is a significant size difference between sexes), the males are more aggressive and are dominant over the females.

That patriarchy and male dominance are, in the "general sense," natural to humans should be unhesitatingly accepted because the survival of human civilization depends on that acceptance. When women are allowed into male hierarchies, the effectiveness of those hierarchies is immediately imperiled. Realizing that the human species is virtually entirely hierarchical in its infrastructure, this becomes more important. For example, corporations are hierarchical, as are school systems, book and newspaper publishing companies, churches, governments (even if elected democratically), etc. The more important or critical the hierarchy is to the success of the society, the greater the peril.

The political scene in Norway shows some of the interconnected effects resulting from the entrance of women into male hierarchies. The first impact is that the male's status within such hierarchies declines, changing the type of males entering such hierarchies. The most capable, aggressive, achievement-oriented and status-oriented men (often those with the most outstanding leadership potential) either leave those hierarchies, or avoid entering them, for this reason alone. This has an immediate compounding effect of lowering the status of the hierarchy itself. Those outside of the hierarchy—especially men—can see the changes, lessening their respect and trust in the ability of the hierarchy. (Unfortunately, this does not necessarily diminish the hierarchy's ability to impact their lives, or have influence over them. Such impact is, as often as not, wielded against the unwilling.) As *The European* has reported, this is what has happened in Norway:

> Political commentators in Oslo see the rise of women in Norwegian politics as a hollow victory. Andreas Hompland, a sociologist and former editor of Dagbladet, believes that men have ceased to compete so hard for political office because they feel that real power now lies elsewhere. Politicians' salaries have significantly declined in real terms over the past 15 years, while their social standing has plummeted.
>
> There is abundant evidence of the general male exodus from politics into more lucrative positions in industry and the public sector.

A key challenger to Kullman Five, for the Conservative Party chairmanship, former Finance Minister Arne Skauge, 43, withdrew from the leadership race, deciding instead to leave politics at the end of the next parliamentary session to become director of a leading bank, at twice the salary. Female politicians have not followed this trend (of declining public office), and there are still no women at the head of large Norwegian companies.

Norway is one of the European countries feminists most often use as an example of a country having the proper balance between men and women in positions of power. However, closer examination of the situation proves this is not exactly the case. In *Why Men Rule*, Steven Goldberg provides that closer examination, disclosing that while there may be large numbers of women in the national legislative body, the real political power of the country lies elsewhere:

> Norway, for example, which has a higher percentage of women in its unicameral house than does any other nation, places an unusual degree of power in the hands of its municipal councils; 443 of 454 municipal council chairpersons are men. Males outnumber females at the judicial level 15:3 (Supreme Court), 63:7 (Appellate Court), and 182:25 (district city courts). In general, "the large disparity in the distribution of women and men in political bodies continues to apply" and, in the Parliament, "the greatest numbers of women are to be found in committees that deal with matters relating to the family, education, and social welfare" (areas with relatively low social status). "The predominance of men is far greater in committees within major economic sectors such as commerce, industry, and oil."

Once a hierarchy becomes bisexual, it is profoundly changed. The public's trust in the wisdom of its leadership is justifiably lowered. Entered by women who desire to interact and compete with men for leadership, and the power influence brings, these hierarchies eventually become filled with a preponderance of status-oriented, achievement-oriented aggressive women, inclined to argue, and disinclined to capitulate or compromise. This is just the opposite of those male members who stay on. Some leave due to the status drop, others due to other factors. For reasons discussed earlier, and to be discussed later, continually arguing with women is something most men avoid for a variety of discomfiting reasons. In any hierarchy, competition exists for high authority positions, and, for men—competition with women is a no win proposition. In competition with women, status cannot be gained, it can only be lost, frequently in humiliating fashion.

For all these reasons, the remaining male members concede to the will of the new female members. In time, there ceases to be conflict within the hierarchy because the men are willing to acquiesce. In time, they frequently even come to think like women. It is because of these basic realities that eventually these hierarchies come to reflect the logic and perceived interests of women.

As previously stated, this has already occurred with the most important institutions of influence in this country. A few bull-headed, unindoctrinated men remain in positions of power within these institutions, but the bulk of such men now reside outside of these institutions, primarily either as independent capitalists or as dropouts.[2]

The impact of women's involvement in all hierarchies can be easily observed in this country. It can be seen that the institutions in which women have been allowed to participate have capitulated to feminist thought. And, whether it be the government, media, academia or the elementary education system, the public's trust and respect for these institutions has deteriorated.

It is a frequently repeated truism that if all the money in the world were gathered together and redistributed equally, it would be a very short time before it all found its way back into the hands of the current owners. The same is undoubtedly true in the case of personal and political power. Men are more driven to seek power of this sort than are women; thus, men will continue to exercise dominance in interpersonal relationships and in society at large.

---

[2] It is worth noting that capitalists are beginning to accede to the logic of feminism, or are willing to promote it for economic gain. Saturn, the new American car company, provides an example of this promotion of feminism in its current advertising campaign:

The Saturn difference really lies in the ability to do things other companies— groups of people working together—only dreamed of. Things like changing the way labor and management interact, or the way a customer is treated when *she* walks into a showroom. Small things really; seemingly insignificant. *Until you add them all up.*

CHAPTER SEVEN

The Role of Self-Esteem

Of all the differences between men and women, the ways in which self-esteem affects the members of each sex may be the most important. Unfortunately, they are among the most misunderstood of our differences. They are also a very big part of what is wrong with the philosophical foundations of feminism, because feminists at nearly every level of commitment deny that any differences exist, whatsoever.

The connections of feminism and women's self-esteem are endless. The pursuit of self-esteem motivated the original feminist leaders to expend tremendous time and energy in organizing and recruiting. The false promise of increased self-esteem has driven countless thousands of women to join and support the feminist movement. And put simply, when feminists clamor for "respect" for women, what they are really clamoring for is self-esteem. But the issue is not simply whether women deserve to be respected and held in esteem—in their own eyes, or in the eyes of others. (Of course, women do.) The real issues are these: 1) Do women need to fill the same roles and achieve the same things as men, in order to gain and maintain positive self-esteem, happiness, and contentment? and: 2) Do women need to be respected in the same ways and for the same reasons as men, any more than men need to be respected in the same ways and for the same reasons as women? The answer to both these questions is no, because men and women are inherently different.

The importance of "inherent," universal, self-esteem differences between the sexes may not be adequately recognized or discussed in any society in the world, including that of our own country. Many men understand this importance intuitively, but for a variety of reasons are disinclined to talk about it, especially in public. In all likelihood at least as many women also understand it, but even fewer of them are inclined toward public discussion. It is almost as though, as a group, they refuse to accept their own knowledge of the truth. Among women, the continual denial of the truth of our differences is primarily the result of the falsehoods common to feminist teachings over the past 30 years.

Self-esteem is very briefly defined by Webster's Dictionary as a confidence and satisfaction in oneself. While this is undoubtedly true, it tells us nothing about how self-esteem is obtained. Nor does it tell us the ways in which the lack of it, the possession of it, or the drive to obtain it, impacts us and influences our daily lives.

Our level of self-esteem is basically a reflection of our opinion of ourselves. This opinion of self is largely determined by whether we feel we have met, or are capable of and likely to meet, our own moral and behavioral standards. Because the standards we impose upon ourselves are both conscious and subconscious, few of us can consciously control our self-esteem. In fact, few of us are capable even of objectively assessing our own level of self-esteem.

The standards we set for ourselves individually are partly determined by both our genetics and background. For most of us, self-esteem will be influenced by comparison to other people important in our lives—parents, siblings, friends, peers, co-workers, and lovers. It will also be influenced by our perception of how those same people think of us. This is the reason such words as "I love you," "Nice job," or, "You look great," can mean so much when they come from anyone on the list of people we wish to impress. Interestingly, this list can even include people we meet only once in our lives.

In general, if we have met the standards we set for ourselves, are content with our proximity to them, or even believe that we will meet them, we will have a healthy level of self-esteem. Conversely, if we have failed to meet these standards (especially if the failure is severe) or have no confidence we will be able to meet them, we will have poor self-esteem. The difference between our standards and our achievements (taking into account our confidence in future achievements) could be referred to as the "self-esteem factor." The greater a person's "self-esteem factor," the more probable it is that he or she will be plagued by the need to increase self-esteem.[1]

For lack of any other standard of comparison, the goals we set for ourselves almost always require that we use others as a measuring stick. Our goals are usually determined by our observations and perceptions of those we relate to on a regular basis—parents, siblings, friends, peers from school or work, and lovers or spouses—or those we adopt as role models.

As children we typically compare ourselves to siblings and friends, while trying to impress and receive approval from our parents. In adolescence we might compare ourselves to friends, as well as trying to impress them, while seeming not to care what our parents think. As young adults we may compare ourselves to friends, siblings, and parents, while also trying to impress them all and gain their respect. If, having measured ourselves, we feel we compare favorably to those we have chosen, and feel we have impressed those we wish to impress, we should at that time have a relatively healthy self-esteem.

The things we must accomplish in order to compare favorably to friends, peers, siblings, parents, and spouses (earning their respect and approval) are numerous, complex, and difficult to achieve. Different societies possess differing lists of typical hurdles an individual must overcome in order to develop self-esteem.[2] These could be referred to as "possible preconditions." Some of these preconditions are universal, even if the lists appear to vary greatly. What an individual needs to accomplish ("possible preconditions") in Japan, to attain positive self-esteem, would not be the same for an individual in the Yucatan. However, there are sex-based similarities.

In America today, the list of possible preconditions we face is changing so fast as to be confusing, or even unrecognizable to young and old

---

[1] The higher the goals, the more a person will need to achieve in order to obtain healthy self-esteem, and vice versa. What might seem a great achievement to one individual need not correspond to the feeling of achievement of another. A Special Olympian may well feel euphoric after high-jumping three feet. The world-class athlete who jumped "only" seven feet would be disappointed. But the person setting the most easily attainable goals would not necessarily have any greater likelihood of maintaining healthy self-esteem, because each of us needs to be challenged to one degree or another.

[2] Some people live in societies that impede the individual's quest, others live in societies that encourage and assist them.

alike. This creates serious problems. The feminist movement's methodical attempts to remove natural sex-roles only aggravates those problems.

The following is a brief list of possible preconditions individuals in our society might face in order to develop positive self-esteem: a reasonable amount of love, security, positive attention and training from parents; academic success in school; toys and clothing comparable to those of peers; adequate numbers of supportive friendships; some degree of athletic achievement; some degree of social success; financial success; spousal and familial success; a level of career or social accomplishment comparable to that of parents; and acknowledgment of success from parents, spouse, family, friends, and peers. All at levels equal, or nearly equal, to inner expectations.[3]

There are many ways in which self-esteem can fail to develop. The development of self-esteem can be compared to the development of math skills. If we do not learn the basics of addition, subtraction, multiplication and division, we are likely to be thwarted in our attempts to learn math skills of increased difficulty. If we are not given the proper building blocks—the early chance in life to develop or build self-esteem—we will likely have greater difficulty with our self-esteem throughout life.

Children who don't receive adequate, ongoing attention and approval from their parents (optimally, *both* parents) are apt to make many unwise decisions and take many undesirable actions in their attempts—either conscious or subconscious—to replace that attention and approval.[4] Recognition and positive attention are the building

---

[3] The above is, of course, an extremely incomplete listing. In recent years, the list has grown enormously in size, and perhaps even more in the difficulty of achievement. Today, a healthy level of self-esteem is needed more than ever, to cope with and overcome the challenges we face in our rapidly changing modern society. Unfortunately, at this time we are experiencing the deterioration of certain traditional support structures, which previously aided individuals in meeting these challenges. This includes the loss of husbands, wives, mothers, fathers, and grandparents; the frequent moving away of friends; the decline of influence from schools, churches, and communities; and the absence of any form of widely recognized morals and values.

[4] From the earliest age, a child may resort to many types of behavior in order to receive attention. Understandably, children may not know, or care, whether the actions they take to garner such attention are positive or negative.

blocks for future development of self-esteem, but are by no means a guarantee that healthy self-esteem will be cultivated.

Frequent criticism, or a lack of parental attention and approval, can cause feelings of not being loved, personal inferiority, and dislike of self that can last a lifetime. If a child experiences a lack of attention because of attention lavished instead on a sibling, severe jealousy, or even hatred can result.

Emotions such as jealousy can be seen to occur universally, and at the earliest of ages.[5] Many of the negative emotions are actually direct offshoots of the need for, and drive toward, self-esteem. Feminists vacillate over whether or not such "instincts" exist. Their conclusions are situational, depending on what point of view happens to be to their advantage in any given argument.[6]

With adulthood, our struggle for self-esteem will not necessarily diminish. In fact, self-esteem may grow increasingly difficult to acquire and to maintain. The reason for this is that our relationships are often deeper—though frequently less secure—and we no longer compare ourselves to other children or adolescents. We now must compare ourselves to the same people we have sought to impress in the past: ambitious, aggressive, motivated, educated, experienced, accomplishment-oriented, working adults. These are our brothers, sisters, friends, peers, and parents. Competing with this group is not easy, though it is necessary and to some degree inevitable.

In America the film industry, television, and other forms of mass media usually serve to increase these difficulties. Television and movies, for example, would have us believe that all men should look like Mel Gibson or Arnold Schwarzenegger; drink Budweiser or Perrier; drive a Harley Davidson motorcycle, a Corvette, an all-terrain vehicle, or a Mercedes; and be strong but sensitive. Women, on the other hand, should look like Jill Ireland; or Christy Brinkley; have jobs with sta-

---

[5] This fact proves that such emotions are instinctive, despite the fact that some such emotions are susceptible to de-programming methods.

[6] If the argument regards a man's behavior (as it relates to self-esteem), feminists will usually deny the existence of "instinctive behavior," seeing it instead as the result of an unnecessary ego problem. If the argument regards a woman's behavior (as it relates to self-esteem), the behavior may be seen as either instinctive, or merely a case of the woman's attempting to overcome the oppression of men.

tus approaching that of Barbara Walters; and be strong, aggressive, confident, liberated, and successful, but sensitive.

But even should we achieve all the goals we set for ourselves, hurdles still inevitably arise. There are numerous examples of how self-esteem can effect even the most seemingly successful, powerful, and contented among us. We have all seen professional athletes feel hurt and unappreciated because they didn't get a pay raise, from $2,000,000 to $3,000,000. Or, they may feel unappreciated and ignored because they failed to be selected for an all-star team. Corporate executives with many years of education and experience, positions of power, and high incomes, can lose their self-esteem if their organization's downsizing causes them to receive termination papers. It is even possible for them to consider themselves failures! The apparently secure individual, believing himself to be happily married and capable of bringing contentment to his partner, may see his self-esteem disappear, possibly never to return, with the arrival of divorce papers. The struggle for self-esteem is still with all these individuals, no matter the level of their previous success.

During a recent championship tournament, the head coach of the Stanford women's basketball team spent a good deal of time complaining that her team wasn't getting the television exposure, or the attention and accolades of the men's team. Hers was just one of the multitude of ways people react to low levels of self-esteem. Sometimes these reactions are conscious, but more often they occur without the individual's awareness of the reasons for their (sometimes strange) behavior.[7]

Among other things, a lack of self-esteem can lead to story-telling. This behavior is usually someone's attempt to build himself up in the eyes of others by telling false stories, making exaggerations about himself or others. Such people sometimes lie even to themselves. They may even be very decent, caring people, with the exception of their

---

[7] Her argument was that her team received less exposure solely because of sexism, which had nothing to do with the comparable levels of talent displayed by the athletes, or fan interest. She ignored the fact her team would be unable to compete with an average high school boys' team, let alone a top college men's team. In this instance, the response and complaints of the Stanford women's coach were relatively simple and straightforward and the reasons for her reacting the way she did are fairly easily understood.

lying.[8] Story-telling is usually a response to the need to achieve, which goes a long way toward explaining why it is predominantly men who exhibit this trait.[9] Men tell the most stories because it is men who most frequently perceive themselves as falling short of their own or others' expectations. It's their attempt at making up the difference, and bolstering male pride.[10]

Low self-esteem can also lead people to become put-down artists. These people belittle others around them, even friends or loved ones. They may criticize others' looks, intelligence, or taste, in an attempt to raise their own position or status.

For better or worse, self-esteem can affect what we eat, what we wear, the cars we buy, the careers we pursue, the political parties we support, and nearly every other aspect of our lives.

Though it can obviously cause problems, the individual need for self-esteem should probably be considered mankind's greatest motivator. The list of accomplishments resulting from man's desire for self-esteem is never-ending. It would not be unreasonable to contend that the world, as we know it, has been built by individual quests for self-esteem. Theoretically, the earliest hunters were driven to build better spears, throw them better, and even to run faster, by an instinctive desire for self-esteem. This same desire would later drive them to better protect and provide for their mates, their families, and their clans. These hunters were the same men who would eventually be driven to invent bows and arrows, to construct houses as shelters, to build boats and ships to explore the world, to invent the cotton gin

---

[8] It is worth noting that the story-teller, or exaggerator, is found in all societies and is predominantly male. There is even a slang word, in most languages, virtually reserved for men. In American English the word is "bullshitter," or perhaps, "teller of tall tales." In Spanish, the word is "pedante."

[9] When women lie it is usually more restricted to covering up something they did wrong, or as a means of getting something they want, and is often a result of failed logic. The lies told in promotion of the feminist movement absolutely epitomize this.

[10] Male pride starts young and leads to many other male traits, competitiveness being one of them. Men have always found things to compete in and challenge themselves with, even if they killed themselves or others in the process. The simple phrase, "the thrill of victory and the agony of defeat," whether it concerns war, work, intellectual pursuit, or sport, has almost unfathomable meaning to men.

and the internal combustion engine, and to discover electricity and the nature of the atom. Self-esteem has been a determining factor, directly or indirectly, in every invention ever devised and fabricated by man.

Henry Ford wasn't motivated to work long hours at the pace he did only from the need to support his family. He had something to prove, to himself and to the world. The need for self-esteem was present in him just as it was in DaVinci, Edison, Bell, and Einstein.

The carpenter who built the house you comfortably live in today surely worked to support himself or his family, but at the instant he was fitting the windows and doors so precisely, he probably was thinking, "I'm the best window and door man on the crew, maybe in this town, maybe even the whole country." That is why windows and doors fit so nicely, if they do. The brick mason thought the same thing, and so did the roofer.[11]

From the climbing of Mt. Everest, to the construction of the Eiffel Tower, the Golden Gate Bridge, and the Hoover Dam, great levels of motivation—resulting from the need for self-esteem—were required.[12]

Perhaps the drive for self-esteem has spiraled out of control in America, but we will need its motivation for our survival. Not only must we work simply to ensure that survival, but many stupendous new achievements will be required if we are to successfully face new problems in the future. Now, as always, the drive for self-esteem fuels the drive for personal achievement. Self-esteem is the only thing that will keep us motivated in perpetuity. Altruism can be a great motivator, bringing its own rewards (and we do need more altruism), but

---

[11] Contrary to the belief of many (including feminists), the drive for self-esteem is not necessarily related to the word "egotist." Self-esteem need not be connected to an individual's tendency to be egocentric. People with either high *or* low levels of self-esteem are capable of possessing egotistic traits. But, whether or not a person has a healthy self-esteem is not what determines egotism.

[12] Of course, many would say that we've gone too far with our inventiveness, constructed too much, climbed too many mountains. Maybe yes, maybe no; but again, we should realize that without technology, industrialization, and the supreme efforts it took to make the transformation, we could never have supported (nor kept civilized) the more than 5 billion people who exist today. Every tree would have long since been cut down just trying to build shelters and keep warm.

pure altruism is not a great motivator for the majority of us. Most people need something more.[13]

An argument can also be made that increased self-esteem is the most important result of the act of loving. In this sense, self-esteem could be considered the greatest gift any person can give to another. When someone says, "I love you," and means it, what they do for their lover's self-esteem (especially if the love is reciprocal) is to give it the greatest possible boost—a boost most of us long to experience.

It is a key hypothesis of this book that vast and inherently different self-esteem needs and drives have always existed between the sexes, and that they are biologically appropriate and will always exist. To continue the attempt to remove them, even using new and increasingly technocratic socialization processes, would be a calamitous mistake, amounting to an attempt at dehumanizing us. Incredibly, many women today seem to have no sense of the pain and harm they are causing men—and in turn society, and themselves—through their failure to understand what self-esteem means to men, or through their cold disregard for it. Feminists also refuse to admit, or fail to realize, that a natural by-product of this is male anger.

The ways in which the sexes respond differently in regard to self-esteem are so closely related to our instinct for survival as to be inseparable. It is for this reason that it is almost impossible to discuss the origins of self-esteem without also discussing the different ways in which the sexes evolved with it.

An instinctive behavior can be defined as a natural or inherent impulse or drive that is active, or activated, without conscious thought. Unfortunately there simply are no proof-rendering measurements of when, how, or even if, specific instincts actually exist. All anyone (including the sociobiologist) has to work with when developing theories on instinctive behavior is observation and the study of history.[14]

---

[13] This is probably a more realistic reason for the failure of socialism than are the laws of economics. The socialist practice of putting all production workers on an equal plane dissuades those who would otherwise strive to be high achievers, by removing the incentives of personal prestige and self-esteem.

[14] One basic feminist contention is, "There are no measurements to prove that men and women are different." This contention is taken seriously, despite the fact that it is ridiculous. An equally ridiculous contention, put forward by aforementioned Major Cornum, is, "There is no measurement that proves non-consensual sex needs to be

Because of this, it is the observation of *universal* behaviors that are of the greatest significance. Since all societies, world-wide, have held some type of religious belief, practiced marriage rituals, lived in patriarchal fashion, and promoted and utilized families as the means of socializing children, such examples can be used as proof that there are instinctive (as opposed to coincidental, or contrived) reasons for their existence.[15]

Steven Goldberg points out the value of the written records that are often the only sources of our knowledge about the universalities that occur in variant societies:

> Cultural anthropology has given the world a priceless treasure, the ethnographic descriptions of many hundreds—or thousands, if one counts less formal works—of societies and the incredible variation they have demonstrated. In the future, when the homogenization of the world has made all societies more alike than different, only these ethnographies will stand against the human ethnocentric tendency to think things *had* to be the way they are.

When a behavior has been recognized as inherent, theories put forth on how, why, or when, this behavior came to be need not (and usually cannot) be put forth with absolute certainty. The test of such theories is in regard to the degree of their plausibility—are they as plausible as other, currently accepted theories explaining the same behavior?

With regard to the differences between men and women, and the self-esteem each achieves from work[16], anthropologist Margaret Mead has been virtually unchallenged on her observation:

> In every known human society, the male's need for achievement can be recognized. Men may cook, or weave, or dress dolls, or hunt hum-

---

painful or traumatizing to women." In line with this type of reasoning, feminists believe that any self-esteem differences presently existing between the sexes are nothing more than coincidental by-products of our socialization processes and should therefore be ignored when planning the future. But even casual observation demonstrates that non-consensual sex *is* traumatizing to women, just as it tells us that men *do* have a greater need to achieve than women.

[15] In fact, any socialization method that flies in the face of these recognized universalities exemplifies a "contrived" effort.

[16] "Work" is the exertion of strength or faculties for the purpose of accomplishing a task that is deemed necessary—something that must or should be done.

mingbirds, but if such activities are appropriate occupations of men, then the whole society, men and women alike, votes them as important. When the same occupations are performed by women, they are regarded as *less* important. (Emphasis added.)

This recognized, universal social pattern serves as proof that "the male's need for achievement" originates from man's earliest existence (there can be no other reason for universalities, as such, to exist), and that within men are instinctive desires to achieve in comparatively grander ways than women. The fact that all societies have been patriarchal is similar proof. Men in all societies have been capable either of enslaving women or of allowing them to do all the types of jobs of which women are physically and mentally capable. But men have never allowed the latter. If we take all societies into account, it is true that men have allowed women to work (or put women to work) at almost every conceivable type of task; but—in all societies—men have saved certain types or levels of occupations just for themselves. This means that even though men could have chosen to ignore the existence of sexual differences in the work environment, and could have chosen to work side by side with women (as equals), it *never* occurred. The male's drive for achievement and self-esteem is the reason.

From time immemorial, men and women have been socialized differently and have had sex-differentiated roles. Because of this, we have developed different behavioral instincts, just as our brains have developed in other strikingly different (and increasingly measurable) ways.

From our earliest history, the roles of the respective sexes were determined by the survival instinct. Survival necessitated the division of jobs and responsibilities by sex. Men's primary jobs of providing and protecting were accomplished by exploring and foraging, by hunting, and by fighting off marauding men from other clans. Because of size, strength, and aggressive tendencies, men were better suited to these tasks and were the only sex capable of performing them. Women's primary, and almost continual, job has been the perpetuation of life: getting pregnant, giving birth, and seeing to the survival of offspring that are, for practical intents and purposes (because of their complete and extended period of dependency), born pre-maturely. Men and women have done these different jobs[17], and developed different physical and instinctive behavioral characteristics over the three and a half billion years of our evolutionary history.[18] The relative recency of the trend toward communal living has not allowed the time necessary for our species to evolve past those instincts (patriarchy, nuclear family, and monogamy), which ensured our survival through the first 99.95 percent of our history. To expect, as feminists do, that our culture can successfully reshape itself—overriding, as it were, our most basic biological instincts—in the span of only one or two generations, is folly of the grossest sort.

By the time our species began to write, 5,000–7,000 years ago, and became civilized, the behaviors that would guide us forward to create documented history had long been deeply ingrained in us. This vast time difference between modern history and pre-history is why men around the world are, realistically, so similar to one another, but so different from women.

Around the world, women read 400 million romance novels a year, in which the hero—seemingly laden with self-esteem—is always bigger, stronger, more successful, more aggressive, even more intelligent than the heroine. In light of this fact, we might do well to remember that the showy feathers on a male peacock developed as a result of female selection. Women the world over are attracted to strong men who appear to possess bountiful levels of self-esteem. It may even be the rewards, which females provide for men possessing abundant self-esteem, that "selected for" those men who appear to possess significant levels of it.

In any case, women were consigned to different roles by biology. Women have never competed with men in the race for "achievement" or "glory" during 99.95 percent of our history, due to vastly different hormonal and physical characteristics. Any strengths or aptitudinal

---

[17] It would be complete idiocy to suggest that one or the other of these sex-related roles was more important than the other. Each complements the other; each is essential to the survival of humankind.

[18] Human evolution is, at best, an extraordinarily slow process, requiring selection processes that take place over the span of many generations, when fundamental changes occur on a population-wide basis. Given an average generation span of 20 years, our species has evolved through approximately 175,000 generations, and during all that time, there is no evidence of even a single culture that has succeeded as a matriarchy.

advantages possessed by women have been of little noticeable service
in a world where the advantages of strength, speed, and aggression
(easily seen to be necessary in providing and protecting) belong in
greater proportion to men.

The old saying, "Behind every successful man is a woman" may
have a more timeless meaning than we know, even if it is not always
true. It is easy to imagine that from our earliest days, women attached
themselves to the "presence" of their men, and assisted in their successes wherever possible. In this sense, women may have developed a
sort of "self-esteem by association."

A different way of fulfilling the need for self-esteem could be part
of the reason women have not suffered a lack of self-esteem in the
past. The different goals and standards women set for themselves may
not have been based so heavily on their own achievements outside
the home (since women were not allowed to compete with males, or
were not capable of it) as upon the success of their mates and families.
The development of the nurturing characteristics historically associated with women, in normal societies, may well be the direct result
of such an indirect acquisition of self-esteem.

Though feminists have continually claimed that there are no inherent self-esteem differences between men and women, and boys
and girls, this claim has not prevented them from using the opposite
claim to make a case for channeling taxpayer funds toward educational
programs that exclude boys, and target girls. One of the better examples of specious studies— commissioned by feminists, to be used as
leverage in their fight to become more than equal to men—is a self-
esteem "study" discussed in depth in the book, *Who Stole Feminism?*,
by Christina Hoff Sommers:

> In 1991, newspapers around the country carried alarming reports a-
> bout the plummeting self-esteem of American teenage girls. "Little
> girls lose their self-esteem on the way to adolescence, study says" (*Chi-
> cago Tribune*), "Study points to stark gender differences" (*Boston Globe*).
>
> The study had been commissioned by the American Association of
> University Women (AAUW), a women's organization . . . dedicated
> to promoting excellence in women's education. . . . Any study bearing
> its imprimatur is assured of wide and serious attention. . . .
>
> Not only did the report make headlines around the country, it led to
> hundreds of conferences and community action projects. Politicians,

educators, and business leaders have been recruited by the AAUW to help America's "short-changed" girls. Fifty congresspersons responded to the alarm by sponsoring a $360 million bill, the Gender Equity in Education Act, to deal with the problems raised by the AAUW study. . . .

Although the self-esteem report is having an enormous impact, a most casual glance at its contents suffices to raise grave doubts about its philosophy, methodology, and conclusions. One glaring example is this major piece of evidence for the difference in boys' and girls' aspirations for success: "Self-esteem is critically related to young people's dreams and successes. The higher self-esteem of young men translates into bigger career dreams. . . . The number of boys who aspire to glamorous occupations (rock star, sports star) is greater than that of young women at every age of adolescence, creating a kind of 'glamour gap.'"

[Hoff Sommers] did a double take on reading this. A *glamour gap?* Most kids do not have the talent and drive to be rock stars. The sensible ones know it. What these responses suggest, and what many experts on adolescent development will tell you, is that girls mature earlier than boys, who at this age, apparently, suffer from a "reality gap. . . ."

The response from the media was gratifying. . . . No one suggested that the AAUW's alarming findings about the plight of the nation's girls might be the product of "advocacy research," research undertaken with an eye to "proving" conclusions that advocates are ideologically committed to and that they find politically useful. Reporters who might normally seek out alternative points of view did not do so in this case. . . .

Despite the sensational and sweeping nature of the findings that girls' self-esteem plummets, as far as [Hoff Sommers] could ascertain, none of the journalists who reported on the study interviewed any social scientists to see whether the poll that reported this was properly designed and its results properly interpreted. . . . Because the media made no effort to look beyond the news releases given them by the AAUW, it was left to skeptics to come forward on their own. . . .

The charge that the self-esteem of the nation's girls was being undermined was made to order for the times. But was it true? That the report was so widely and uncritically credited cannot be taken as a sign of its soundness. The journalists and their readers, the concerned politicians and their constituents, did not know that the AAUW is yet another para-academic organization that has become highly political and ideological in recent years . . . its present leadership has changed the association into an activist arm of . . . feminism.

The AAUW is happy to accommodate anyone who wants to see the . . . readily available materials (which) summarize the "findings." Getting hold of the actual Goldberg[sic]-Lake self-esteem study—the hard data on which all the claims are based—turned out to be far more difficult. . . . When the full report finally arrived, after several weeks and three more phone calls, [Hoff Sommers] saw immediately why AAUW was so cautious. For one thing, it contained nothing like a definition of self-esteem, or even an informal discussion of what they meant by it.

The concept of self-esteem is generally considered to be unstable and controversial, yet few psychologists doubt its central importance. The instability and fluidity of the concept makes it ill-suited for a pollster approach. Polling firms are good at tallying opinions, but self-esteem is a complex personal characteristic, and people's expressed opinions of themselves may have little to do with their sense of inner worth. Yet the AAUW/Greenberg-Lake procedures relied almost exclusively on self-reports.

Self-esteem and a host of related personal characteristics such as self-love, humility, pride, and vanity have been under study since Aristotle. The scientific study of self-esteem by developmental psychologists and sociologists is in its infancy. At the moment, there is little agreement about how to define it and far less agreement on how to measure it. . . .

Of course, boys must learn to be thoughtful and respectful of girls, but they are not culprits; they are not silencing girls or lowering their self-esteem, and no one should be sending the boys the message that they are doing any of these things.

Due to the influence of feminism, the ways women are being encouraged to measure themselves today, with the intent of gaining self-esteem, are changing rapidly. The ways women live their lives are also changing rapidly, in response to self-esteem needs. But the type of self-esteem women increasingly seek is that currently advocated by strident feminists of the sort who head the AAUW, feminists who seek validation for the choices they themselves have made—that of "career at the expense of everything else." Women are increasingly measuring their success, not by the success of the family but by their own achievements and successes in the work force.

As can be seen, self-esteem, or the lack of it, can have any number of negative effects on an entire race or culture. The need for cultural pride is widely known and accepted. In the same way, pride—or the lack of it—can also affect an entire sex. This is happening today, with both sexes. It is time to recognize that men and women are not clones of one another. It is time to recognize the impact that the restructuring of this society is having, individually and collectively, on men and women. This culture is becoming subversive to the biological needs of both men and women. It is also time to recognize that self-esteem's impact on individuals has a subsequent, cumulative impact on society as a whole.

If we do not recognize these things (even should we avoid complete degeneration and anarchy), we will eventually lose—completely —some of our most distinct, albeit sex-specific human characteristics. Without any uniquely male pride, there will eventually cease to be any uniquely male honor. Male honor is a natural motivational force, but it is also a force that serves to restrict certain natural tendencies and appetites that are detrimental to civilization. Without any uniquely female pride, there will eventually cease to be any uniquely female honor. As in males, female honor is not only a natural motivational force, it is also a force that serves to restrict certain natural tendencies and appetites that are detrimental to civilization.

Absent these traits, only a virtual police state will be able to deal with men and women who haven't the inner honor to control themselves. This is true in public life, and even truer in private homes.

Self-esteem is only a word. Its meaning, however, is critically important, so important that it is our basic measurement of self and self-worth; it is our reason for being—our motivation for living. Self-esteem is a part of all of us throughout our lives. To greater or lesser degrees, it fluctuates continually within all of us, regardless of the level of success we may achieve.

What we absolutely do *not* need are experimental, wholesale plans to solve everyone's quest for self-esteem. What we *do* need is a habitable social environment in which love, caring, compassion, and other positive human traits, can flourish. This can only begin to happen when we recognize the vast differences between the sexes, and the different needs that result from them.

CHAPTER EIGHT

Incompatibility with Religion

Attempting to write about the perils of a social movement as large
and influential as feminism, without ever bringing religion into the
argument, would be nearly impossible.[1] Religions have existed in every culture throughout history. Their function has been to unite the
members of society under a given set of beliefs (generally, but not
always, concerning the existence of a supernatural being). Religions
also provide moral codes (mores) or guidelines (philosophies) by which
people may govern their lives.

In many ways, feminism can be compared to a religion. Though
it does not concern itself with the existence of a supernatural being,
it definitely advocates a philosophy by which its followers live. Feminism certainly meets a part of Webster's Dictionary's definition, "a
cause, principle, or set of beliefs held to with ardor and faith." As
with religions, the followers of feminism can be extremely evangelic,
intolerant of other viewpoints, and willing to lay guilt on disbelievers.
The widespread all-powerful zeitgeist of political correctness proves
this.

Though feminism is similar to religions in those ways and others, it is the differences between its principles and the principles of
all religions that are crucially important, and which point to its illogic. Instead of looking to men like Buddha, Jesus, Mohammed, or
Confucius for words of wisdom to live by, feminists ridicule them. Instead, they look to the commandments of The National Organization
of Women, the American Association of University Women, college

---

[1] Introducing the subject here is not an attempt to advocate any specific set of religious beliefs, but rather to demonstrate for the reader some of the parallels and contradictions feminism poses to traditional religious thought.

professors and students involved in Women's Studies Programs, *Ms.* magazine, The National Gay and Lesbian Task Force, and other gay- and lesbian-dominated organizations, etc.

The tenets of feminism reject those of all religions. Because of this it is impossible for the individual to believe in and practice feminism, while believing in and practicing any major religion. The primary reason for feminism's rejection of all major religions is that they conflict with a key principle of feminism in the most profound of ways, and are therefore in competition with it. Feminism attempts to refute all scientific and historically observable evidence of the significant differences between sexes, and that there is any need for sex-differentiated roles, while every major religion throughout history has recognized and accepted the existence of significant differences between the sexes, and the need for sex-differentiated roles in families and within society. As feminism has adamantly rejected those principles common to all religions (which result from their recognition of these differences), its followers have been left with virtually no choice but to reject all other religions. The evidence of the rejection of religious principles by feminist followers is obvious in this country, as it is in other feminist-dominated countries. The more dominant feminism becomes, the more complete is the rejection of any other religious philosophy.

Religions openly give people codes to live by, and openly pose restrictions upon their immoral or unacceptable behavior. At first glance, feminism gives us few codes or mores to live by, except that we should refute the existence of sexual differences and the need for sex-differentiated roles. Feminism also pretends to oppose intolerance of any sort, and to propose no restrictions on personal freedoms.

The fact is that feminists are not tolerant. Nor does feminism equate to more personal freedom. Should feminism become predominant, it will put upon us a wider range of rules and coercive, freedom-limiting regulations than any major religion ever has—only in much different ways. Feminism may continue to preach freedom and tolerance, but it will impose the desires of its followers in such ways as to be almost unnoticeable to all but the most perceptive observers. For example, tax mandates (following the Swedish model) will pay to cover women and children for regular health care, abortion, food subsidies, housing subsidies, and daycare for infants and children. Feminism itself will not be seen as responsible for imposing such mandates, but will have worked behind the scenes to promote them.

Christianity, Judaism, Islam, Hinduism, and *all* major religions, encourage men to love their wives and children. They all seek to compel men to provide for their wives and children and not abandon them. Feminism does virtually nothing to encourage men to love their wives and children and not to abandon them. Feminism places no value on the nuclear family. The principles of most religions are the principles of self-reliance. Despite their claims to the contrary, the principles of feminism are the principles of dependency—dependency on society at large, to avoid dependency upon family.

Perhaps it is time to redefine feminism as a religion. Defining feminism as a religion will allow us to first recognize its gospel (as we now recognize its modus operandi), and then to enlist the aid of the courts to invalidate it, using the same methods feminists and atheists have used in their efforts to invalidate the principles of Christianity.

The arguments of feminists parallel those of atheists when feminists argue that no one in the decision-making processes of government should be guided by their religious beliefs, in any way. Both groups claim that any such influence, ipso facto, leads government officials into depriving someone of their freedom, or being intolerant of someone's chosen lifestyle. A key hypothesis of this book is that, for a variety of reasons, our freedom ends up being more compromised when feminist principles come to dominate, than when religious principles do.

Even most of those who don't make religion a conscious part of their lives would probably have a difficult time imagining an America without the presence of Christianity, and other historically traditional religious influences, which feminism seeks to extinguish.[2] Sociologist

---

[2] Eventually, there would be no churches across our nation. There would be no deacons, no rabbis, and no priests; there would be no choirs, no masses, no sermons; there would be no Sundays of rest, no Christmas, no Hanukkah, no Easter, no Thanksgiving. We would have no religious schools or teachings of any sort, no christenings or religious baptisms, no Bar Mitzvahs, no funerals, and no prayers for guidance, help, mercy, or forgiveness. Though formal marriages might still occur, there would be no white dresses (or any ceremonial wedding gowns, as we know them) or any other symbols of chastity. IN GOD WE TRUST would, of course, be removed from our money.

But more important than the elimination of any of those things would be the fact that we (especially children) would never hear words such as "Thou shalt not kill,"

Emil Durkim has posed a maxim: "When mores are sufficient, laws are unnecessary. When mores are insufficient, laws are unenforceable." One of the root problems of feminism, as compared to a religion, is that it provides no valid, comprehensive mores—at least none ever utilized by any previous society. "Mores" are the fixed, morally binding customs of a particular group of people. Feminist mores would be limited to only a few things: 1) individualism is right, so long as the whole of society is androgynous; 2) sexual choice is unlimited; 3) everyone pays their taxes to support the results of following feminist philosophies; 4) everyone has equal rights, unless their rights as individuals interfere with feminist policy; and 5) we must all be tolerant of everything that feminism holds to be in our best interest.

At the time most of the sacred texts were written (the Bible, the Koran, the Talmud, the Vedas), we possessed little or no technology, no birth control, no ability to abort infants, and no equal rights laws. We had only been cultivating crops for a few thousand years. Because the writers of these texts were part of a simpler and more natural environment, they were closer to the earth and in tune with it. They had a much better understanding of nature, and an easier job of observing their fellow man exhibiting true human nature—including the very obvious different nature of the sexes. These were aids in giving them a type of intuition or wisdom that many people no longer possess. When it was written, for instance, "Neither shalt thou desire thy neighbor's wife, neither shalt thou covet thy neighbor's house. . . ." the writers knew that these were troublesome temptations. But they also knew that temptation could be avoided by anyone who would treat others in the same way they would like to be treated. There is no reason that anyone should need to believe in a specific religious doctrine for anthropologically demonstrable guidelines like these to have value. But there is also no reason that we should now discard the guidelines because they were written by someone who did. Without

---

"Thou shalt not steal," "Thou shalt not commit adultery," and "Do unto others as you would have them do unto you." These are Christian Commandments (and appear here only because they are the Commandments the author is most familiar with). But this is not an argument in favor of any specific religious faith, only an attempt to point out that some type of moral code or ethical structure is necessary in every society, so as to provide mores for people to live by.

doubt, the principles of Christianity and other major religions make far more sense than the feminist alternatives we face today.

Columnist Richard Cohen wrote, "It borders on the whimsical to suggest that America's problems are basically spiritual when they are more importantly economic and social."

To this, Samuel Francis made a pertinent reply:

> To Cohen and his species, it is inconceivable that economic and social "problems" might have spiritual roots or "solutions." But when stated as baldly as Cohen states it, the proposition that such problems are not in some sense "spiritual" or moral is absurd on its face.
>
> If the social and economic problems caused by the glorification of instantaneous self-gratification—through sex, drugs, power, money, murder, rape, assault, abortion, divorce, and desertion are not "spiritual" in the ordinary meaning, then what are they? If these are not our major social and economic problems, what are? And if literati like Cohen don't quite see their causes, what do they—and what can they—see?

CHAPTER NINE

Conclusion to Part One

The first part of this book has been an attempt to reveal how feminism and feminists have come to gain such influence and power over this society, and how great that power is. It has attempted to at least make clear that what is happening in America today is not just a simple case of "this being what the people knowingly want." There is a long list of factors that has brought us to the present point.

Feminists have planned, plotted, contrived, and habitually lied about the past and present, fostered hatred and mistrust in women toward men, engendered guilt in men whenever possible, employed political correctness, manipulated the media and educational systems, virtually rigged the debate process, and have successfully forwarded their agenda.

Because of technological developments and feminist influences, three institutions that have historically and universally been our primary sources of influence (religion, government, family) have, to varying degrees, been undermined by feminist thought, succumbed to feminist thought, or both.

Religious teachings and principles, are increasingly becoming a non-factor in the lives of Americans and the future of this country. Why? Because—in conjunction with the fact that feminism simply has a more pervasive influence on us and society today than any religious philosophy—feminism is its own religion, with its own rules, and feminists are intolerant of any person or institution that stands in the way of their agenda.

Our government itself is now becoming an agent of feminism. As the first draft of this book was being written, a year or more before the elections of 1992, it included a passage that said, "The political leadership of this country is, in effect, the last major established institution impacting our lives, whose influence has not, for a certainty, been superseded by the dictates of the women's movement." (Though, in some ways, the movement's leadership at that point could already be described as more influential than our government itself, because as a part of the feminist master plan, it had captured the media and academia and, therefore, the minds of many in our society. This, of course, means voters.) Today, it would be appropriate to say that feminist thought has taken control of the White House; and this is not simply intended to warn the reader about Hillary Clinton's presence there. Bill Clinton is a feminist, as will be the majority of those thousands of men and women he will appoint over the course of his term. Barbara Boxer and Dianne Feinstein, both strident feminists, hold the only two Senate seats in the most populous and influential state in the union, California.

Can the family be used as a rudder for society, instead of the principles of feminism? Thanks—in large part—to feminism, the nuclear family is dying. Even where it technically exists, parental and familial influence as a whole are increasingly supplanted by feminist-dominated factors within society, factors such as the media and educational systems.

Academia can no longer be looked to as a rudder for society, because it is controlled by feminists. Nor can the media be used as a philosophical rudder for society, because feminists control it, as well. (It is because of the unnatural and unprecedented role the mass media has played in determining our thoughts and actions—more than any other reason—that the modern women's movement can never be considered a natural social reorganization.)

Feminism's modus operandi equals psychological warfare, which Charlie Reese describes, in the *Conservative Chronicle*, as being:

> the deliberate campaign to convince masses of people to accept a falsehood in order to manipulate them for selfish, often secret, reasons. In peace, psychological warfare is called public relations.
>
> A psywar operation, to use army jargon, is not a simple lie. It is an elaborate, complex campaign involving many elements. To be effective, it must seem not to be a campaign. Rather it must seem to be the natural coming together of a consensus. It involves the use of language, authority figures, and specious studies, many of them seeming to be unrelated, for added credibility.

It is well past the time to acknowledge the power feminists wield over us, and to "respect" the movement's pre-eminent role in determining the future of our society, and how we will lead our lives.

It is time to take a serious look at the different directions in which the movement is pushing and pulling us, because the course of recent history has proven that, with few exceptions, the visions of the leaders of the feminist movement do become historical fact.

Only now, after well over 20 years of sheep-like behavior is there a sense that a public awareness, a "conscious" questioning, and hopefully a soon-to-be-conscious resistance, are forming in regard to the feminist movement's agenda. Only when we realize the extent to which we have been, and are being, manipulated by feminists can logical progress toward finding the solutions to our problems begin.

PART TWO

CHAPTER TEN

The Consequences of Androgyny

By this point in the book, it is probably clear to the reader that despite all the rhetorical claims about fairness, justice, and equality, the actual, primary goal of feminism is—quite simply—a shift in the balance of power. This is the case whether feminism is considered in the workplace, in the home, or in society at large. In every arena —journalistic, educational, sexual, domestic, political, business, religious, athletic, finance, real estate, and all others great or small— feminism seeks to transfer power *out* of the hands of males and *into* the hands of females.

While there is every reason to believe that the goals of the movement have evolved to this point, there is little reason to believe that such a dramatic and complete shift of power was the original conscious intent of those first few feminists who set the movement into high gear during the early 1960s. Likewise, the establishment of a matriarchy within the United States was most probably not a part of the agenda of those early feminists. Rather, they pursued and promoted changes which they thought would shift *more* power into the hands of women. Today's feminist leaders, however (the most influential leaders of the most influential sociopolitical movement in America) are successfully promoting changes to create a matriarchy, though (for obvious, conspiratorial reasons) they don't discuss it in public. It's an interesting situation, one which Philip Jenkins *inadvertently* described perfectly in *Chronicles* magazine when discussing an entirely different issue: "We therefore find the curious situation that a hugely influential theory of social organization and reform survives only by virtue of not being discussed." This is a conspiracy in which innumerable groups of different types—media personnel, academics, politicians, employers, human resources departments, and even clergy—are all pawns.

Matriarchy itself, the ultimately desired state of today's most strident feminists (a state in which women would essentially have garnered *all* power for themselves), has only recently become a possibility, and then only because of the recent successes in promoting androgyny. Androgyny may, at first, have been seen as the state that would enable women to *equally* share power in the widest possible number of arenas where they would be competing with men (to include the domestic competition for authority). But as the movement's goals evolved and widened, and as the process of androgynization met with more success, it became apparent that widespread androgynization would open the door completely for a matriarchic America.

During the early stages of the movement, feminists rarely made open denials of the differences between the sexes. As the scope of their goals increased, however, feminists began to realize that in order to rationalize many of these new goals, they would have to promote radical new ways of thinking about the sexes. One of those ways—the outright denial of significant, inherent differences between the sexes —has subsequently become a principal tenet of feminism. That feminists now wholeheartedly believe in this tenet is evidenced by their consistent claims that there are absolutely *no* behaviors that should not be indulged equally by men and women, except those behaviors which should be eradicated completely.

One of the most profound changes promoted by the feminist movement is that of androgyny. The feminist commitment to the androgynization process originally sprang from a key assumption about sexual behavior—that women should have as much freedom to explore and enjoy their sexuality as men. A larger truth, though perhaps no more important, is that androgyny is promoted for the simple reason that when girls are socialized to become traditional women (and boys to become traditional men), those adult women are incapable of filling many of the roles envisioned for them by feminists—specifically those roles traditionally belonging to men. Feminists have understood for many years that if women in the workplace are to compete favorably with men, if women are to vie for at least "equal" authority in heterosexual relationships, if women are to succeed in becoming equally influential in society at large, both boys and girls must undergo conditioning programs which will override their hereditary, genetic predispositions. This, of course, also necessitates eliminating any cultural reinforcement of the natural predispositions of either sex, reinforcement that has occurred universally across all cultures and which, thus, also deserves to be labelled "natural." In other words, boys and girls must *artificially* be made to be clones of one another, that being the actual—though carefully unspoken—feminist definition of equal.

Androgyny, by its nature, weakens male characteristics in men while strengthening those same characteristics in women. Thus, like other concepts feminism promotes, androgyny works against patriarchy and will be effective in helping feminists create a matriarchic or equiarchic society. Women will not possess the drive, the aggressiveness, the education, the experience, or the other qualities necessary to fill traditionally male roles—or to participate fully in the desired equiarchic or matriarchic society—unless they are socialized in the same ways men have been socialized throughout history. Similarly, men, to every degree possible, will have to be trained to accept the propriety of women's new roles. (This new program of socialization necessitates silencing dissenters as much as possible by using the tactics of guilt, ridicule, and condemnation referred to earlier.)

Regarding home life—what they envision of it—feminists realize that they must instill in women an increased willingness to reject the importance and status of traditional female responsibilities, such as wifehood and child-rearing. Simultaneously, men must be emasculated. In a letter to the editor, arguing the necessity of career as a means to fulfillment, feminist Priscilla Oppenheimer recently went so far as to say: "Wishing that wives could be like Donna Reed is as abhorrent as wishing that African Americans could be like *Aunt Jemima* and *Uncle Tom*" (emphases added). Contrary to her opinion, many women have voiced—and still do voice—their happiness at being able to fill the roles of housewife and mother. Nevertheless, it is important to note the tactic by which Oppenheimer attempts to condemn traditional womanly character. By referencing the dark period of American slavery, she implies that women of the 1950s and 1960s were similarly enslaved, and she also attempts to place any reaction against feminism into the same category as racial discrimination. She thus attempts to silence dissent through ridicule and guilt.[1]

Prior to this era, no known society has ever attempted to create an androgynous population by teaching and socializing men and women in the same ways. Even in the relatively recent past, if someone were to have suggested that men and women should be socialized identically, in preparation for filling the same roles, "because men and women are essentially the same," that person would very probably have been considered insane, regardless of the culture from which he or she came. Until recently, the idea of men and women having identical responsibilities in the home, as idealized by feminists, has never been a serious consideration anywhere.

Webster's Dictionary defines the androgynous person as "having the characteristics or nature of both male and female." One who is androgynous is called an androgyne. In the normal individual, opposite-sex traits always exist to some small degree. In the androgynous person, however, behavioral traits heretofore known as masculine or feminine are blurred, becoming present more or less equally in the individual, regardless of sex. (A "sexually transcendent" person would be one in which both masculine and feminine traits disappear).

In other words, in the androgynous culture a man could act in what has been traditionally considered "a feminine manner" ninety percent of the time and what has been considered "a masculine manner" only ten percent of the time, and be considered a "normal person," rather than being considered feminine. For women, the reverse would be true.

In the androgynous society, words such as masculine and feminine eventually lose their meaning, based as they are on the two sexes and the noticeable behavioral differences between them. That this situation is increasingly the case today is easily observed. Virtually any behavior that was formerly considered masculine—whether good or bad—is now practiced by any number of women. The same is true of men with what was once regarded feminine behavior. This is due primarily to the influence of the feminist movement.

Though it goes far beyond this, some might say that there have

---

[1] It would not be difficult to compile an entire book consisting of nothing more than comparable examples of the feminist use of such tactics.

always been aggressive women and passive men, which is true, but there are differences between yesterday and today. In the past, the unassertive man was still very much "a man," and perceived himself as being a man in many ways. He would have identified himself with other men. As a child, regardless of the society from which he came, he would have been treated differently than his sisters and different things would have been expected of him. As an adult, he would normally have had many masculine roles to fill in his home (as a husband, a father, and as the head of his family), and at work (as the family breadwinner). He would have known of his manhood in the same way that the aggressive waitress or the head nurse knew she was still "a woman," with feminine roles and a feminine side to her personality. The fact that such women were rarely in direct competition with men served to temper tendencies toward true masculinity, and such women were seldom (if ever) encouraged to take on masculine roles and behaviors within domestic relationships, or in other areas of life such as sports, academic endeavors, or careers, etc.

Others might ask what is wrong with encouraging (through the socialization process) the sexes to freely exchange roles. For one thing, it is unnatural on its face, discomfiting to anyone forced to undergo such socialization. Attempting to make the sexes fill identical roles in society and within relationships is akin to socializing naturally left-handed people into right-handers. But far more important are the problems androgyny causes within the context of individual and familial relationships and, consequently, within the larger context of society.

In the earliest stages of their attempts to integrate the work environment (a process not yet completely successful anywhere in the world) feminists discovered that men didn't want women in certain male domains (for reasons which will be discussed at length in a later section). They also discovered that the work world of men was a rough, demanding, and sometimes almost brutally competitive place.

Those women who initially attempted to assume a place alongside men in traditionally male jobs found that they were unable to cope with many aspects of the situation, or to compete in many ways. Recognizing this to be the case, the feminists' first response was to encourage women to integrate by becoming more masculine, by adopting more masculine postures in dress and mannerism. They thought, for instance, that if the wearing of ties was essential to men's success in business, women could wear ties and would then succeed alongside those men. And, for a time, it was not unusual to see women in business environments, dressing in two- and three-button business suits, wearing vests, with white shirts closed to the neck, and neckties arranged with four-in-hand or Windsor knots. They also made conscious efforts to become more assertive, more decisive, and more independent—in other words, to resocialize themselves in more masculine ways.

The plan failed. Women did try, with limited success, to become more masculine in the work force, but men still didn't want women working at or above their own level. And even when women did get the opportunity to work among men, feminists realized that beyond the fact that men still didn't want them there, men were still just too tough—even for the "recently" adjusted breed of woman.

This realization served to spawn a new and far more serious type of discussion among the then-still-small coterie of feminist leaders. As a result of these discussions, they concurred that the trial period was over, and that the original plan was unworkable. It had been far too simplistic. As early as 1970, the leaders of the women's movement were realizing that women would never be able to compete with men; nor would men welcome them as competitors, so long as men were socialized as men—no matter how the women were socialized. The playing field was still uneven, and it was a field upon which women were not wanted. Feminists realized that many more changes would be required, some of them quite radical. Indeed, during their discussions, feminists concluded that their only hope for "equality" lay in emasculating men through the socialization process, while continuing their efforts to masculinize or de-feminize women to an even greater degree. They also concluded that such work had to start early in the life of a child to be most effective. It was at that time that their plans began to take on a new and more consciously motivated complexity.[2]

---

[2] Though feminists undoubtedly devoted much time and thought to planning strategies that would help in achieving their "new" and "visionary" conceptualizations of society, they applied very little time or thought to evaluating the negative effects of what they had already accomplished. No-fault divorce laws, and the exercise of women's "sexual freedom," both of which feminists sponsored, were just two factors that had started America down the path toward soaring divorce and illegitimacy rates, toward

By March 4, 1973, Betty Friedan had published an article in *New York Times Magazine*, in which she gave a brief description summing up what she and other feminists had decided needed to be done:

> The changes necessary to bring about equality were, and still are, very revolutionary indeed. They involve a sex-role revolution for men and women which will restructure all our institutions: child-rearing, education, marriage, the family, medicine, work, politics, the economy, religion, psychological theory, human sexuality, morality and the very evolution of the race.

Though new, untested, and unproven, feminist leaders concluded that the socialization process needed to make things "truly equal" for men and women was androgyny. Androgyny would be the goal, and Sweden would be used as a role model.

After receiving wide coverage and support from the feminist-dominated mass media, these goals—known shortly before to only a few—soon became part of mainstream feminism. An advanced and far more invasive and coercive type of feminism was about to begin in this country.

Before long, Friedan had written another highly influential book, appropriately titled *The Second Stage*, which documented in great depth many of the earlier discussions of radical feminists, and outlined their plans for achieving their revolutionary goals.

The repercussions of such "revolutionary changes," in terms of human suffering, are not easily calculated. Feminists variously insist that any suffering that results is justified by the greater rewards to follow; or that any suffering is the responsibility of men, who "oppressed" women for so long; or that there has been no suffering or degenera-

---

single-parenthood, and toward societal degeneration. These trends (which can definitely be labeled repercussions of feminism) *did* get noticed by feminists, but rather than recognizing them as warnings that their actions were inappropriate to the health and welfare of American society, these very problems were then added to the list of rationalizations they were using to promote their agenda, under the guise of meeting women's "necessities." More divorces meant that fewer women could count on family economic support; therefore, women *needed* careers for income (they no longer had to rest their demands to work shoulder to shoulder with men on the argument that such work was the only means women had of obtaining fulfillment). Women *needed* access to abortion in order to be free of pregnancy so they could preserve their freedom to work. Women *needed* daycare centers, where they could put their children while they went to work to earn a living.

tion at all as a result of feminism. Regardless of this, it behooves us to proceed with extreme caution and a wary respect for the influence of feminism, because almost all of Friedan's projected changes are in the process of becoming realities, at a time when there is unparalleled social disintegration in America (a fact which has not escaped the notice of all other major countries around the world).

Friedan's new prophecies were adopted by the movement so quickly because, as illustrated by the publication of the *New York Times* article itself, the personnel of the media and academia seem to have listened to her every word. Subsequently, a multitude of articles, books, and specious studies sprouted up to support her completely unproven concepts. Before long, we had her advice (and that of other feminists) on what schools should be teaching students, what parents should be teaching their children, how families should live, how we should interact at work, how adults should sexually interact, what the role of religion should be, and what psychological theory should consist of. The damage that resulted from the popularity of these feminist positions took its toll on individuals and relationships, and began to undermine the family. The decline of the family, in turn, increased calls for help from the government—calls that, once answered, served to even further endanger the family.

Even before that time, the federal government had charted the course of additional changes. In 1967, President Lyndon Johnson ensured that women would fill an ever larger role in the work force by signing Executive Order number 11375, which mandated affirmative action in the government and for contractors of the government—intended to "eliminate job segregation by sex." In *From Cottage To Work Station*, Alan Carlson noted J.E. Buckley's observation that:

> between 1968 and 1971, the EEOC (Equal Employment Opportunity Commission) "converted Title VII into a magna carta for female workers, grafting to it a set of rules and regulations that certainly could not have passed Congress in 1964, and perhaps not a decade later, either."

No one realized that these early laws would lead to the myriad regulations that exist in today's workplaces—laws and regulations that may accurately be described as attempts at behavior control—nor was anyone aware that the necessity of enforcing all these regulations would place the government in the position of having to become "Big Sister," by the decade of the 1990s.

Ours is an interesting period because on one hand many people have no idea what androgyny is, or what it would mean to our culture—and would certainly be against it if they knew. On the other hand, though it may be hard for some to believe, the creation of an androgynous culture is now a conscious goal for many (if not most) "recently educated" people in this country. This is particularly true of the most "in the know" and influential feminists, those who openly classify themselves as feminists, but also true of a high percentage of those working in academics, who classify themselves as psychiatrists or social scientists, but who, in reality, are feminists—by virtue of their roles in perpetuating feminist ideologies. In social science departments at universities across the country, it is now widely taught that the androgynous society is the highest ideal and should be a goal for our society.

Interviewing the second of the two female University of Minnesota, Duluth, undergraduate psychology students (who answered the ad for a research assistant) was as eye-opening as the first had been. After a lengthy, but polite conversation on the subject, she became flustered and blurted out, "We're taught to be androgynous, because that's the best way to live life." Then she hung up.

In fairness to the university, her feelings probably emanate from more than just her academic education. Feminists have put forth just as much effort to paint a picture denying the idea that a woman can exhibit femininity and still be taken seriously, as they have to painting pictures denying that a man can be inherently masculine and be a good human being at the same time.

But, regarding academia, in *Family Questions: Reflections on the American Social Crisis*, Alan Carlson has pointed out that androgyny has already had a significant impact on psychological theory:

> As of 1980, 72 percent of mental health professionals—the persons responsible for counseling adults and children regarding proper adjustment—described a "healthy, mature, socially competent" adult as androgynous. Only 2 percent labeled a feminine woman as healthy, mature, and competent. Psychologist Jeanne Marecek saw androgyny as the means of psychologically institutionalizing the joint revolutions

in sexuality and lifestyles, replacing masculinity and femininity as the norm for men's and women's behavior.

Why the sexes have always been socialized differently and have had different roles in every culture ever existing are simply not topics for discussion on today's politically correct campuses.

Having first convinced academia that androgyny is the only suitable way for intelligent adults to live in contemporary society, feminists then encouraged academicians to create studies to support this belief that androgyny is the *best* way for all of us to live. Simultaneously, they were telling media people these same things, and encouraging the use of as many of the studies from academia as possible, so as to confer credibility upon this new philosophy. They knew they were going to have to sell this to everyone, including those with children. And they knew that the earlier they could start educating children the better it would be. Before long, guidelines for daycare and elementary school teachers were in place.

And so it has come to be. Daycare teachers are trained to treat little girls and boys the same way, and to give them extra encouragement to play together. Teachers are told by modern psychiatrists that little boys wanting to play among themselves is not healthy or natural, and that such behavior must be discouraged—it could potentially lead to a desire for male bonding, and everything male bonding entails, later in life. Similarly, historically normal female bonding is discouraged. All of those games that American girls once played together at school recess, hopscotch, jumprope, jacks, are now discouraged unless they are to be played by both groups. Virtually all school books now project this outlook.

Carlson addresses this specific problem in *Family Questions*:

The androgyne revolution has carried over to school textbooks. In a recent analysis of over 100 such books in current use, Paul C. Vitz of New York University reported that "by far the most noticeable ideological position in the readers was a feminist one." Not a single story or theme celebrated marriage or motherhood as a positive experience. Sex-role reversals and the mockery of masculine men were common. ("For example, there is a story of a princess who sets out to slay the dragon in her kingdom; she invents the first gun and with it shoots and kills the dragon. The slain dragon turns into a prince who asks the princess to marry him.") The obvious goal is to pave the way for the androgynous order.

While, for Carlson and Vitz, it may seem that such a scenario represents no more than an inroad toward androgyny, a closer evaluation of this storyline suggests that it does more. True, the princess setting out to slay the dragon is nothing more than a reversal of sex roles, suggesting to little girls that they, too, can be decisive, strong, resourceful, and physically aggressive, just like boys. The metamorphosis of the slain dragon into a prince, however, who then asks the princess to marry him, implies that the male persona (the dragon/beast/marauding destroyer) will be grateful, loving, and tamed, after it is physically conquered. In this story, the male ethos is completely—and properly—dominated by, and subjugated to, the *new* female ethos. Can there be any doubt that what this, and other, similar stories promote is matriarchy rather than androgyny?

In any case, books that conflict with the androgynous vision have been removed from the educational environment, with little or no debate, at the behest of the "experts." The reader will remember an earlier statement to the effect that pictures of women in traditional roles have been removed from textbooks as part of promoting the Big Lie; the promotion of androgyny is another reason for this censorship. The only permitted pictures of women with children portray the mother, leaving the child at a daycare center on the way to her work, pictures that imply she is employed in a career position of high status, or one with great altruistic rewards.

Little girls are encouraged to compete with boys in every way, including athletics. They are encouraged to dream of being truck drivers, firefighters, police officers, fighter pilots, and politicians. Little girls, with the support of their parents and the media, are suing for the right to participate in Little League baseball, Pop Warner football, even Boy Scouts. Simultaneously, they are subtly or overtly encouraged to disdain roles traditionally chosen by girls or women. Competitiveness, aggressiveness, and achievement orientation receive praise, and are recommended as values for girls to possess. In the meantime, boys are told to "get in touch" with their feelings, be tolerant of any wishes of females, and that it is okay if they want to become nurses, secretaries, and waitpersons. The message *boys* get is, "*don't* be so competitive, aggressive, and achievement oriented."

A casual study of the media, and the journalistic media especially, shows that the vast majority of women receiving positive press coverage generally possess what have previously been known as masculine traits—aggressiveness, ambition, confidence, and strength. The majority of men receiving positive press coverage tend to possess traits that have, in the past, been considered feminine, or they are supportive of feminist causes. The messages become ever stronger: acceptance and encouragement of masculine behavior for women is "in";[3] acceptance of feminine women, or masculine men, is "out."

Though some may doubt that an androgynous society is possible in the United States, evidence is beginning to show that if we continue in our current direction the sexes could be deprogrammed so that we *will* become androgynous. Sex-differentiated roles and behaviors will simply cease to exist. Sweden and certain other Northern European countries exemplify those in which androgyny is closest to becoming complete. This is precisely because feminist philosophy has, for so long, dominated those countries.

Sweden, for example, has already taken parenting out of the hands of biological parents, on a national level. After years of formulating policies which served to undermine the existence and autonomy of the nuclear family, their government has largely usurped this role, including the rearing of children, which it utilizes to further promote androgyny. In 1989, over 70 percent of Swedish children under six years old were not being cared for by their mothers, but instead by "municipal" daycare systems.

At first glance, the idea of "social parenting" through governmental daycare systems may appear to have little to do with the concept of androgyny, but this has not been the case anywhere it has been practiced, and is certainly not true in Sweden. Sweden's government is

---

[3] Reference the State Farm insurance company advertisement featuring a photo of the U.S. Olympic Women's basketball team that reads "These days, *little girls* don't live down the lane. They drive down it. Talented, tenacious and tough to beat."

Listening to and reading the commentary on the recent Olympics, one would have been led to believe that women are actually better athletes than men. Alexander Wolff, in the July 22, 1996 issue of *Sports Illustrated*, ended his article with this clear example, insulting the male Chinese athletes: "Beware the day when, in sports, China's men will be able to do what its women already can."

openly indoctrinating and pro-androgyny, and its citizens seem to follow its wishes in sheep-like fashion. A clear example of this appears in the official and widely distributed governmental statistics handbook. A question regarding the roles of the sexes is posed for Swedish citizens, and then *answered* for them in a definitive way:

> How can we end the separation into a woman's and a man's world? Sex-specific educational choices *must* cease.
> In Sweden: Equality of the sexes has a quantitative as well as a qualitative content . . . Equitable distribution in this context refers to a group composition of women to men of 40%–60% or even nearer 50%. If women constitute more than 60% of a group, it is woman-dominated. If there are more than 60% men in a group, it is man-dominated.

The importance of such a public policy statement is that *all* jobs, all occupations, are under government mandate to reach the goal of 50 percent female participation and 50 percent male participation. In other words, the government has decided that no occupation, regardless of its nature, may remain dominated by either sex or more importantly, regardless of the combined inclinations of the private and public sectors of the populace! The government has decided that "sex-specific educational choices must cease," regardless of what the wishes of its citizens might be.

We are showing our vulnerability to making the types of changes that Sweden has already made, by allowing feminist ideology to dominate our behavior and the social policies that affect us as a nation. At the state level, laws mandating multicultural, non-sexist education continue to be passed. Laws such as these, notably, do not spare regulation of private educators, such as religious schools. Non-sexist curriculums are in place in daycare centers and from elementary school through college. And one would be hard pressed to find a single activity, occupation, or athletic event, where men compete or simply interact among themselves without feminists striving to enter the fray, if it is humanly possible for them to do so. If feminists are allowed to continue dictating the social policies of this country through their influence over the mass media and educational systems (all the while gaining ever-greater political and judicial influence), the trend toward androgyny will continue—barring complete social breakdown and anarchy.

One by one, all institutions which historically have been all-male domains (and which thus serve to prevent or slow any trends toward androgyny) are being forcefully desegregated at the hands of the courts and Congress. The laws originally intended to prevent discrimination in the work force are now being interpreted as going far beyond dictating the rules of the workplace. The December 1990, "Phyllis Schlafly Report" addressed this issue regarding all-male colleges:

> You would think the Department of Justice would have enough to do, dealing with our nation's many legal and criminal problems, but on a slow day in 1990 it filed suit against Virginia Military Institute, charging "sex discrimination" because VMI does not admit women.
>
> The purpose of this mischief making lawsuit is not to enable young women to be called Brother Rat. The real purpose is to force VMI to feminize its educational system and conform to the androgynous society demanded by the radical feminists. The statutory language and legislative history of Title IX's rule against sex discrimination clearly exempt military schools and undergraduate colleges that have been traditionally single sex. The feminist suit should be laughed out of court. Every woman in Virginia is within a few miles of at least one of Virginia's 40 colleges or universities. Five of them are exclusively for women.

The availability of institutions solely for women isn't good enough for feminists. In short, they cannot stand to contemplate the existence of one single "place" strictly for men, because they know this will perpetuate differences between the behavior of men and women. One of the latest and most ridiculous examples of the attack on all-male domains regards the recent court ruling allowing Shannon Faulkner into Charleston, South Carolina's famous all-male military college, the Citadel (VMI's sister school). Fathers have been recommending (and young men have been choosing) this 151-year-old college for aspects unique to it that can *only* be maintained with an exclusively male student body.

This, of course, matters not at all to feminists like nineteen year old Shannon Faulkner. The case is discussed in the August 1, 1994 issue of *The National Review*, in an article written by Elizabeth Fox-Genovese:

To destroy this alleged bastion of male privilege, the opposition advanced the purportedly moving claims of poor Shannon Faulkner, the young woman who had been "stigmatized" by her exclusion from The Citadel's corps of cadets. Miss Faulkner, you will recall, had applied to the Citadel, having first persuaded her (high school) guidance counselor to remove all indications of her sex from her application and transcript. She received a provisional acceptance, which The Citadel, when it discovered she was female, withdrew. What a blow to her self-esteem! All this was widely reported. What was less widely reported, if at all, is that Miss Faulkner applied to The Citadel only because she accidentally discovered that it did not admit women, that she plans to become a teacher of young children, and that she has secured a Hollywood agent.

The folly of it all doesn't just end with her entrance. After claiming (on the basis of her sex) that there was no reason for her not to be allowed entry, Faulkner immediately went to court (on the basis of her sex) to have the rules of the institute changed! Her new battle? To change the long-standing Citadel tradition of shaving the heads of new recruits to exclude women. The judge who granted her the right to entrance, U.S. District Court Judge C. Weston Houck, said that the college could shave Faulkner's head, as it does all first-year male cadets, because he found no legal basis for grooming standards based on sex. Who's on her side? only the U.S. Department of Justice, headed by feminist Janet Reno. Their argument is that shaving her hair would "altogether denigrate Faulkner's identity as a woman."

Essentially, Faulkner has been talking out of both sides of her mouth, saying, "There is no reason I should not be allowed because there are no real differences between men and women—no justifiable reason men should want to attend a school that does not admit women"; but then saying, "I'm a woman—different from men —and should not have to undergo the indignity of having my head shaved, which would help to eliminate the differences that separate me from men." It's another example of a feminist wanting to have her cake and eat it, too. (Rarely mentioned is the fact that the physical performance standards for cadets had to be altered—exclusively for her—because from running, to pushups, Faulkner was incapable of meeting the requirements set for all the men.

In hearing testimony for Faulkner's suit to be admitted to The

Citadel, the court zealously took into account a variety of "expert" opinions about the "sexist nature" of the institution. Fox-Genovese goes on to report:

> One of the expert witnesses for Shannon (Faulkner) actually announced that she considered the reluctance of the Citadel cadets to use obscenity in front of women as conclusive evidence of their sexism. So much for manners and civility! The low divorce rate (3 per cent) of VMI graduates produces a similar response: VMI men must be dominating, if not abusing, their wives.

The observations of Andrew Van Sant, a physician and graduate of Annapolis, in the *Conservative Chronicle*, indicate that the judiciary is not alone in its commitment to ending the separation of the military roles of men and women. That commitment has become standard at even the highest of military levels:

> Having briefly served on the staff of the Presidential Commission on the Assignment of Women in the Armed Forces, I read R. Cort Kirkwood's "Life on the Front Lines" (*Vital Signs*, March 1994) with interest. His report on the commission is exactly correct. Particularly depressing is that so many of the Naval Academy and Military Academy graduates on the commission considered equal opportunity to be more important than military readiness. Even more depressing is that no senior military officers are now willing to voice any opposition to current plans to put women in combat.

Failing to realize that the next generation will be subject to feminist indoctrination from the day of birth right on through to adulthood, some might believe that what they see is an insignificant trend. But the next generation will not have the types of role models that previous generations have had, to give it examples of the types of behaviors that are seen universally. The next generation will grow up among its elders (us), who will be far more androgynous than our generation's elders. What kind of models will that new generation provide for the generation following it? A question such as this might seem rhetorical, but its answer warrants careful consideration. Our society has become extremely sensitive to these issues, and so contentious that confrontations are arising in environments that should, more properly, be focused upon other matters. One such confrontation occurred recently in a public high school, concerning the dress code for its students. The *San Jose Mercury News* newspaper reported:

They wore flowery, flowing skirts. Skirts with moon patterns. Plain ones. Plaids.

A handful of Nova High School male students Thursday put on a show of solidarity with one of their buddies who was sent home two days earlier for wearing a skirt.

"Girls can wear pants, so why can't guys wear skirts?" asked sophomore Jesse Itzkowitz, 16, who strolled to classes in a green skirt with tiny flowers, a green and yellow checkered shirt and gray high-top sneakers.

"It's not right. It's flagrant sexism, and we don't feel we should be tormented with that in a learning environment," he said.

Actually, the boy being sent home had nothing to do with sexism. Assistant principal C. Dege Robertson said she based her decision to send him home solely on the basis of rules in the code-of-student handbook, which says students have the right to wear stylish clothing, as long as it isn't a distraction.

"I felt that the clothing would cause undue attention. It's important to have as few distractions as possible." Robertson said she plans to bring up the issue of skirt-wearing male students at the next administrative staff meeting.

Skeptics of the potential for an androgynous United States might ask, "What about human nature? Men and women have always acted so differently that sex differences must be natural. Androgyny would be going against Mother Nature. How could we ever make men and women act alike?" It would be against our nature, but recent history can give us examples in which basic tendencies of our human nature have been either exaggerated (via the socialization process), or—at least for a time—socialized away to insignificance. If we simply look around us we can see that, in many ways, ours has already become an androgynous society.

It may be true that men have been socialized in ways that seem to make some of them overly competitive, aggressive, and achievement-oriented. Nevertheless, it is a worthwhile cost to pay, because some degree of male competitiveness, aggressiveness, and achievement orientation (over and above what is normal for women) has been customary in all societies, and can be looked upon as having been essential for many reasons.

What has happened, in recent years, to what we have always known as the maternal instinct is an example of how instinctive behavior can be socialized into insignificance. It has always been widely accepted that women (like all other maternal mammals) are instinctively driven to protect their babies, whether already born or still in gestation. Despite the fact that no mammalian species regularly practices maternal infanticide, women in this country, having been socialized to the degree that they believe there is absolutely no reason to feel guilt, now voluntarily abort one out of every four pregnancies. It used to be said that mothers derived the greatest enjoyment when their children were small and vulnerable, that mothers were so driven to protect their children, that they even had "eyes in the back of their heads." Today, ever-increasing numbers of mothers contentedly deposit their infants (as young as three months) in daycare centers of every level of quality.[4] These are examples of women being socialized to ignore their maternal instincts in favor of doing "more fulfilling things."

The demise of the family that must inevitably result from the desertion of women from their role as mothers will only contribute to androgynization. The increases in the rate of illegitimacy and the number of divorces brought about by the feminist-inspired social revolution, ensure that young boys will increasingly be raised by their mothers, institutions, and day-care centers, without the benefit of a full-time male in the home as a role model. (Even if there is a man "in the house," a young boy may be less likely to wish to emulate him than if the adult were his biological father.)

Women are obviously becoming more competitive in all facets of life, increasingly involving themselves in all the competitive pursuits feminists have so long chastised men for indulging in. Feminists would typically claim that racing incredibly powerful, fast, and dangerous race cars around a track is ridiculous—until a woman got into the race. War was considered a strictly male undertaking—no woman would get us involved in one, and no woman would fight in one. But British Prime Minister Margaret Thatcher led England into a war, and some female troops are seemingly champing at the bit to get into ground combat—even being on a ship or in a plane isn't close enough.

---

[4] There is a huge number of "mothers" waiting in line for government-provided daycare so that they can do the same thing without having to pay anything: deposit their infant children in daycare for ten hours a day and longer.

Roughly coinciding with the granting of equal employment rights, the advent of modern birth control methods, including abortion, served to complete the double whammy that enabled and encouraged feminism to become what it has.

In the mid-1950s, the birth control pill was invented, *Playboy* magazine arrived and, before long, men were told (by other men) that they were stupid to commit themselves to one woman. Though not many really believed it, men were told that marriage was an institution cleverly devised by women—so as to virtually enslave men to do their heavy labor for them by denying men sexual opportunity unless a permanent commitment was made. Men were also told that, with the pill, not only was the danger of accidental pregnancy going to be a thing of the past, so was the need for making a commitment. At least until a man was "really" ready.

Incredibly, it wasn't long before women were being told almost the exact same things, by feminists, but with the exact opposite viewpoint. Feminists began telling women that marriage and monogamy were the creations of men, so that each man could have "his own personal servant and sex slave." Feminists began referring to wives as "unpaid prostitutes," and it went on and on.

In line with their refusal to admit other differences between the sexes as they promoted androgyny, feminists began to deny that men and women are different even when it comes to the sex drive. Feminists insist there are no inherent differences in drives, emotions, or anything else regarding sexuality. If differences presently appear to exist, they only result from the ways in which women have been socialized (under the patriarchic rule of men), and are therefore meaningless. This has translated to the feminist viewpoint that if a woman feels like having sex she should indulge her desire in the same way men do, without reservation. "Why shouldn't she?" we are asked. The personal and social ramifications of such behavior (which result from actual physiological differences regarding our sexuality) have amazingly gone unconsidered by feminists.

CHAPTER ELEVEN

Promiscuity: The Hidden Dangers

From its very beginnings, the feminist movement has served as a promoter of sexual promiscuity. Today (after 30 years of feminist-supported "sexual liberation"), with the teen pregnancy rates significantly higher than ever before, with illegitimacy rates at almost 30 percent, with one out of four pregnancies being aborted, with a number of sexually transmitted diseases reaching epidemic proportions, and with family disintegration at an all-time high, feminists still refuse to admit that there might be even a single virtue to the notion of chastity, especially feminine chastity. They still refuse to advise or promote restraint or abstinence, at any level, for any reason.

Among other ways, feminists promote promiscuity by denigrating Christianity and other major traditional religions, and the moral codes of behavior religions seek to instill in all of us. (This is perhaps the most significant area in which the feminist denial of traditional religious values causes harm.) They argue that children—adolescents —have "rights" in sexual matters, and they insist that all stigma be removed from sexual activity. They insist on the need for sex-education classes, which have promoted sexual activity among younger and younger children everywhere they've been implemented. They continually deny that any differences exist between the sex drives of adolescent boys and girls.

The statements of former U.S. Surgeon General, Joycelyn Elders, exemplify the feminist position on sexual activity among children: "I tell every girl when she goes out on a date—put a condom in her purse." When hearing the news of two extremely young girls becoming pregnant, one 8 years old and the other 9, Elders proclaimed that this was further evidence of the need for governmental sex education —not to teach them to abstain at that age, but so that they could be knowledgeable of the variety of birth control methods available to them.[1]

A newly coined term, now used to describe the highly promiscuous, epitomizes the legitimizing of promiscuity by feminists. The term is "Wild Girl." By referring to highly promiscuous girls as "Wild Girls" (instead of the traditional derogatory labels, "loose," "bad girls," and "sluts"), the stigma that was formerly attached to such behavior is replaced with its opposite. "Wild Girl," as a descriptive phrase, is meant to bring to mind thoughts of harmless, fun-loving rebelliousness. The problem, of course, is that such thoughts actually condone and encourage the type of behavior associated with the new, positive phrase. In this case, by historical standards, such encouragement results in a higher level of promiscuity.

Some degree of feminine chastity has been considered virtuous in all societies, as well as being necessary. Words like "whore" and "slut," with negative meanings, have sprung up in all languages (as a protective measure) and have lessened the tendency toward promiscuous behavior by stigmatizing it, thereby protecting the stability of society. Forty years ago, the young women who are now defined as "Wild Girls" would have been labeled "sluts." Today, the slut can be called a "Wild Girl," and can even be considered a role model. If not superior to the woman (particularly the young woman or girl) practicing virtually any sexual restraint, the "Wild Girl's" behavior is regarded as at least normal. The "Wild Girl" is portrayed as "getting what she wants," rather than as being taken advantage of.

The point here is that feminists promote promiscuity while denying the array of perils to individuals and society that can so easily be associated with the behavior. Seemingly, in the minds of many feminists, promiscuity is just an example of the process of androgynization becoming reality—girls are swearing, competing, fighting, drinking, and smoking just like boys. Lost on feminists, however, is the fact that

---

[1] Related to feminism's promotion of promiscuity through its refusal to tolerate calls for abstinence from any quarter, is its attempts to remove any stigmas that have traditionally been attached to promiscuous behavior (not to mention abortion). Anyone calling for a degree of chastity is labeled "out of touch," "intolerant," or a "repressive, religious zealot." For example, Elders, defending the number of abortions resulting from promiscuous behavior, chastises the Catholic church by saying that it has got to get over its "love affair with the fetus."

unlike boys, they're also getting pregnant at ages when they are completely unequipped to mother their offspring, in a feminist-dominated society that does nothing to correct this shortcoming, but acts in such a way as to perpetuate the practice.

CHAPTER TWELVE

What's Happening at Work

As discussed, when feminists initially failed to realize that working on equal terms with men and competing with men on all levels would necessitate the androgynization of society, they were essentially guilty of lack of foresight. But since that time (after more than 20 years of teaching women to emulate men—especially in the realm of work, as though that were a necessity), they are guilty of more than a lack of foresight. By choosing to ignore, and attempting to refute, all the universally observable, historical evidence pointing to work having special meaning to men, they are guilty, among other things, of promoting many lies. They are also guilty of absolute cold-heartedness. And, by undermining the roles of men, they are guilty of putting society, their own future, and the future of our children at risk.

Despite all their attempts at indoctrinating men to behave otherwise, it is obvious that real, normal, masculine men around the world, regardless of the culture from which they come, simply do not want to work alongside women at the same jobs. Feminists, though, still refuse to acknowledge even the possibility of real, inherent reasons for these obviously deeply held reservations of men. It is for fear of the truth that feminists refuse to admit or discuss the possibility that work has special significance in men's lives.

As discussed earlier, from our very beginnings and in all societies ever studied, men and women have had different roles in all areas of life. Nowhere is this more true than in the realm of work. In all societies, men have chosen to work among themselves, in one way or another, at any variety of tasks, and have always held the high-status positions across the various planes of occupations. Despite such compelling evidence, feminists still deny even the possibility that there might be instinctive reasons for this. Realistically, feminists are only able to cling to this argument because, as of now, there are still no scientific means of determining whether or not such "instinctive" drives exist within man. Feminists are as if blind to the fact that all observable and historical evidence shows that they do.

Because there is not, as of now, an accurate method of *scientifically* measuring instinctive behaviors[1], theories involved in substantiating the existence of instinctive behaviors are based on the observation of individual and cultural traits, existing universally. The reasons for the universal existence of such instincts can only be theorized. (This is one reason modern psychology cannot truly be called a science).

It is important to note that universals existing *prior* to modern methods of mass communication can be said to have special significance for two key reasons. First, through their heightened abilities to influence, methods of mass communication enable all sorts of rapid changes to occur within a given culture that wouldn't be possible in more natural states of existence. Second, and perhaps of greater importance, is the fact that cultural values can be effectively transferred from one culture to another so rapidly.

The point is that it was impossible for *prior* universals to be the result of mass media indoctrination and, lacking widespread communication, impossible for one society to transfer its universals to another society. This means that the universal behaviors of each society sprang spontaneously from within. And, of course, given the number of cultures that have been observed and studied, universals are not coincidental. Nor are they even accidental.

Most theories regarding the special meaning of work for men revolve around the noticeable fact that men everywhere have related to the idea of work, and have taken pride in their work, in ways different from women. In his book, *Sexual Suicide*, George Gilder notes that feminists, "cannot recognize that while women may work because they have to—or because the job is interesting and meaningful—men usually work to validate their very identities as males." He theorizes that men, as a group, have evolved to subconsciously perceive work as being the main reason for their existence. Margaret Mead theorizes that women have had no reason to evolve in that direction, because

---

[1] "Instinctive" behavior can be defined as a natural or inherent impulse, or a drive that is active, or activated without conscious thought.

they have always had a built-in reason for their existence: giving birth. For women, other achievements in life are comparatively like frosting on the cake.

In 1948, Margaret Mead wrote:

> If any human society—large or small, simple or complex, based on the most rudimentary hunting and fishing, or on the whole elaborate interchange of manufactured products—is to survive, it must have a pattern of social life that comes to terms with the differences between the sexes. . . .

Echoing that belief, and expanding upon the reasons for it, George Gilder took up the same topic in *Sexual Suicide*:

> Apart from the diversity of mankind, this is perhaps the clearest lesson of the anthropologist. How a tribe manages its sexuality—its births, matings, kinship ties—determines the nature of the tribe and its durability. . . .
>
> One of the concerns of every society is how to respond to the essentially unprogrammed form of male sexual energy. . . .
>
> A man who is oriented toward a family he loves—or wants to create —is apt to work more consistently and productively than a man oriented toward his next fix, lay, day at the races, or drinking session with the boys. A man who feels affirmed sexually by his work environment, and his relation to other men and women in it, will produce more than a man who finds his job sexually erosive and confusing. A man who is integrated into a community through a role in a family, spanning generations into the past and future, will be more consistently and durably tied to the social order than a man responding chiefly to a charismatic leader, a demagogue, or a grandiose ideology of patriotism. . . .
>
> A man's commitments to his job, his career, his family—his deferred gratifications and his sacrifices for the larger community—are not the product of a simple calculus of cost and benefits. Rather this behavior pattern is motivated by a system of sexual relationships and affirmations. . . . Crucial is the desire, conscious or unconscious, for progeny with a specific woman, who subjects the male's sexual drive to long-term female patterns.
>
> Because the father's role is a cultural invention rather than a biological imperative, however, the civilizing impulse of love is psychologically fragile. The subordination of male sexual rhythms to the long-term cycles of female sexuality is constantly subject to erosion by short term male impulses: to give up the job, the family, and pursue a life

of immediate gratification. The husband's commitment thus needs external props.

The sexual constitution has long afforded three principal props. The first is the insistence of most women on some degree of monogamy. In general, a man still cannot get sex easily and dependably with women he likes unless he foregoes others, or undertakes some deceitful drama of love that is a strain on his conscience. The second support is marriage. The culture still exalts it with religious ceremony and affirms it with legal sanctions and social pressures. Third is the male role as the essential provider. This gives the man a position in wedlock to some extent commensurate with the woman's. Otherwise he is inferior. In social terms the family is formed to create a stable home for children. The woman's role is clearly indispensable while the man's is secondary. The whole sexual constitution is based on the maternal tie.

. . . paternity, as a cultural invention, will not serve to give the man a durable role in the family; and there is virtually no society that successfully relies on it to keep the man actively present. To keep the man present and to preserve the nuclear family as the prevailing institution, even love will not long suffice. He must be needed in a practical and material way. . . .

In these terms, the sexual role of most jobs is far more important than their economic function. In its extraordinary complexity, modern civilization is also extremely vulnerable to the outlaw—whether the alcoholic driver or the hijacker, the guerrilla or the drug addict, the mugger or the assassin. The real contribution made by individual men in their work rarely exceeds the real damage they can do if their masculinity is not socialized or subjected to female patterns. . . .

Crucial to the sexual constitution of employment is that, in one way or another, it assures that over the whole society, class by class, most men will make more money than most women . . . in essence, the additional pay is part of a tacit social contract by which men are induced to repress antisocial patterns. On the immediate and superficial level, justice and efficiency—so stressed by the feminist—have little to do with it. . . .

A male's money . . . is socially affirmative. If the man is unmarried, a much higher proportion of his money than a woman's will be spent on the opposite sex. His money gives him the wherewithal to make long-term sexual initiatives. It gives him the courage to submit to female sexual patterns, for he knows he will retain the crucial role of familial support. His sexual impulses can assume the civilizing rather than the subversive form. . . .

. . . the [women's] movement is striking at the Achilles' heel of civilized society: the role of the male. They are correct that it is a cultural contrivance and that it can be destroyed. But they are wrong to suppose that men, shorn of their current schemes of socialization, would mildly accept the new roles provided by the movement. New roles can work only if they come to terms with the sexual inferiority and compensatory aggressiveness of the male, only if they afford a distinctive male identity that accords with the special predicament of male sexuality in civilized society.

The existence of such emotions in men does a great deal to explain why they have always been reluctant to let women enter their work domain.

Such feelings may seem outdated in today's world (in which it is increasingly women, and our governmental support structures, rather than individual men, that fill necessary protector and provider roles). But ours is a society in which increasing numbers of women believe that their individual survival can, theoretically, be accomplished without a male partner. Simultaneously, the male role is further undermined by the fact that many or most of today's jobs don't require male strengths or qualities for satisfactory performance. Seemingly unconsidered is the fact that, after eons of having filled these roles, protecting and providing are instinctively perceived by men as being reasons to exist.

Not only does a man take pride in his work, he also takes natural pride in his gender, and in his being a member of it. Consequently, when women attempt to enter his work domain in direct competition with him, more emotions are affected within him. Not only is he, as always, competing for his sense of personal pride in his work, but he's now also competing for the pride he has in his gender.[2]

---

[2] Does his taking pride in being a man seem ridiculous? Or the fact that a main source of his pride in himself comes from his work? They shouldn't, because taking pride in one's individual or group attributes is an ordinary part of human nature.

A brunette, for instance, will tend to be more irritated at catching her husband admiring a blond than she will another brunette. It is apparent that many men are highly attracted to Asian women. It is equally apparent that this infuriates many Caucasian women and Asian men. On a grander scale, the U.S.—with almost unanimous approval of its citizens—raced to send men to the moon before the Soviet Union, mainly for the sake of pride and the chance to win a good, competitive race. In a great example of racial or cultural pride, and capitalistic motivation, the railroad builders of the 1800s were able to get the Irish and Chinese workers to work in vigorous competition to

Men are resentful of women entering their spheres of work for many reasons, pride in gender being one of them. To be in direct competition with women on a daily basis at work, where they have universally derived their pride, sense of accomplishment, and feeling of worth, is incredibly threatening to men's self-esteem. For women, work outside the home has always held much less personal significance (as proven by the lack of competition among them).

Nor is working among men (when competition arises) threatening to women, in terms of self-esteem. This is primarily because women are the habitual underdogs.[3] They have nothing to lose. On the contrary, when women do get to compete with men, their status rises for no other reason than being beside men. The opposite is true of men. Men's status is instantly lowered by the presence of women as competitors. Men have the pressure of being the favorites, and are expected to win the race. Because of this expectation, they know winning will bring little or no real reward, no increase in status. Losing will bring shame. (Under such conditions, we should not be surprised that more and more men simply choose to quit the race, upon doing cost/reward analysis.)

Certain jobs and occupations are non-competitive by nature, or are self-rewarding. Consequently, these jobs don't generally pose problems if men and women work together as equals. For example, teaching, nursing, and administration are occupations that are inherently non-competitive, and are unlikely to promote competitiveness in an individual. This is probably one reason why women were allowed to work at, were funneled into, or chose to enter into these occupations, even before the word self-esteem was commonly used. Lacking a competitive environment, people in these occupations often find

---

see which ethnic group could lay the most track each day. (Women left to their own devices would never think of, or do such a thing, because women don't think like men. This is not to say that women don't take pride in their gender, or don't sometimes relish competition with men. Nevertheless, in work, competition and achievement don't have the same meaning to women.) Though leery of looking for actual, specific—and possibly gender-related—reasons, even feminists often agree that men are inherently more competitive, and motivated by competition, than women.

[3] Terming women the underdogs isn't ridiculous when we consider that men have been ruling the world since time immemorial. If all were equal in the rat race and men had as much to gain by competing against women as women gain by competing against men, women would be the underdogs for good reason, they would lose.

other ways to challenge themselves in their attempts to find added motivation. The primary competition in job areas such as these is the competition for promotion.

Once women have decided to enter the work force, many changes are necessitated. Women are going to have to deal with discrimination, which is inevitable. It is so much inevitable that laws are needed to prevent it. But once these laws are enacted they must be followed by laws that prevent harassment of those women who get jobs by virtue of the anti-discrimination laws. The truth is that regardless of the number of laws enacted, these problems cannot be legislated out of existence. Discrimination and harassment are often men's way of trying to let women know they are not welcome as direct competitors in men's domains. Even with such laws in place, discrimination and harassment against women will continue to occur wherever women actively seek to compete against men as equals.[4]

That, though, is just one source of the male anger currently being expressed toward women in our society. While feminists believe or pretend that this anger is unjustifiable, it isn't. On the contrary, it's universally a normal response; i.e. a natural response to the discomfort caused by women's attempts to undermine the role and status of men. It is an example of men being angry for a very real reason, rather than for no reason at all. It is compounded by the fact that most women do know of the discomfort they cause, and sometimes intentionally make it worse.

---

[4] Whatever sexual misconduct occurred at the Navy's Tailhook Convention, for instance, happened because those women were integrating themselves into the Navy hierarchy with men. In so doing, they were, ipso facto, lowering the status of the male officers, whether they recognized it or not. Any mistreatment of female officers could, in whole or in part, be attributed to resentment. If those Navy women had not been in direct competition with men, it wouldn't have happened.

CHAPTER THIRTEEN

The Undermining of Relationships

The ways in which androgynization of the sexes imperils individuals, relationships, and society are so numerous as to nearly defy clear description. Even briefly discussing a limited number of them (as is done here) is all but impossible without seeming redundant. Additionally, the reader is asked to keep in mind that although many of the perils attributable to androgynization may *appear* inconsequential, it is the fact that they have a cumulative effect that makes them dangerous. In other words, though a specific peril may affect only a small percentage of relationships, given a long enough list of such perils, the overall effect becomes significant to a large percentage of the population. As examples, such phenomena as our sky-rocketing divorce rate, and the rapidly growing number of adults who will never marry at all, can be seen to stem from the process of androgynization occurring in the United States at this time.

In much the same way feminists failed to recognize that full integration of the work force would necessitate the androgynization of the sexes, they failed to foresee the array of detrimental effects the androgynization of the sexes would have on relationships. They also failed to foresee the impact that weakened relationships would subsequently have on individuals and on society. It is these weakened relationships that constitute, perhaps, the greatest peril of androgyny.

It is a truism, with regard to love relationships, that opposites attract. This seems particularly true of the emotional and physical "chemistry" that binds couples together, but it is also true of the roles and responsibilities that partners adopt, with regard to one another, within the relationship. In fact, whether we are discussing emotional relationships or business relationships, complementarity is the cement that allows partnerships to survive and to thrive.

Androgyny is perilous because it undermines the mutual attraction between men and women (which most often initiates love relationships), *and* the needs for one another that normally provide the practical basis for an ongoing relationship. The further women move toward masculinity (and men move toward femininity) the fewer are the characteristics that set them apart and make them attractive to each other. Through its tendency to make men and women interchangeable, androgyny also reduces the ability of each sex to fill the other's needs through complementary abilities and behaviors. Women, by assuming roles within relationships that have historically been reserved for men, neutralize men's prerogative of filling those same roles and of embodying and exhibiting normal, masculine characteristics—those same characteristics that have historically attracted women. At the same time, these women decrease their attractiveness to their mates, or potential mates (healthy, typical men, despite any claims to the contrary by feminists or anyone else, are attracted most to women who need them). Men, by relinquishing roles within relationships that have historically belonged to them, may realize some slight gain by seeming up-to-date or "modern," but do not gain an amount of respect and attractiveness commensurate to what they have lost by becoming less masculine, in the eyes of most women.[1]

Simplistically speaking, men have traditionally led, protected, and provided, and have filled these roles to varying degrees within all societies. As opposed to leading, women have been the receptive sex, and as opposed to protecting and providing, have nurtured family and cared for the home, assuming many variations of these responsibilities in all societies. This provided each sex not only with defined responsibilities, but with the opportunity to give and receive the rewards that come with giving and receiving. This give and take included both physical and emotional dimensions of the relationship, though these two are interrelated. The person who has become androgynous via the socializing process, on the other hand, is something of a self-sufficient entity. The woman's need and desire to feel sheltered, protected, and cared-for diminishes or disappears, just as the man's need and desire

---

[1] Men's assuming traditionally feminine roles may have less overall impact on heterosexual relationships than women's assuming traditionally masculine roles, because those men strongly inclined to exhibit feminine traits are frequently more sexually attracted to other men than they are to masculine women.

to fulfill her needs diminishes or disappears. What feminists refuse to recognize are the impacts this has on men.

One of the primary aspects of relationships that is seriously impacted by feminism, and its promotion of androgyny, is the distribution of authority. This is not only brought about by the removal of sex-differentiated roles and responsibilities, but by the open insistence of feminists that men should never possess anything resembling final authority over their partners within the relationship.

Another factor undermining relationships is the extent to which the androgynous society adapts itself to filling roles that have historically been filled from within self-reliant families by their members. It does this not only by providing an array of financial supports for the now-larger number of disenfranchised, family-less individuals, but also by caring for children. As this happens, women become ever more self-sufficient. And as the need to make sacrifices for their men is reduced, women increasingly become unwilling to make such sacrifices. From the man's viewpoint, he becomes ever more expendable and he adapts to this and to the subsequent removal of any social pressures to stay and make sacrifices for his family. Increasingly, men will not stay and make sacrifices for women, who have increasingly fewer incentives to make any sacrifices for them. In this way and others, androgyny turns the concerns of individuals inward, promoting selfishness, self-centeredness, and the pursuit of immediate gratification.

There has been much discussion of the reluctance of today's men to commit to today's women, and of their inability to honor that commitment when they do make it. There has not been a corresponding amount of discussion of the real reasons for this failing.[2] What little has occurred has emanated from people fantasizing about how men feel or are supposed to feel. In tune with the politically correct climate of today, men have been blamed—they're either this or that, or have something called a "syndrome." In any case, the upshot of such discussions is inevitably a specious list of ways in which American men should reform themselves, and a great deal of clamoring about the

---

[2] The displeasure of American feminist women with American men has received inordinate attention in the popular press and elsewhere, while the feelings of American men about the opposite sex and relationship problems have gone largely unexplored and ignored. For this reason, it is not a goal to give the feminist point of view equal time here.

need for society/men to provide more benefits and services to replace the men who are unwilling to do the right thing or are deprived of the opportunity of doing the right thing.

In an environment which is making the veneer of femininity thinner and thinner, until it is veritably only skin deep, it would be more informative to ask, *"Why should* a man make and keep a commitment to today's woman—particularly to today's feminist-influenced career woman?"

Just as it is impossible to deny feminism's promotion of promiscuity, it is equally impossible to deny that the loosening of sexual behavior and feminism's encouragement of androgyny have had tremendous impacts on short- and long-term relationships.

The perils of disease, teen pregnancy, and illegitimacy are increasingly receiving the attention they deserve. Unfortunately, the emotional impacts to individuals and relationships that result from promiscuity do not receive equal attention. As with other aspects of androgyny, even if the perils of promiscuity to the individual seem minimal, and even if they could be further reduced, promiscuity would still negatively affect the development and maintenance of long-term relationships.

What has not been contemplated seriously enough is the fact that only modern birth and disease control technologies, combined with decreasing female reliance on men, have allowed women to become so promiscuous—more promiscuous than in any of the mythic "free love" societies ever dreamed up by feminists or anthropologists. Feminists promote promiscuity either in the name of sexual freedom—in the belief that it enhances feminine power (which it sometimes does, in the short term)—or as a means of rationalizing their own sexual misbehavior, as E. Michael Jones pointed out at length in his book, *Degenerate Moderns.* Referring to a modern screenplay, entitled *Blue Lagoon,* about two adolescents alone on a Pacific island paradise, who find their sexual lust for each other unconstrained by even modern conceptions of morality, Jones labels the feminist-created tall tales about promiscuous societies as *"Blue Lagoon* anthropology."[3]

---

[3] Efforts by feminists to rationalize promiscuity have even led to their inappropriately attempting to compare humans to certain other groups of primates. "Inappropriately" because, as legitimate study has shown and Donald Symons, author of *The Evolution*

Regardless of the fact that condoms, abortions, sexually transmitted diseases, and birth control pills change some factors regarding our sexuality, they do not, and cannot, change others. Promiscuous sexual behavior is still going to impact us in many ways. For argument's sake, however, let us assume that we were eventually able to control all of the potentially negative physical consequences of promiscuity —principally unwanted pregnancy, cervical cancer, and disease. Additionally, let us assume that feminists got their wish, and all public stigmas regarding promiscuous behavior could be removed, and were removed.

Even, or perhaps, especially, if the above were true, a significant number, perhaps even *most* girls in early adolescence—regardless of how many sex-education courses they receive in public school—if sexually active at all, are going to be *very* active. At such young ages, it doesn't make sense to expect restraint from sexually active girls, simply because they lack the ability to form sound judgements. Also, boys at that age are going to take whatever they're given and whatever they can. Assuming that a *significant* number of adolescent boys will show sexual restraint in the presence of available girls is unrealistic.[4]

In this era of feminism, sexual liberation, and the acceptance of the natural impulses of boys and young men, it cannot be doubted that a significant number of young girls have lived through scenarios much like the following: Beginning sexual relations early in adolescence, they enjoyed the results so much that they became very promiscuous. They quickly realized that boys liked and wanted them, and they naturally liked this. A natural progression of events led them to recognize that they could get boys to do things for them, which they also liked. Many discovered there were some boys with wills stronger than their own, who could manipulate them, which some of them also liked (at

---

of Human Sexuality, has pointed out, even the "happily promiscuous, nonpossessive, Rousseauian chimpanzees turned out not to exist."

[4] Feminists seem to be in a state of denial about, or simply unable to understand the sex drive of—or the importance of sex to—the typical adolescent male. Even more so in the case of the *highly sexed* adolescent male. The highly sexed, highly aggressive adolescent male is the male likely to have, by far, the most sexual conquests, and is likely to feel the fewest emotions and concerns for his partners while enjoying the pleasure. John Engleman has pointed out a cold reality that especially applies to adolescent sexuality. "For teenage boys and men, sex is not so much an expression of affection as it is the impulse of an appetite . . . male sexuality is frequently violent and exploitive."

least for awhile). During this stage in the lives of sexually active girls, the formation of personality is influenced to a much higher degree by sexual experiences and peer-group concerns than is the case with sexually inactive girls, whose personalities are influenced to a greater degree by emotional stimuli from other relationships—such as friendships with other girls and boys, teachers, grandparents, mothers and fathers.

In time, these girls realize that the main reason boys—or perhaps, by now, men—have been interested in them at all, has been their sexual accessibility. Beginning to understand (both consciously and subconsciously) the lack of genuine respect they have received during their formative years, they begin to be affected. Their self-esteem (very possibly negatively affected) will determine their reaction. They may become confused; they may become bitter, and develop a dislike or distrust of men. They might very well continue to seek relationships based on their previous behavior. In such cases, they may marry abusive men, and have personalities that almost invite abuse. Or they might look for a way out by finding the proverbial "nice guy." Given their sexual experiences, and their emotional state, neither partner is likely to satisfy the other, creating matches doomed to failure. In any event, their lifestyle and future choice of partners will be affected to a higher than normal degree by their adolescent sexual experiences. There can be little doubt that women who exhibit highly promiscuous behavior in adolescence suffer higher than normal rates of physical and emotional abuse from their men. The increase in reports of spousal abuse, as well as the increased rates of divorce, point in concrete terms to the perils of promiscuity. And this does not even take into account increases in rates of abortion, increased incidence of sexually transmitted diseases, and increased use of drugs and alcohol among adolescents.[5]

The reality is that it is one thing for girls to get married in more primitive, or less complex, cultures and to become sexually active within such marriages, between the ages of 12 and 17 years. It is quite another for girls to become sexually active outside of marriage,

---

[5] Note that whether promiscuity fosters increased usage of drugs and alcohol, or the other way round, there can be little argument that the two behaviors are statistically linked.

in a society as complex and confusing as ours. In short, the perils of promiscuity are felt early in life, and for the great majority will have lifelong impact.

One of the commonly unconsidered impacts of promiscuous lifestyles among young women has to do with their future choice of mates. It is common knowledge that men are easier to satisfy sexually than are women. The promiscuous woman, having had more experience on which to judge the sexual performance of a given partner, may find herself in a position where other factors important in a mate (honesty, morality, work ethic, and the importance of family, to name only a few) are given relatively little consideration—at great cost to her future stability and happiness—compared to the case of a less-experienced woman.

On the other hand, a second potential problem arises when an "experienced" woman makes her choice of mates based on traits other than sexual performance. Having done so, she may well find herself dissatisfied with her partner because she remembers other partners whose sexual performance was more satisfying to her. Should such a situation occur, her marriage is at risk if she cannot be content with the mate she has chosen and forget those others.

Should a man choose a woman who has led a promiscuous lifestyle, he may spend an inordinate amount of time wondering whether his performance measures up satisfactorily to that of her previous partners. The woman is less likely to find this the case, because she knows when she has satisfied him. This is not to suggest that *all* men are uncomfortable or insecure with women who have had many lovers. Given the role sex plays in contemporary society, some men would actually prefer wives who are "experienced." In such cases, particularly if he believes that the majority of men are not more expert than he, the husband may feel reassured that his mate will know what she is *not* missing, but the number of these men is undoubtedly relatively small compared to the population at large. Virginal women have been the cultural ideal throughout history, and men's insecurity about their sexual performance is at the core of this fact.

Male sexual jealousy and insecurity are universally strong. So strong and so universal, in fact, that in many countries (and even in some places in this country, until 35–40 years ago) if a man found his wife committing adultery and killed both her and her lover in the act, few juries would convict him of murder. In light of this, it is foolish to imagine that a woman's pre-marital experiences are unimportant or unconsidered by the man she eventually marries.

Also regarding male sexual insecurity, if feminists claim there should be no such emotions in men on the basis that there is no evidence of the need for them, then, again, using that same feminist logic, there is no reason for the emotion of jealousy, or even the feelings of love, regarding other aspects of relationships. They are equally immeasurable emotions; therefore, there is no reason for them to exist—they have only arisen out of the socialization process. Feminists would ask, "Why should men feel insecure about the number of partners their potential mates might have had?" In the same way, they'll soon be asking, "Why should a man or a woman ever need to feel jealous of another person, even if that person is sleeping with his or her partner? What's the big deal?" According to feminist logic, they shouldn't. This is not mere conjecture. Feminists get what they want, and many of today's leading feminists do, in fact, advocate open marriages—if not the end of marriage, love, trust and family (as we know them) entirely. The leader of N.O.W., Patricia Ireland, openly lives an alternate lifestyle: husband *and* lesbian lover.

To varying degrees, in a varying percentage of cases, sex can make us fall in love. At least, it can make us believe we are in love. When this happens, we obviously become inclined to make our opposites believe that we are in love with them, regardless of reality. What untold number of divorces ended marriages that resulted from sexual infatuation? These were relationships that were built on true lust, instead of true love.

As opposed to earlier times, how frequently do women make men "fall in love" with them by satisfying them sexually, as opposed to using other feminine attributes they possess? Perhaps, for the modern woman, this is necessitated by the withering of those other attributes. Or perhaps, women simply fail to recognize the possibility of men falling in love for this reason. Unfortunately, when either the newness of the sexual experience wears off for the man, or the female's receptivity drops sometime after commitment is achieved, the results are somewhat predictable if what the man felt wasn't really "true love." Things begin to deteriorate, and she is left to wonder why.

Habitual promiscuity also gives rise to unfortunate situations in which the woman believes that sexual access to her body is all that is required of her (or at least the major part of what is required) to "satisfy" her partner. The woman not granting sexual access (or not depending upon sexual behavior to guarantee her partner's interest) during the dating process must rely on other of her charms in order to maintain the relationship—a tendency that may well extend far beyond the dating process and into marriage.

Many, while recognizing the perils of "Wild Girl" type promiscuity, still advocate premarital sex, so long as love is present. The problem with this is that men, consciously or unconsciously, respond to this in ways detrimental to women in the long run. Because of the differences of sex drives, it is ultimately women who must individually set the boundaries of accessibility. Even prior to being legally married, after romantic break-ups, many women feel "used," that their lover never *really* loved them, but just pretended to so that he could use them. Probably just as frequently—given the influence of sex on the male psyche—he was at least partially or intermittently in love. And when he left, he may very well have left because—other than sex—his needs were not being satisfactorily met. If they had been, *then* he might have truly fallen in love. (This is not meant to hurt anyone, but simply to note a reality).

Because making a lifetime commitment to another human being is, to a degree, analogous to agreeing to work at the same job or for the same company for life—or living in the same home or city for life—there need to be some awfully compelling reasons to make the commitment and to stand by it. Once a society becomes non-monogamous past a certain point, men's reasons for committing, and inclinations toward staying committed, are drastically reduced in several ways.

In reality, sex has always been one of the most "compelling" reasons, if not the primary reason for men to form a lifetime relationship. Even love and the desire to perpetuate the "lineage" (the family name) may be less compelling reasons (though they may be equally essential). In the past, the great majority of men around the world may have been pushed to make a commitment in order to obtain a reasonably reliable source of sexual satisfaction. But today, because of the change in women's attitudes toward sex—ironically spawned by feminism—reasonably attractive men can frequently, if not generally, obtain the same level of sexual satisfaction without the need to make a long-term commitment. In many cases, their level of sexual satisfaction is actually increased. This can be true for several reasons.

If a man has no commitment to stay, and his partner values his presence, she will often make a greater effort to bind him to her by satisfying him sexually and emotionally than the woman who has a binding commitment from a man. This becomes something of a continuation of the dating process, in which both partners may exhibit excellent behavior. (This obviously has widely varying time limitations, depending on the individuals involved.) The temporary type of arrangement also allows him to easily change partners, which is incredibly tempting for most men, especially in a society of promiscuous women.

Additionally, without a marital commitment (or *meaningful* marital commitment), a man need not fret how the future attractiveness of his mate might change, because if it changes for the worse, he can simply change mates. What this means is that a marital commitment may no longer provide a man with his best chances for the highest levels of sexual gratification. On the contrary, many men may think of themselves as receiving a great deal more sexual satisfaction by refusing to commit and leaving their options open. Given the importance of sex to men, the significance of these things cannot be measured. They all become extremely important to contemplate when we recognize the feminist promotion of the non-monogamous society, and remember the vastly increased numbers of available, single women.

Love and feminism hardly belong in the same sentence because, in reality, they almost cannot co-exist. Most people are either in love, or would like to be in love. Tellingly, most of those who claim they have no use for it are feminists.

In addition to men's sexual reservations, there are many other factors that have changed their outlook toward relationships with women. Seemingly unnoticed by feminists is the fact, sad but true, that men today are less likely to fall deeply in love, and receive love's rewards, than men were 20–30 years ago.

There are many reasons for this, and most of them arise out of the illogic of feminism and its impact on women. One of the most important is that American women seem to have lost all ability to understand men, or comprehend their needs. In fact, in probably no other area has the illogic of feminism been more bankrupt than in its failure to comprehend men and their needs. Another reason is that women now behave so much more like men that men need them less, and find them less attractive. The result is that several primary needs of men—within the realm of love—are ever more frequently unfulfilled.

Regarding women's misunderstanding of men, first, it has been feminism's open viewpoint that men have no needs unique to them. Second, women—having been told daily for the past 30 years by feminists that they have all been victims—have largely come to believe in their status as victims. Perceiving themselves in this way has diminished the feminine inclination to care, commiserate, or attempt to understand. Third, as women themselves have increasingly become less secure (as a result of having been encouraged to abandon roles natural to them in favor of emulating men), they have had less time to devote to understanding men. Female insecurity has also grown in correlation with the increase in failed relationships. Increases in female alcoholism, drug addiction, child abuse, and the lack of a sufficient number of psychiatric couches are all evidence of declining female mental health and security.

Feminists cannot seem to realize that the male need to be understood by women is more on the deeper emotional level of "acceptance" than on the rational level. Men don't need to be "analyzed" by women—as seems to be in vogue today. Men can sense, without much contemplation, whether or not they are understood on an emotional basis by women. In the old days, when men were accepted for what they were—as "just men," unchangeable by women—being misunderstood was less important. Now that women are challenging the way men are, rather than accepting it philosophically, many men are unhappy about the repeated demands to discuss their feelings, but are no more ready to do so. (We are, by nature, focused outward toward the world instead of inward toward ourselves.) This is why men don't always like talking about certain subjects, or feelings. And, when men *are* understood, they may not want to talk about it all night, since there is no misunderstanding. Too many of today's feminist-influenced women (those in heterosexual relationships) fail to understand what can be understood through simple day-to-day living, heeding their intuition, and caring about the real concerns of their men instead of satisfying their own curiosity.

In regard to today's women, there is definitely something lacking in their understanding of men. All of the contemporary books and psychology often cause the "new woman" to misdiagnose virtually all of men's feelings. A prime example of contradictory opinions about today's men—seemingly held by the majority of women—is that, on the one hand, men are afraid of making themselves vulnerable, and on the other hand, women are tired of having to "mother," or "nurture" them. If a man is willing to let himself be mothered, and nurtured, he must be willing to make himself vulnerable.

The fact of the matter is that if a man rejects a woman, out of a lack of feeling love for her, there is a distinct possibility that it is due to her inability to understand or accept him for what he is. Without understanding and acceptance there can be no compassion, no caring, no nurturing, not even any meaningful communication.

Perhaps it is men's need to give love—and the ways in which they go about fulfilling this need—that is most misunderstood by women. One of men's greatest needs is to be needed—to have an outlet to give of themselves, to express their love on a daily basis (and, thus, have a reason to exist)—even if this is only accomplished by bringing home a loaf of bread. Women, of course, also want to be needed, but there is no reason that they must do the same things as men in order to be needed or appreciated. There are many reasons for mounting divorce rates, single parenthood, and growing disregard among men for their families, but there can be no doubt the usurpation of the male role is one of them. (Other reasons will be discussed later.)

The result of feminism's influence is that today's women are less likely to receive the types of gifts men gave in the past, and that today's men find fewer ways to express their love and fewer women worthy of loving. Opportunities and inclination are in decline, as is the likelihood of long-term commitment.

In regard to men's roles in filling the needs of women, there is a great amount of observable evidence pointing to men having the desire, need, and typically the responsibility to fulfill the role of "entertainer" (for lack of a better term) within relationships. One thing this means is that when a man looks at a woman as a potential mate, consciously or not, he wonders, "Can I content her?" (i.e. Can I entertain her sexually, emotionally, with humor, and make her confident in me.)

On the woman's part, observable evidence points to the reverse being true. Women—whether conscious of it or not—don't usually set out to be the entertainer so much as to be entertained, and are generally not attracted to men who aren't entertaining. It is unlikely that any woman ever sets out to find a boring mate. Perhaps this is why women so frequently seem attracted to "storytellers." Even the stereotyped "strong, silent type" of man does not represent boredom for women, since they characteristically set out to determine what is going on inside that silence. If they discover that he is silent because he has nothing to say (or, God forbid, because he isn't very intelligent and, so, says nothing) they rapidly begin to look elsewhere for their entertainment.

No one can be certain as to the origins of behaviors such as the entertainer, but there are any number of possibilities. One is that this behavior developed as a part of courtship, as a necessary effort by individual males to differentiate themselves from other males competing for the same mate. In most species in the animal kingdom, males are the aggressors in courtship rituals, and in many species females require flamboyant displays of physical and behavioral prowess before accepting the male. The male peacock's plumage and the beautiful display he creates by spreading it are actually the result of female selection.

Though in Part One the phenomenon of storytelling was discussed in relation to men's self-esteem, storytelling could also be a part of men's filling the entertainer role. Possibly such behavior is an extension, or by-product, of men's outwardly directed behaviors. As men hunted, waged war, explored surrounding lands as potential sites for migration, and so on, they would naturally have had interesting stories to tell; men have—up to our contemporary era—always been the natural gatherers of news.

This information, when brought back to the home, the tribe, or the village, was invariably received with great attention, and its bearers reaped great benefit for the risks they incurred in gathering it and for the stories they wove about it. In many cases, of course, those risks became exaggerated in the telling, simply because there was little danger of exposure for the teller and because the rewards—admiration, awe, and probably even sexual recompense—increased in proportion with the risks. The river across which the bridge was built invariably became a "swollen torrent" with the passage of time and repetition. In any event, storytelling became a time-honored tradition of men— a situation rarely seen with women.

It is also possible that the entertainer role developed, at least in part, from the sex act itself. Given the normal roles assumed by men and women during sex, the man has to be—to a degree, at least— the aggressor; and to use an old cliché, is more the performer (entertainer) than the instrument.

Men's role as entertainer may even have developed in conjunction with their need to be respected and accepted. By going on adventures, then telling stories about them (making certain it was understood that they were the heroes in most of them) they kept practicing their roles as entertainers. The entertainer role may have been—it certainly is today—one way a man can increase the esteem with which he is regarded by others.

Women are attracted to strong, confident men exhibiting signs of abundant self-esteem. This has been true since the first time a hunter killed a lion by himself and became a hero, as well as an attraction, to the women of his clan. Since then, men have all been trying to do the same, or at least talking about "the one that got away."

Rarely is a woman referred to as "entertaining." Surely, women are frequently called charming, but this usually (at least for men) relates to their ability to listen to a good story and make appreciative commentary, rather than creating their own good stories—in other words, because they like "manly" stories, or are at least good at pretending they do. Again, human nature is immeasurable, but women want to be "entertained"—it is universal.

The point is that the entertainer role represents one more difficulty that arises when women enter "a man's world" in every area of endeavor. Not only does a man not want to come home to a woman who has a better story than his, but she doesn't want to come home to a man who doesn't have a story. He also doesn't want to come home to a woman who *thinks* she has a better story (or more troubles) and feels she doesn't need to listen to his. (Two things I constantly heard about from men while discussing this book.)

The woman who has accomplished equality with her husband may feel good about having done so (may even feel that she has the right to gloat, since she is the "underdog" in that "man's world" and has made her presence felt in the face of tremendous odds). Her husband, however, realizes he has been equalled. This may not seem to mean much, but when we contemplate how few women select mates with less power, confidence, influence, money, or strength, we realize that not many women truly wish to be equal or superior. Nor can they ever be expected to. Just one more nail in the coffin of the chemistry of male-female relationships.

Among other things, feminists have been telling women for the past 25 years that mothering is for the brainless; it is not challenging; it is not important to their children; and it cannot be looked upon as a reason to exist. Consequently, women's problems have been increasing during this period, and they have begun to feel many of the same emotional needs that have always been associated with men.

As women increasingly feel the need for competitive achievement, rather than relying on the successes of their husbands and children as measures of their own success, men are increasingly asked to provide the kind of nurturing for their wives and children that wives and mothers traditionally provided. Not only are these roles not inherently suited to them, but the extra demands placed on these men guarantee that they receive less of the same kinds of emotional reinforcement from their wives that they are now asked to give. This has far-reaching consequences for the relationship in that, despite being asked to take on added responsibilities, there is often no corresponding decrease in the other duties and responsibilities that they are expected to perform within the relationship. In other words, men are often giving more while receiving less from their relationships.

Self-esteem in an individual—or more aptly the lack of it—is a burden that has an incredibly wide variety of effects upon that individual. As discussed in the self-esteem section of Part One, one effect is that it can lead some people to put down others around them, in an attempt to build themselves up. Attacks on a person's self-esteem are also used as a means of inflicting pain in bouts of anger. This, of course, may happen in both directions between sexes, particularly in stressful times, but such attacks have tended to have greater negative effects on men, for several reasons.

First, women typically tend to be more capable of using this weapon because of their awareness of the vulnerability of this aspect of the male psyche. Perhaps this understanding has grown out of necessity, because women are (and always have been) less able to rely on strength as a means of "persuasion." Girls can be seen learning to manipulate, or "persuade," their fathers from their earliest ages—about one year and up. An American woman (especially a feminist) denying these facts, or her expertise, would also be denying the truth. (Strident feminist and popular singer/songwriter Helen Reddy produced a hit song from the 1970s, entitled, "Should I Bring Him Down," that may be familiar to the reader. The lyrics deal with just this ability in women.) So the capability is there and, due to ready availability of the movement's line of propaganda, has even grown and developed. (Unfortunately, the "new man"—a feminist creation—who can accurately be referred to as a "man"ipulator, is also developing these capabilities.) Self-esteem is either a man's sweet tooth or his achilles heel.

Second, many of today's women have lost certain "feminine characteristics." Perhaps the characteristic that most applies to this area of discussion is "compassion." A compassionate regard for men and their problems is rigorously avoided by those adhering to the feminist philosophical stance to even the most minor degree (a result of their "perpetual victimhood").

Third, things are changing (out of necessity), but Western man has —as discussed—generally relied upon woman's nurturing of his self-esteem to a greater degree, and is consequently very vulnerable to attack, particularly from the person who has normally been so important to its preservation. (Even most feminists won't deny that women have historically been the nurturing sex).

Fourth, men are usually less apt to "mess" with a woman's head. Men are well aware that emotional attacks on their partners' self-esteem will hurt women more than they understand (or intend), and will adversely affect future relations, sexual and otherwise. Also, men generally suffer fewer mood swings—especially the severe type such as those resulting from hormonal fluctuations causing PMS—than women, and are thus less likely to lash out emotionally at those around them. Unfortunately, these attacks appear to be occurring more and more frequently in our "stressed-out society."

As discussed above, women are obviously experiencing their own self-esteem problems as their needs grow, regardless if they are single or in a relationship. Whether they realize it or not, most unattached women miss the love they might be receiving from a husband, as it benefits self-esteem; but even when a relationship exists, their increased need for personal achievement interferes with the self-esteem that they would derive from a more traditional relationship.

The behavior of both men and women is highly affected by the need for self-esteem, but in the past it was men whose self-esteem needs (shortcomings) influenced behavior most noticeably—if not to a greater degree than women. The differences were obvious in their relation to men's need for success and achievement in the competitive worlds of work, sports, etc. Unfortunately, in America today, the need for success and achievement (which can become obsessive) is becoming an equal opportunity disease.

CHAPTER FOURTEEN

Defining the Family

Beside the way androgyny undermines the attractions between the sexes—and the devastating impact that it has on individual relationships—there is a long list of other reasons feminism imperils family. High among these is the fact that the leaders of the movement are as anti-family as the philosophies and policies they promote. Though not always (or even usually) admitting it, they know that the prevalence of the nuclear family will be destroyed by the impact of their agenda. They are not bothered by this, though. Some, because they believe that maintaining a lifetime relationship is an impossibility. Some, because they believe the family to be an unnecessary institution. Further, some believe the family to be an institution inherently harmful to its individual members. Some, because they believe family has been the cause of their own psychological problems or unhappiness. The main reason, though, is that they believe the family to be a barrier to achieving their short- and long-term goals. This is also the main reason the leaders of feminism can so frequently be heard scorning and ridiculing the family—they see it as being a direct threat to carrying out their agenda.

For our purposes here, there are only three types of families, and they do *not* include the many feminist-advocated alternatives described today as families. All three types of families defined here involve one man and one woman, who are legally married to each other. There may or may not be children in these families, though the assumption will generally be made that there are. All three types are "nuclear families," but there are differences between them, and they are important differences.

The traditional nuclear family is one in which the "primary" income earner (not necessarily the sole earner) is the man, and the "primary" provider of child care (not the sole provider) is the woman. The most significant physical responsibility of the man (but not his only responsibility) is earning enough income to support the family. The number one physical responsibility of the woman (but not her only responsibility) is to care for the children (if there are children), her husband, and their home. This family either has had children of their own, has adopted, or has children from some combination of the two. Sex-differentiated roles and behaviors exist. This family, overall, provides the most beneficial living arrangement for its members, for its community, and for society as a whole.

The non-traditional nuclear family is defined the same way, except for the fact that the man isn't the primary income earner, and other sex roles and behaviors become blurred for a variety of reasons related to this.

The third type of family, the nuclear step-parent family, is one in which either the man or woman bring children to the marriage from previous relationships. Any further definition would depend on the chemistry of the relationship, as with those above. The man may or may not be the primary breadwinner. Sex-differentiated roles may or may not exist. While this family is not the ideal, it is the inevitable result of the fact that there will always be cases of illegitimacy, divorce, or death, which prevent or destroy the other two forms of nuclear family. The creation of this family type is the best solution for those inevitable, but unfortunate, circumstances; it deserves respect and promotion in the sense that such families are needed, and because they are a far better alternative for everyone involved than those solutions or alternatives advocated by feminists.

One of the feminist perils to families is their ridiculing of these definitions of family, while they attempt to expand the definitions of family to include virtually any type of living arrangement imaginable. Simply doing so serves to undermine families.[1] There are a variety of

---

[1] In the same fashion, we might attempt to undermine the importance of humans by broadening the definition to include all animals having two legs, two arms, two eyes and ears, and some ability to solve problems. However silly this might seem, at first, it is used here to illustrate a rather simple point. If we were to broaden the definition of "human" in this way, we would thereby include chimpanzees, and possibly a few other primates. The problem is that, were we to do so, such a decision would ultimately result in many changes in our thinking about *humans*, and the acceptance of many changes in

reasons that feminists do this, but the first reason is that they want their own definitions of family—which basically encompass all "alternative lifestyles"—to gain credibility, so that the actual "alternative lifestyles" (which they believe to be equally beneficial, or which at least meet their own needs) can gain acceptance and encouragement. Once this is accomplished, benefits and rights for these lifestyles can then be fought for. Feminists want people to say to themselves, "Any lifestyle I choose is as good as any other, and any lifestyle I choose is as deserving of support as any other."

Feminists also ridicule true definitions of family as part of their efforts to claim the moral high-ground by making advocates of nuclear families appear to occupy the moral low-ground. This is done by attempting to put people in a position in which it becomes difficult to praise or promote nuclear families without appearing to criticize, or lay guilt on, all those who don't belong to such families. Defending nuclear families—and the proper definitions of them—becomes difficult when we are constantly asked, "What is wrong with *me* and *my* family?" (or alternative lifestyle, as is actually the case) and are, as constantly, told, "You have to accept the fact that divorces, homosexuality, and single-parenthood, are going to occur, and that these are people, too." No attempt is made here to lay blame or guilt on *all* of those who do live in alternative lifestyles, because many people who fall outside the categories described here as "nuclear families" are not living the way they do as a matter of preference (contrary to what feminists would have us believe). Moreover, many—particularly children—have absolutely no choice about living in such conditions, though we all know what their true preference would be if they did have a choice.

And, of course, many people in these lifestyles—including children from them—do well. But, as a whole, they do not do nearly as well as those from nuclear families. Virtually every statistic available demonstrates that people from nuclear families do better than those from al-

---

our behavior. For every animal-rights activist who would see this as a way of extending benefits to non-human primates, there exists someone out there who would see it as a way of allowing us to treat our fellow humans as if they were no more than apes.

The point is that by expanding the definition of "family" to include unmarried couples, gay and lesbian couples, single-parent households, and any of a number of other alternative lifestyles, we demean the meaning and importance of families!

ternative lifestyle "situations," or from broken families. Though there are fewer statistics available, the same is true of the traditional nuclear family, when compared to the non-traditional nuclear family. There are many reasons for the success of people from traditional nuclear families (beyond the fact that divorce rates are much lower in families in which the man is the primary provider), but the main one is that in traditional nuclear families the children are generally a higher priority to the adults. It is because of the vast and growing evidence that, on the whole, feminist alternatives don't do well enough that judgmental attitudes are warranted and remain morally justified. Spouses whose behavior or attitudes are so intolerable to their wives or husbands that divorce becomes the only solution deserve our moral condemnation. Mothers or fathers who are the cause of divorce, or other unnecessary pain to their children, deserve our moral condemnation.

As for the family being considered an impediment to achieving feminist goals, there are many reasons that this is true. The immediate goals of feminism are androgyny, socialized child care, and a far greater degree of socialism. These are goals that feminists see as essential to achieving their desired state of absolute female self-reliance (with no personal responsibility to anyone else), and the ultimate goal of achieving total female power.

Feminists see the nuclear family—especially the traditional nuclear family—as a threat to their goals of androgyny and female power. First, they realize that these families are not only the most likely to remain intact (their success, thereby, a threat to the selling of feminists plans), but that they are the families most likely to be composed of a feminine woman and a masculine man capable of turning boys into men, who are then capable of imposing societal patriarchy. The masculine role model alone is a threat to feminists. Another reason for their contempt for this type of family is that they abhor the fact that the woman in these families is not only reliant (to a degree) on her man—and capable of being satisfied with her dependence—but that she is also capable of actually wanting to make sacrifices for him. Feminists cannot tolerate even the thought of a woman trusting or relying on a man. It runs counter to everything they believe in, which is one reason they abhor and denigrate feminine women almost as much as masculine men.

Freedom from responsibility and freedom from reliance on men are the main reasons they so strongly support socialized child care (which will be discussed). Socialized daycare allows the woman to "become free," so free as to have to care only for herself. Daycare eliminates the problem of caring for the children, which has traditionally been one of the primary responsibilities of the woman (but has also required the aid and cooperation of a man). In the eyes of feminists, reliance upon a man equates directly to loss of power. Daycare relieves both problems at once, thereby moving the woman farther from the need to rely on a man—or a family—and, subsequently, from having to make personal sacrifices for either of them.

Another reason feminists deny the value of families is related to their general perception of themselves as the victims of men. Today's psychology (dominated by feminist thought and advanced by the media) not only constantly encourages women to perceive themselves as victims, and to find imperfections in their lives, it also provides a long list of probable causes—most of which supposedly result from relationships with men. Because of this, their perceptions and recollections of their own childhood and family are all too often negatively affected. Perceiving oneself as a victim, the goal naturally becomes to find the incident that caused the victimization and to place blame upon someone for it. Doing so allows the "victim" to avoid any personal responsibility for her own problems.[2] The concept of recognizing fault in oneself—or the fact that life will inevitably be less than utopian—is seemingly foreign to influential feminists and their followers. If the (female) feminist cannot recall incidents of her own abuse or victimization from her childhood, then it must have been her mother who was somehow abused, deprived, or neglected. If the feminist has had an unsuccessful marriage, she must either look to the man or to the institution of marriage itself as the cause.

Though it would be denied by some feminists, from the very beginnings of the movement they have strongly questioned the need for the nuclear family. Early feminist Germaine Greer put it bluntly:

---

[2] There is a growing body of evidence which indicates that false memories—with a markedly feminist orientation—are now regularly being implanted through the technique of suggestion, by "expert" psychologists, psychiatrists, counselors, etc.

A housewife's work has no results: it simply has to be done again. Bringing up children is not a real occupation, because children come up just the same, brought or not.

Kate Millet, another highly influential feminist in the early days of the movement, wrote:

The care of children is infinitely better left to the best-trained practitioners rather than to harried and all too frequently unhappy persons with little time or taste for the work of educating minds, however young or beloved. The family, as that term is presently understood, must go.

And feminists have been attempting to make the family, as the term is "presently understood," go away ever since, just as assuredly as they have attempted to deny the need for it.

As was noted in Part One, the media has been only too willing to help them in these efforts. The reader will recall the *Life* magazine article in which writer George Howe Colt, after admitting that "families are essential in a world turned increasingly impersonal and harsh," attempted to redefine the family:

a young couple awaiting the birth of their first child, a mother who kidnapped her son from her ex-husband, two gay men, and a divorced couple whose children sleep every other night in a different parent's home.

Though these are supposed to be descriptions of families, what is clear is that they are far from universal norms, and far from what the writers of the United Nations Universal Declaration of Human Rights had in mind when they correctly proclaimed that the family is "the natural and fundamental unit of society." What is rarely recognized is that articles like this are not only influential in determining what will be acknowledged as "family" by society, but that when society acknowledges these arrangements as families, the acknowledgement then serves to influence public policy. (The authors of such articles, however, are very well aware of this.) Additionally, there can be no doubt that such definitions are more than just coincidentally in line with the feminist agenda, just as is the insistence that homosexuality be accepted as "normal."

As early as 1979, the 50 page program of the N.O.W. (National

Organization of Women) New York City conference had described the family as follows:

> The family is that climate that one "comes home to" and it is this network of *sharing* and *commitments* that most accurately describes the family unit, regardless of blood, legal ties, adoption, or marriage. (Emphasis added.)

It is the obvious and inherent lack of continuity of alternative lifestyles, which equate so completely to a lack of *commitment* and point so strongly to lack of selfless *sharing*, that makes one wonder how N.O.W. can even put those two words together in the same sentence—especially a sentence with the word family in it. Several of the people mentioned in the *Life* article obviously lacked the commitment and selfless sharing necessary to maintain their original families intact.

The April, 5, 1991 edition of *U.S.A. Today* gave space to Ivy Young (the Director of the National Gay and Lesbian Task Force's Families Project) to echo the new definitions proposed by *Life* magazine:

> What you see is diversity: domestic partnerships, including unmarried heterosexual couples and gay and lesbian families; single parents; dual-income families; teen-age, step-parent and extended families.
>   And just because my family looks different from yours does not mean it should be any less valued, respected or protected.

The question begging to be asked is, "Why *should* they be equally valued and respected, when virtually all studies show that these alternatives to "traditional nuclear families" are causal in the transmission of diseases such as AIDS, herpes, gonorrhea, syphilis, and other sexually related afflictions?" If they perpetuate all types of psychosocial misbehavior, criminality, and social dependency—and it is proven they do—why should they be equally valued and respected? (Another interesting aspect of her statement that warrants questioning is her referral to unmarried heterosexual partners as "couples," but gay and lesbian partners as "families." Why the discrimination?)

The "relationships" discussed in the above articles are now described as families in national publications, such as those just quoted, and by academia and an increasing number of politicians, as well. But if history and language have any meaning, these are not families (with the possible exception of the first-mentioned, expectant couple in the *Life* article). The types of groupings in these articles can best be described as broken families or temporary mating arrangements. The record shows that these are all too frequently dysfunctional units that can far more accurately be described as breeding grounds of pathological behaviors, unlike the traditional families that feminists attempt to denigrate by (frequently) labeling them "dysfunctional."

When the author of the *Life* article didn't mention whether the expectant couple was married or not, he was implicitly declaring that whether they are or are not legally married is completely irrelevant to their status as a family, and that legal marriage itself has no meaning. The failure implies, for that author at least, that there is no difference between the more safe, stable, and secure home life provided by legal marriage and the transitory, insecure home life resulting from simple cohabitation.

If we accept feminist definitions of family, and allow "alternative lifestyles" to be legitimized as equal to nuclear families in status and worth, the behaviors leading to broken families (and the individuals who live alternative lifestyles) will soon become legitimized. Once legitimized, they are only one short step away from being promoted. Feminists know this applies to many areas, which is why they expend so much effort fighting the vocabulary wars they initiate. As Thomas Fleming has observed, "Obfuscatory language is the product of dishonesty," which explains feminism's continual reliance upon it.

Recognize also that the definitions of family associated with acknowledged feminists are now being used by political leaders not normally associated with, or considered, feminists.

Such feminist writings as the *Life* article promote the belief that the definition of a family has nothing to do with the bearing of children, or the permanent adoption and raising of them, by two heterosexual parents who have formed a life-long, legally sanctioned partnership (intended to last through both good times and bad).

They promote the belief that homosexuality is neither a biological nor a cultural accident but normal behavior, and that its lifestyle can be considered familial—that it is equal to the heterosexual family in its production of healthy, happy, contributing, and self-reliant members of society. And that, therefore, this lifestyle should be supported (as the traditional family has been in the past) and encouraged equally—

whether that support comes in the form of recognition, tax benefits, or equal rights (including the right to adopt children).

They promote the belief that the practice of children sleeping every night in a different parent's home should be accepted as "normal"; that these children are likely to have happy childhoods; that these same children are as likely to grow up to be healthy, happy, contributing, and self-reliant members of society as their peers who have had the benefit of living a stable life with their biological or adoptive parents as members of nuclear families.

Such pro-feminist articles promote the belief that the separated parents of these children are going to be content, contributing members of society, equal to their peers who remain married for life.

They promote the belief that a mother who kidnaps her son from her ex-husband is behaving normally, and that she and her child are as likely to be healthy, happy, contributing, and self-reliant members of society as are the mothers and children of nuclear families.

What they do nothing to promote is nuclear families, either from the beginning, or via remarriage. Nowhere is anything said in favor of women attempting to find new husbands to love, to help them with child-rearing, or to help provide financial support.

It is primarily due to the influence of feminism that to "stigmatize" a behavior or idea is now looked upon as if it is something harmful, or even evil. If a person possesses a politically incorrect viewpoint, however, then it is okay to stigmatize that person as well as his viewpoint. As is the case with so many words in our language that are currently used to connote negative images, "stigmatize" is a term that was formerly used to describe a process having very positive social consequences. To stigmatize something has always meant to mark it as being negative, or even disgraceful, with the intent of producing positive consequences. The stigma attached to a given behavior discouraged anyone who wanted to be perceived in a positive light from behaving in that way. For instance, everyone knew and accepted the fact that if a man abandoned his wife and family he would be considered immoral and irresponsible. From that time forward, fewer respectable people would consider associating with him. This had a deterrent effect upon many men who might otherwise have considered divorce because their marriages were less than perfect. It also had the desirable effect of teaching the young people in the community that marriage was a long-term commitment, not to be treated casually, nor run from simply because it became familiar or uncomfortable. Such a stigma did not completely prevent abandonment and desertion, but it definitely lessened its frequency. Better, in those days, not to get married at all (and to be thought abnormal) than to get married, abandon one's spouse and children, and be considered immoral. Today, if anyone were to stigmatize a woman for divorcing her husband or even abandoning her family, they would most likely be labeled "intolerant" by feminists and ridiculed for "passing judgement."

A recent article on the present state of American families in the *San Jose Mercury News* newspaper had a simple headline that said, "1 in 2 kids live with mom, dad." The article then had the all-too-typical, glorifying, feminist tone ("see we told you so, and isn't it great!") on the present state of American child-rearing. The headline should have read, "One in two children no longer receive benefits of being raised by both parents." The sub-headline could then have read, "Couples having difficult times holding together in difficult times," which is certainly the truth.

The majority of people in America—and around the world, for that matter—would still, as always, agree that homosexual couples are not families. Rather, they are homosexual unions. Parents living in one area while their children live in another are not members of an "extended" family, they are members of a broken family, or victims of illegitimacy. An extended family is that part of a person's family outside of the immediate nucleus (the nucleus being mother, father, sisters, and brothers), including grandparents, aunts, uncles, cousins, and in-laws.

Many (or perhaps even most) members of broken families deserve our sympathy and our compassion. What they do not deserve is to have their broken families glorified or praised as equal in worth to traditional nuclear families. To do so is to promote their broken families and to encourage others—whose families are still intact—either to take those actions that cause their own families to become broken, or to fail to make the sacrifices necessary to keep them together. This is true in the same way that it is true of promiscuity. To promote broken families and promiscuity is neither a way of being a compassionate human being nor of promoting a truly civilized society. Broken families must be acknowledged to be "broken families," not glorified as "alternative lifestyles," just as highly promiscuous adolescent girls or young women must be acknowledged to be "morally loose," not glorified as "wild girls." In other words, the stigmas attached to these situations must not be allowed to slip away. If anything, our moral condemnation of these situations should increase.

The denigration of traditional nuclear families, and the attempted legitimization of all "alternative lifestyles" (in large part, by redefining them as families) are policies feminists promote in their efforts to gain power by undermining the existence of nuclear families.

CHAPTER FIFTEEN

Defending the Family

Feminism's support of the removal of sex roles "within" the family context is just one more way in which it attempts to undermine families. Jim Fordham has noted this in his book, *The Assault on the Sexes:*

> While the language of [women's] lib[eration] emphasizes "equality" and "freedom," what is actually occurring at the psychological and social levels is the breakdown of the sense of commitment and duty that husbands and wives, parents and children, feel for one another. This begins with feminists who try to destroy the confidence of women in the protections of marriage and the security and value of their wifely status in the home. Once the wife is persuaded to shift the focus of her life away from home, husband and children, the sense of mutual commitment between family members tends to evaporate as they come to spend little time together and the home becomes less significant as a primary focus of concern and sustenance. As the wife withdraws her confidence in the husband as breadwinner and protector, he in turn often feels less called upon to perform traditional duties, and gradually the sense of living with a group of independent agents affects everyone.

The man's desire to be the "protector and provider," however, is more complex than is stated by Fordham. If he is not needed to protect and provide, man is deprived of the opportunity to give love through his labor; he thus loses a valuable motivation for working, and also loses the rewards that result from giving. Being needed is one of the reasons men and women get involved in romantic relationships in the first place. One reason that the old saying is true—about opposites attracting—is because each has different needs and desires that can be filled by the other. Feminists, of course, would call this a "co-dependent relationship," but using psycho-babble to disparage healthy heterosexual relationships doesn't alter the fact that mutual dependency is one of the normal bases for most, if not all, successful relationships.

The removal of the protector and provider roles within the family lessens men's opportunity to give and receive love within relationships and is one more negative impact on them.

Equally important are the predictable changes in a woman if the man isn't needed. Feminists theorize continuously about men being ungiving or selfish when they retain financial power for themselves, yet these same feminists are loathe to discuss the impacts on women of gaining financial power within the relationship. The fact is that when women gain economic power, they still retain innate manipulative skills, including the right of refusal in regard to the couple's sexual activity. These two things together are quite likely to severely reduce the physical comfort, equality, and esteem of men. The combination forces men to attempt to develop their own manipulative skills to offset a very substantial power imbalance, or to cede authority (if they wish to remain in their relationships) as women become more assertive and authoritative. Many men, under such conditions, will choose to terminate their relationships rather than become subservient.

Of all the feminist dreams, socialized child care poses one of the greatest threats to the family, and even to humanity, as we know it. Despite this, socialized child care is difficult to argue against and, as usual, feminists continually make attempts at laying guilt on dissenters. Unfortunately (though also as usual), a majority of people have no real understanding of the complex array of its long-range, but predictable, consequences.

In regard to programs like government-provided daycare, it has been said: "If you want more of something, subsidize it; if you want less, tax it." Once daycare becomes widely *subsidized*, there will be *more of it*. Not only will there be more of it, but there will be more single mothers because it (daycare) subsidizes them, also. Women will have more power over men because it subsidizes that, as well, by serving to remove one of women's primary needs for men. Women (in accordance with the principles of feminism) will retain their leverage over men; men will lose their leverage over women. These are all reasons that, in socialized daycare states, the marriage rate can be expected to decline further, and the divorce rate to rise higher. Once socialized child care becomes available, it eventually becomes the rule (whether or not, by choice), as do many ramifications related to it. Feminist-dominated countries, like Sweden and Denmark, exemplify these changes.

As in Sweden, once socialized daycare begins to take hold, the direction ceases to be one of choice, and becomes coercive, a situation in which maternal care of small children becomes increasingly difficult for everyone, and financially impossible for the majority. This is why, in Sweden, over 70 percent of the children between the ages of one and six are in daycare, the great majority of these being in government centers. It is also a big reason that as of 1991, over 50 percent of Swedish children were born out of wedlock. With socialized daycare, men are much less necessary, hence there is less need for commitment or sacrifice.[1]

As a way of getting their foot in the door toward socialized child care, feminists ask, "What about the poor single mothers?" Without considering the fact that we have enough of them already (the result of other liberal handouts, such as welfare, and feminist encouragements, such as promiscuity), they ask, "Shouldn't we provide them with child care, so that they can work and become productive citizens (just those poor single mothers and not married people with children)? That wouldn't hurt anything would it?" No, we shouldn't because,

---

[1] In Denmark, the impact of daycare (and the psychology promoting it) has been very similar to that in Sweden. *Time* hailed Denmark as a country with one of the most highly developed daycare systems in the world: "Nearly 44 percent of Danish children younger than three and 69 percent of those between ages three and five are enrolled in a public facility." Professor Matthiessen, a Danish demographer, notes that between 1971 and 1984 Danish divorces outnumbered new first-time marriages by fully 10 percent. Over 40 percent of Danish births now occur out of wedlock, compared to less than 10 percent in 1965. His conclusions are definite:

> The improved economic position of women—a result of their increased participation in the labor force—has probably contributed to the decline in the number of legal unions (marriages). The woman's earning ability has made marriage less important as a means of support. . . . It is also probable that the women's improved economic position has contributed to an increase in the dissolution of marriages which have failed to meet the expectations of the couples concerned.

predictably, what we would then get is a bunch of single mothers who would stay single permanently, or "shack up" rather than marry—even if they might otherwise prefer to marry. Why? Because getting married certainly isn't worth losing the $400–$500 per month that daycare can cost. So, the marriage rate begins to drop. The drop in marriages encourages feminists to cry out for the government to respond with programs to fill those needs formerly filled by intact families. In short, subsidized child care for single mothers encourages young single women to become mothers—without getting married—because of the benefits available; it encourages out-of-wedlock mothers to remain single because of the benefits available; it encourages divorced mothers to remain unmarried because of the benefits available; in a variety of ways, it acts as an enticement for married mothers to become unmarried because of the benefits available. Until, finally, some insightful government official realizes that the money provided by the government for daycare has set up a disincentive for couples to marry. Then, the government decides that in order to eliminate that disincentive, they should expand the availability of the program to allow married couples the use of daycare services, too. In this way, eventually, the government replaces the family in the rearing of children, further reducing everyone's need for the family.

Human nature being what it is, and the records on welfare and subsidized child care (wherever it has been provided) being what they are, make the truth of these projections absolutely inevitable.

To provide widely available daycare requires huge tax increases. (Sweden's taxes are nearly 70 percent.) As taxes increase to pay for direct and indirect costs, the take-home pay of the single breadwinner diminishes to the point that two incomes increasingly become a requirement—spurring further growth in daycare—spurring still higher taxes. The net result of feminist/governmental efforts to increase women's choices is inevitably that women lose their "choices."

If socialized daycare should become reality, the nuclear family will virtually cease to exist, or will cease to have significant meaning in the socialization of human beings. What could do more to undermine the existence of the family than attempting to replace it or make it unnecessary? For all the reasons discussed here, a socialized child care facility in every neighborhood has become one of the very highest-priority goals of the feminist movement.[2]

Socialized daycare will do nothing for women who like being women, love their husbands, love their children, and want to care for their own children and homes. In reality, it will only serve to make this more difficult. And, as discussed, socialized child care will also contribute to the feminist dream of a unisex, gender-free society by removing one more "sex role" responsibility (motherhood) that has typically been more important to, and prevalent among, one sex than the other. It will also enable the feminist socializing processes to be started on boys and girls at much younger ages.

Socialized daycare is just another example of the fact (as discussed throughout this book) that virtually every policy and vision the feminists promote is, or would be, detrimental to the family.

Dr. Eric Brodin, a scholar and a native of Sweden, spoke of the coercive nature of Sweden's governmental policies on child care (which are exclusively pro-feminist) at a conference sponsored by the Eagle Forum Education & Legal Defense Fund. His comments are recorded in Phyllis Schlafly's book, *Who Will Rock the Cradle?*:

> With virtual monopoly control of the electronic media (two television channels and three radio stations), the government can ensure that its policies receive wide diffusion. In fact, the law requires that 40 percent of air time be devoted to explaining and demonstrating the virtues of the welfare state. Programs may, for example, be documentaries that ridicule the mother at home. In 1970 the Minister of Finance Gunnar Straeng said: "We don't want to force the woman into the labor market; she should have a right of choice. If she wants to stay home and have a lower living standard, she should be allowed to do so."
>
> Radical voices in Sweden, and especially in the last few years the shrill voices of the feminists, like to characterize the mother at home as living an "unworthy parasitic life." The feminists assert that her isolated life at home makes her into a "spiritual cripple."
>
> Yet . . . in a book entitled *The Woman in Sweden in Statistics*, it was shown that, of married women with children under age ten, only seven percent wished to be employed full time and 33 percent wished to be

---

[2] Because of the abundant evidence that widespread socialized child care—and it becomes widespread, once it is socialized—so severely undermines the family, their simply promoting it serves as further proof that feminists believe there is neither hope nor need for family.

employed part time, whereas more than half, 53 percent, did not want to be employed at all. . . .

The entire taxation system (up to 68 percent income tax) relies upon both parents working full-time in the paid labor force and contributing payroll taxes to support the welfare state. To elect to stay at home is actually viewed as a disloyal act. For years the Social Democratic housing policy encouraged the building of very small apartment units. Owning one's own home was ridiculed as bourgeois middle class. Small apartments helped to reduce family size, as well as to exclude grandparents and other relatives, thus creating one-generation households. This policy upset tradition so that the people could be much more readily manipulated to fulfill the objectives of the socialist welfare state.

The motivations for such policy decisions must seem obvious to even the most politically liberal American: the feminist-dominated Swedish government is primarily interested in perpetuating and extending its own power—even at the expense of the wishes of its citizens. (Though, of course, they believe that they know what is best for the citizens, whom they increasingly treat as children). Brodin offers a further example of how this governmental self-perpetuation is promoted in a quote (which also demonstrates how the subtle use of language can disguise the true nature of a policy) on the role of schools in shaping the lives of citizens, from one of Sweden's "pedagogic experts":

> "One of the difficulties which the school has to face is that the homes do not respect the principle of the freedom of religion and the child's human rights. In many homes the parents seem to think it is their duty to bring up their children in the Christian faith. . . . The children are inveigled into the conception that there is a personal, omnipotent God, that personal salvation can only be obtained through Jesus, and that there exists a personal life after death. With these peculiar notions the child arrives at school and gradually discovers that there are other views than those of his parents, conceptions which may even have more validity than those the parents taught. The children may refuse to listen to these new views and thereby be hindered in their free development. The children may also absorb the new views resulting in an inner conflict which the authority-bound education of the home is responsible for."

According to this "expert," it is the duty of the schools to "liberate" the children from the yoke of their parents' teachings. In 1968, this sentiment was expressed even more directly, Brodin points out, by a former chairman of the People's Party youth group:

In his book *Child in Sweden*, Pehr Garton declaimed:

> "The parental monopoly cannot be broken solely by indirect measures—the State must intervene directly by, for example, taking the children from the parents during part of their growing-up years, perhaps a few hours each day, so that a balance of power is more clearly expressed. . . . It is for the best for the children and society that a universal and compulsory preschool program become clearly indoctrinating, thus enabling society to intervene more directly when it comes to the children's values and attitudes."

With anti-family views such as these by Sweden's leading intellectuals (Brodin asks), is it any wonder that the moral bankruptcy of Sweden is evidently almost complete?

Simultaneously, the physical needs for family are undermined. The children are "cared for" and the family loses importance and influence, and frequently ceases to exist. It is at this time that some outside entity (not under control of the family)[3] vastly increases its influence in determining human behavior, usurping the influence formerly wielded by the family. The large-scale demise of the family is assured after the physical needs for it are removed.

As recorded in *Who Will Rock the Cradle?*, economist and author George Gilder offered his own commentary on governmental programs in America, in an address to the same Eagle Forum Education and Legal Defense Fund conference on child care:

> Irving Kristol has written that "the unintended effects of social policy are usually both more important and less agreeable than the intended effects." The advocates of massive new federal child care programs imagine that they are providing options for beleaguered mothers. They claim to offer necessary preschool training for disadvantaged children. They purport to be saving latchkey children from a dangerous and depraved life on the streets. Their intentions seem good. Even some conservatives have succumbed to the siren appeal of helping children.

---

[3] The "outside entity" most likely to gain influence at this time is government. (Where religions are concerned, their efforts can be seen instead to focus on strengthening or promoting families.) What is not so obvious is the philosophy that drives or encourages government to formulate policies and programs that inevitably result in the demise of the family. That philosophy is feminism. This is the reality in Sweden today.

But perhaps never in the catalog of government programs has a proposal entailed a greater gulf between its intentions and its likely consequences than the current government daycare initiatives.

This is a strong statement. The marmoreal buildings of Washington provide a veritable street map of the hell that can be paved by federal good intentions. Health and Human Services (HHS), Housing and Urban Development (HUD), Education, Justice all ring with high purpose and compassion. But HHS is the source of welfare policies that have given America at once the richest and most wretched poor people on the face of the earth. The Justice Department heads a system of criminal justice that is a holy terror toward small Christian colleges and deadly toward police departments with single-sex squad cars, but that fosters a rate of violent crime 62 times higher than Japan's patriarchal society.

HUD is the source of public housing so afflicted with crime and drugs that a resident or visitor would be safer in Beirut or Belfast, Soweto or Sinai. . . .

The Department of Education symbolizes a U.S. school system in which the top one percent of 18-year-olds perform less well in mathematics achievement tests than the average Japanese, while spending far more money than Japan per student. In some cities, moreover, this public school system boasts some 400 times as many administrators per capita as Catholic schools that perform far better.

The good-intentioned array of governmental programs against racism and poverty, covering a gamut from affirmative action and black studies to workfare and AFDC (Aid to Families with Dependent Children), have inflicted more damage on America's blacks than centuries of slavery. But the dire achievements of government in the ghetto probably pale before its achievements on Indian reservations. For the catastrophic results of liberal good intentions, it is hard to imagine beating the record of the Bureau of Indian Affairs.

Now, in a new climax of liberal presumption, the same people who paved the road to hell in America's inner cities want to take care of your small children. It is an outrage. And yet, it is perhaps the most seductive of all the liberal offers. Conservative Senators and Congressmen, tough-minded with terrorists and only rarely intimidated by the *Washington Post*, go weak at the knees and wet in the eyes when confronted with feminist staffers proposing a new program of daycare centers.

You've got to admit it sounds appealing. Small children are one of the enduring problems of life. They constantly make demands, disrupt projects, spill food on your word processor or new copy of *National*

Review or Phyllis Schlafly's newsletter. They bawl and shriek. They distract you from important work. No way around it, small children are a major problem. All of us from time to time may be tempted to let the government solve it for us.

It is in fact the ultimate liberal temptation.

To the average sexual liberal, the role of women seems so routine that it can be assumed by a few bureaucrats managing child development centers. To the current advocates of a gender-neutral society, both the work of the world and the duties of the home are so undemanding that they can be accomplished with part-time effort.

It is foolish to imagine that the complex domestic and social roles of women can be assumed by outside agencies. The woman's role is nothing less than the hub of the human community. All the other work —the business and politics and entertainment and service performed in the society—finds its ultimate test in the quality of the home.

Just as the female role cannot be shared or relinquished, the male role also remains vital to social survival.

. . . the facts of life. A single-parent family is almost always a broken family and a burden on society. Both the man's role and the woman's role remain indispensable to a civilized and prosperous nation. The advocates of government administering daycare in a gender-neutral society live in a dream world. No government program in the world, however expensive, can make up for the economic and emotional disaster of broken homes. No daycare scheme can enable most single women to both raise their children successfully and earn incomes above the poverty level. In most cases, female-headed families cannot even begin to discipline teenage boys or provide role models for them; in many families that I have interviewed, the mothers are actually afraid of their teenage sons.

Governments grow by the pretense of solving problems. By solving the immediate problem of where to park the kids, government daycare creates an illusion that families may break down without major damage —and an illusion that women can bear children without marrying the fathers. By solving the immediate problems of female-headed families, government thus creates the deadly long-term problem of a society full of them.

The broken families of America already constitute an insoluble problem that can absorb unlimited funds and efforts and provide a pretext for unlimited expansion of government. The current welfare programs already do all that the state can do to provide minimal care; an enrichment of these programs with job training and daycare will further accelerate family breakdown. With every new initiative of the state, the problem will grow inevitably worse and demand ever more extreme government action.

The new government daycare proposals will tax families that care for their own children in order to subsidize families that place their children in another's care. The more the state subsidizes the breakdown of family responsibilities, the more families will break down. But there is no way on earth for government to supply the love and attention and self-sacrifice that mothers spontaneously offer their children. There are not enough resources on this entire planet to raise a new generation of civilized children if mothers defect.

The government has been paying for divorces and broken families. It has been paying lavishly for illegitimacy. It thus should not be surprising that it has been getting more broken families and illegitimate children. The government has been paying women to leave their families or refrain from marriage, and to enter the workforce. It is not surprising that women follow the dictates of these powerful government incentives.

The stable families of America both sustain the American economy and raise virtually all the nation's productive new citizens (most of the rest are immigrants from stable families overseas). The female-headed families of today create an unending chain of burdens for tomorrow as their children disrupt classrooms, fill the jails, or throng the welfare rolls. Then they gather as bitter petitioners and leftist agitators seeking to capture for themselves the bounty produced by stable families.

The competitors who give trouble to American firms mostly come from the patriarchal family structures of Asia where women take care of their children and where schools teach physics and calculus rather than sex education and Indian rights.

Two things are clear about Japanese families. From the point of view of Americans, they are entirely patriarchal. But women are in charge of young children and the women stay in the home in the early years.

It is perhaps the feminist viewpoint regarding the need for the nuclear family—and all it entails—that best exemplifies both the coldheartedness and the illogic of feminist thought. It is also almost solely because of the influence of feminist thought (as opposed to the influence of some religion, or governmental leadership) that the worth of the nuclear family must now be defended.

Defending the nuclear family is such a ridiculous argument to have to make that it is difficult to know where to start or end, because the argument could go on almost forever. Midge Decter said it well, though, when she said that "defending the family is a little like defending breathing." Saying that we don't need family is saying we don't need mothers or fathers, sons or daughters, husbands or wives, grandparents or grandchildren, aunts or uncles, nieces or nephews. It's also akin to saying that we are all capable of functioning in a social and emotional vacuum and don't need love, because a society of people without families will eventually cease to know the meaning of giving love. Without meaningful families, society will either degenerate and fall apart, or (should government "succeed" in adequately replacing the family as the key directional and motivational agent in our lives, and filling the survival needs of individuals) we will become robots under the control of technocratic masters.

What is meant by the phrase "meaningful families" can best be explained by considering what feminists believe to be an out-dated, unnecessary institution: marriage. In an article entitled, "Poor Suffering Bastards," anthropologist David W. Murray discusses the necessity for marriage:

> Marriage is the very basis of society because it creates kinsmen out of strangers. . . . By uniting with outsiders, marriage helps families multiply their economic capital—and, perhaps even more important, their social capital. You and your wife's uncle may not like each other very much, but marriage imposes a set of reciprocal obligations on you; you are at least partly responsible for looking out for each other's well-being.
>   . . . Consider how the word "bastard" has come to mean someone heartless, cruel, or prone to cheat. We are not alone in this judgment. A Navajo saying captures well the universal stigma that attaches to illegitimate offspring. *Do Ahalyada*, they call them, "those who care for nothing." The worst social characterization the Navajo can offer of a thoughtless, deviant man is the charge that "he acts as if he has no relatives. . . ."
>   A man with no relatives, the Navajo feel, is a man with no concern for the shame or honor that his behavior might bring upon those he loves. He acts, therefore, without control or humanity.

Though the family is, of course, needed by children, all too frequently the argument that families are needed focuses *only* on the needs of children, neglecting the effects of singleness—or the impacts of divorce—on adults. Feminists attempt to convince women not only that there aren't any good reasons to get married, but that when a marriage has been consummated, there aren't any good reasons it shouldn't end in divorce. Their viewpoint is that the unmarried are just as well off in every way as the married, and that divorce need not be painful in those cases where a marriage was consummated in the first place. Further, the programs they promote are such that single and divorced individuals actually appear to be just as well off —or even better off, in some ways—than those who marry.[4]

Yet, virtually all studies show that married men and women are healthier, both physically and mentally, than their single, or divorced counterparts. Married people enjoy better sex lives. Married people do much better financially. Writing recently in *Social Science and Medicine*, Catherine K. Reisman and Naomi Gerstel observe that "one of the *most* consistent observations in health research is that married (people) enjoy better health than those of other marital statuses" (emphasis added).

In a study presented to the American Public Health Association, researchers found that, "in spite of the recent changes in American marital patterns, there was still a clear association between being well and being married in 1987." This study further suggests that the "surge in divorces" in recent decades has imposed "hidden health costs on the population" that should be recognized. Indeed, a 1988 study at Ohio State University found that divorced men are less healthy and exhibit weaker immune systems than married men, even if their personal health habits are identical. According to Peggy Thoits of Indiana University, "married persons have significantly lower anxiety and depression scores than unmarried persons, regardless of gender."

It is the mental health aspect of marriage that is arguably most important, because we are a species seemingly, and certainly more so in these "liberated times," prone to neuroses. Single men and women are far more prone to it, and to greater degrees, than are the married. The single and the divorced of both sexes are far more likely to become drug dependent, to need psychological help, and far more likely to become homeless.

---

[4] But despite what feminists frequently tell us, singleness isn't the road to happiness or health, even if they've come to believe it in their own minds. Who really wants to come home to an empty house or apartment? Who really wants to sleep alone? Who really wants to have no one to care for? Who really wants no one in their life who cares if they are sick or well, unhappy or happy?

Single and unmarried people are far more frequently involved in committing crimes, and are far more likely to have crimes committed against them. Domestic violence is just one example of the vulnerability both sexes endure as a result of being unmarried. The great majority of incidents of domestic violence, whether against women or men, occurs in households in which there is no legal marriage (still the minority of households). Rape is another problem mostly concerning single and unmarried people. The great majority of all rapes are committed by single men. Most of the victims of rape are unmarried.[5]

Feminists don't wish to acknowledge that there are links between rape and men who are sexually deprived, because feminists don't wish to acknowledge that the nuclear family is the best means for civilizing men and keeping them that way. Feminists don't want to acknowledge anything that might be used to rationalize the need for the nuclear family. Their cure for rape is to "civilize" men via the feminist, androgynous, socialist, technocratic, male-neutering system. The problem is that this approach is likely to create as many rapists as it cures because it devalues men and their natural roles, engendering frustration and anger among them. Most of this anger and frustration will be directed toward women. When combined with sexual deprivation, these feelings can be expected to culminate in acts such as rape.

The fact of the matter is that married men are not roaming our streets raping women. Another fact is that a non-monogamous culture will always produce greater sexual inequalities—meaning a greater number of men will not be sexually satisfied.

Nearly everyone would agree that the great majority of American men—with good reason—prefer to choose women without ex-husbands and without children. The proliferation of divorces and illegitimate births makes this preference increasingly difficult to satisfy.

---

[5] The American public has been told continually by feminists, and others, that rape is solely a crime of anger and violence, and has absolutely nothing to do with sex. But, if rape and the male sex drive have absolutely no link to one another, why are married men less prone to become rapists? And why isn't this question asked by feminists?

In the majority of cases, married men are sexually satisfied to an acceptable degree. The reason we don't we read about them raping women is that it's a very rare occurrence. Men who are the members or products of intact families—particularly families where love, caring, and respect for one another are the rule—do not generally become rapists.

In the situation where a man does consider marrying a woman with children by another marriage, he can sometimes bond to the other's children as if they were his own; but it cannot be ignored that, often, this is simply not possible. Age and personality factors may be responsible. Or, the children may simply reject the would-be "father."

Additionally, whether or not the man hears about him from his prospective wife, children are a reminder of the ex-husband, who may be a presence for many years during the child-visitation process. In such situations, many a man will wonder if she really loves him, or if he is just a savior.

The concerns facing a woman who is divorced and has children are different from the man's, but revolve around many of the same issues. Her first husband may have turned out to be less than perfect, but at least she had a choice, and she picked him. He must have had some redeeming value. Now she may be starting to realize that many, or most men are reluctant to get "involved" with her, largely because of her children.

If she hopes to get a decent man, her appearance and her sexuality may have to play a significant role. With children as part of the equation, a "nice" personality may not be enough. This is not intentionally cruel, these are just the facts of life.

In a culture where promiscuity is the rule (such as ours is rapidly becoming), rather than the exception, a divorced woman with children will have fewer ways to attract a man as a mate, because single women are just as available but have none of the limitations brought about by the presence of children or ex-husband. Because of this, a non-monogamous culture will guarantee that great numbers of women will face old age alone.

Some of the more obvious reasons children need intact traditional nuclear families are apparent, even to those who argue against the value of such situations. First, the great majority of incidents of in-home child molestation and physical abuse, involving men, occurs at the hands of live-in boyfriends or, less frequently, step-fathers; only a small percentage occurs at the hands of biological fathers (who are the majority of fathers). Second, the acknowledged fact that peers do not make the best role models proves that every child needs the presence of both parents (an intact family).[6]

Donald B. Rinsley, M.D., F.R.S.H., Clinical Professor of Psychiatry at the University of Kansas School of Medicine, is an authority on child development and personality disorders. His views on this subject are recorded in *Who Will Rock the Cradle?*:

> As is well known, the human being requires the longest period of parental guidance, discipline and nurturance among living organisms before the young one is capable of mature, independent life. No substitute has been found, nor is ever likely to be found, for the natural two-parent family to serve as the vehicle for the optimal training and socialization of the human child.

Yet many feminists believe that children do not really need two parents (as demonstrated by the growing number of women willfully choosing to have children without the benefit of a permanent male partner). Many feminists even go so far as to say that daycare is a positive substitute for the family.

Brenda Hunter is the author of *Beyond Divorce* and *Where Have All the Mothers Gone?* Like others addressing the Eagle Forum Education and Legal Defense Fund conference, her beliefs are recorded in *Who Will Rock the Cradle?* She reports having spoken with many in the mental health profession:

> who wonder if we are not foolishly experimenting with a generation of children when we, in this country, advocate daycare for the very young. One, who teaches at Harvard Medical School, told (her) that he predicts that many hospital beds in psychiatric wards of the future will be filled with those currently growing up without a close bond to parents.

The bond of children to their parents is undoubtedly as important as Rinsley and Hunter claim. But it is a bond whose benefits extend in both directions, as Murray points out:

> That women domesticate men who marry them has been widely noted. . . . In addition, children domesticate both men and women.

---

[6] A father is needed, as is the rest of the family, to provide discipline and role modeling. For small children, that means needed more than between 6–8 P.M., after their having been in daycare for eight, nine, or ten hours. And—for the children of divorced couples—it means more than every other weekend.

In American cities the presence of children has become a "miner's canary" for social health; where we find children playing, there we find safety for ourselves. . . . There is a relief that comes from seeing (young males) hand-in-hand with a young child. We recognize instinctively that males caring for children are not seeking violence.

Neighborhoods without fathers, by contrast, are seedbeds for predators. Without a female *and* a male who consider themselves responsible for children, the stable features of continuity are not constructed. . . . Children are any society's greatest hope, at the same time that they are its greatest threat. Since citizenship, as with any art, is made and not born, children are the most consequential social investment.

As discussed previously, feminists love to euphemize. They love to use metaphors. They love to distort the language completely. (They also love to cast themselves in a positive light and put guilt on others.) So it is only too predictable that when feminists argue for children's rights, they are actually arguing for their own.

What kind of "children's rights" are they talking about? If you're an embryo (even an embryo developed enough to have a heart and eyes, and to be sucking your thumb), they are talking about the right to abort you. But, of course, they've only got *your* "best interests" in mind. As Margaret Sanger, the founder of Planned Parenthood, said: "The most merciful thing a large family can do for one of its infant members is to kill it."

If your mother has decided to give birth to you, you can rest assured that feminists are working hard to eliminate your need for a father. This is in case your mother has no idea who your father is, or in case he was such a rotten pig that she can't stand the sight of him, or in the case she simply decided it was time to have a baby, but didn't want any strings attached. So, don't worry about possibly not knowing who your father is; he isn't needed anyway (which is exactly what feminists attempt to tell us). And, of course, this applies to the possibility of your parents divorcing (with which there's nothing wrong, either). You may begin by sharing your home and life with your father, only to have him removed at some point, but this should not be an inconvenience. And if he falls out of love with you, or decides not to make child support payments for some other reason, he will be tracked down and forced to pay.

You will also have the right to be put in daycare when you're three months, six months, or one year old, in case your mother doesn't know where your father is, or in case she wants to have a "real" job. They are talking about putting you in school for ten hours a day, all year round, instead of seven hours a day, for just nine months of the year, so your mother's work schedule won't be affected. But this will, of course, only help you in becoming better educated more quickly. You'll soon learn not to worry about identity problems. Whether you're a boy or girl, you're going to be brought up and taught the same things in the same ways by the daycare/school system, because you are the same—boys and girls have no differences.

In actuality, the woman who willfully (and without need) puts her young child in a daycare center is not only shirking one of her fundamental responsibilities as a human being, she is also ignoring a responsibility (her child's care) that is the primary reason for her existence.

Suppose, then, for the sake of her child, the young feminist mother decides that she will make the sacrifice and stay at home with her newborn for a year or two. Isn't that what the evidence suggests she should do? Surely, that will be enough? No, it is not enough.

Though feminists claim that preschool and early formal schooling provide the best basis for successful socialization of children, there are many reasons to doubt just how humanitarian it is, in addition to how successful it is. Martin Engel, director of America's National Day Care Demonstration Center in Washington, D.C., has observed that:

> The motive to rid ourselves of our children, even if it is partial, is transmitted more vividly to the child than all our rationalizations about how good it is for that child to have good interpersonal peer group activities, a good learning experience, a good foundation for school, life, etc., etc. And even the best, most humane and personalized daycare environment cannot compensate for the feeling of rejection which the young child unconsciously senses.

It must be realized that even in the best daycare center there will never be more than one worker per four children, and those four children will never receive equal care. There will almost inevitably be at least one child out of those four who receives a disproportionately small amount of time and attention. (Perhaps the best reason daycare should be rejected is because it creates a situation in which the caregivers have no personal investment in their charges. Each child becomes only a statistical unit. Success for each child becomes dependent upon how well that child avoids being different. In other words, daycare promotes intellectual and temperamental mediocrity.)

Most people have probably noticed the situation in which a parent bonds more with one child than another; in fact, this appears to happen on a regular basis. Now, imagine the effects of divorce on the child who has his most-attached parent removed from the home environment due to divorce. Such a situation is, in itself, one more significant reason to increase our efforts to slow the dissolution of the family.[7]

Beyond the impact to a young child of having one parent removed from the day-to-day environment, divorce has any number of other ramifications. If the father is removed from the family, it is very uncommon that the father's family (his parents, brothers, sisters, aunts, and uncles) will maintain the same importance or presence in the child's life. This is particularly true in cases where either the father or the mother leaves the area. As the distance increases, or the familiarity decreases, between the child and these relatives, the child's ability to count upon the help and support of these relatives diminishes.

For the child's parents, the effects may be similar. As long as they remain married, they are likely to be considered relatively "stable" by their respective families. Relatives are far more comfortable providing help to family members who are married than to those who are no longer married. Beside which, as long as the marriage is intact, there are twice the number of relatives upon whom to rely. As David W. Murray says:

> American men and women today have many sources of personal identity and relationships other than family, of course. . . . Yet it is patterns of kinship which most often cover us in our undertakings, provide us market opportunities, and even shield us from the importunings of the state. We do not hope to receive tuition, childcare, or a kidney from a business associate, but we do from relatives. Marriage is that device

---

[7] In cases where divorce does occur, feminists would have us believe that young children subjected to a procession of various stepfathers or live-in boyfriends will either not bond to them at all, or will suffer no ill effects when they do. The truth is that, in these cases, there will almost inevitably be pain—either during the stepfather's presence, upon his departure, or perhaps both.

which extends to us a social security network of obligated kin. . . . For many traditional cultures, marriage may contain romance, but the institution serves primarily to "arrange" the structure of society.

Marriage provides a kind of capital. Married couples, more than single parents, have parents and grandparents as a resource. House loans, emergency aid, car payments, and job opportunities come disproportionately from these relatives. Over one-fourth of all new home purchases depend upon gifts from parents. . . . There is little question that having four parents and eight grandparents attached to every marriage broadens the base of economic support. . . .

But the plight of the single mother, isolated from kin, can be economically grim. One reason is the simple mathematics of relationship. With fewer people tied in a committed and socially-sanctioned way to the obligation of support, the single parent is hobbled from the beginning. Single parenthood that passes through more than one generation, from unwed mother to unwed daughter, results in an almost exponential collapse of the number of supporting relatives.

Despite all this evidence, feminists continue to claim the nuclear family is unnecessary.

In the society feminists envision for us, where daycare is the rule for all children, everyone will suffer the presence of children (now grown into adults) who behave in antisocial ways. What America needs, instead, are adults who are well-behaved, productive, contributing members of a healthy society.

Schlafly's book, *Who Will Rock the Cradle?*, provides the testimony of another expert in the field of child development. Dr. Harold M. Voth received his medical degrees from the University of Kansas School of Medicine, the Menninger School of Psychiatry, and Topeka Institute for Psychoanalysis. He is a charter fellow of the American College of Psychoanalysis, and a fellow of the American Psychiatric Association. He speaks nationally on social issues and has testified before many Congressional committees. Dr. Voth puts it this way:

The creation of people (who make good citizens) depends in great measure on the quality and quantity of care the child receives from birth forward into youth. No period in life is more crucial to the future of the individual and to mankind's future than the first few years of life, for what you become determines to a substantial degree what you believe and what you do, including the values you create and live by.

Mothering is the central factor of this period. How the child is mothered—good mothering—leads to a variety of human qualities and personality development. There is no adequate substitute for a mature, psychologically healthy mother who is bonded to and loves her child.

For the mother to function best, she should have a good man by her side whom she loves, to whom she is committed and who loves her, provides for her, is committed to her, and so on. Men have a direct impact on child development during the first three to five years of the child's life, but not to the extent of the mother. Men can carry out maternal functions to be sure, but their effect on the child is by no means comparable to the mother's. Men should be good fathers, not try to emulate mothers, as seems to be the vogue these days.

It is hard for me to believe that a civilized society such as ours treats millions of children the way we do. Child care in the United States is shocking. Our own society is paying a high price, not only in terms of the personal suffering these children are experiencing and will experience throughout their lifetimes, but also in terms of the damage they do society and what they do not do for society. They will crave input of all kinds into their psyches. They hunger for material possessions, drugs, alcohol, freewheeling sex, instant pleasure, in short, narcissistic gratification of any kind. Others lead slothful, unproductive lives and become a serious drain upon society.

If I have ever seen a self-destructive life course—and I have seen many in my 40 years of professional work—I am now seeing such a course taken by our country. . . .

I can tell you with absolute confidence that we in the United States must soon restore the family, and thereby ensure better rearing of our children, or our country will fall into an ever decreasing status among nations.

Murray ("Poor Suffering Bastards") explains it this way:

Marriage links us to two sets of relatives who are our best allies. Moreover, to the extent that the families invest in us, their own interests, economic and social, become entwined with ours. . . .

When a Husband acquires a Wife, however, he acquires, for better or for worse, all of that entangled wiring that constitutes her structural position as Daughter, Sister, Niece, Aunt, Granddaughter, Heiress, and obligated actress in the domestic rituals of matching, hatching and dispatching. She, this multiple social "person," also brings into the relationship that complex of relatives "in-law" that we can acquire by no other route than by wedding. This entanglement is stabilizing not only in the life of the couple and their children but in the life of the neighborhood.

Such kinship figures are missing from the lives of the bastard. To be brought up without male authority in the household is a deficit. But . . . missing from the lives of the impoverished, these spouse-less mothers and troubled children, are not just male authority figures, role models, or wage earners. Important though these are for the well-being of society, the absence of (the biological father) from the home is not the central loss.

What are missing from these families are Fathers and Husbands as well-defined social statuses. Many people, as it were, and not just one, are missing whenever a Father is absent, for Fathers bring Brothers, Uncles, Grandfathers, Sisters, and even Mothers-in-law. And it is this network of attachment and affiliation that finally enables Fathers, and not boyfriends, to transform bastards into Sons (and Daughters). In a home where there has never been a Father/Husband, there is, no matter how valiant and strong the Mother, a crippled unit, condemned to isolation from society's opportunities and to predation from society's brutal.

It is mainly because of the shortcomings of feminist alternatives to families that feminists promote such an array of social supports for these alternatives. Books such as *Feminism and Socialism*, written in 1972, by Linda Jenness, have long been produced by feminists, and are staples for feminist philosophers. For this reason, and others (related to their dislike of family), feminism and socialism always have been— and always will be—intricately and necessarily interlinked. The prevalence of the nuclear family makes socialism unnecessary, its absence makes socialism inevitable.

Because of its impacts on relationships and its role in the breaking down of the family, an androgynous society can never be anything other than socialistic. A meddling form of socialism is the only alternative to the family, but socialism itself is fatally flawed, and will never be a lasting replacement for the nuclear family.

If we become androgynous, the family as we've known it will cease to exist due to a lack of need for each other and a lack of attraction between men and women. Socialism will be forced to fill not only the physical needs of individuals that the family once provided, but also many of the metaphysical needs. Men won't be teaching their sons how to be men, nor will women be teaching their daughters how to be women. Socialized daycare facilities, the educational system, the media, etc., will replace the family. These institutional replacements for the family will essentially be run by technocrats who have the influence needed to create policy and the power needed to enforce it. Technocrats are technocrats by choice. They *want* to run people's lives and tell them how to think and behave. They are driven by the belief that they know best. The technocratic "socialization process" will do away with the male's need and drive to achieve for personal reasons, his need and drive to protect and provide for his family for personal reasons. The technocratic "socialization process" will attempt to replace these with the desire to work for the state. The technocratic socialization process will promote the end of the female's maternal role to her children in the same way. The state will be number one, children number two. This may be hard to imagine, but it is already happening here, and it is the reality in Sweden.

As George Gilder reminds us in his book *Sexual Suicide*:

> Individuals no longer so closely tied to mother, family, and sexuality become more open to a totalitarian state.
>
> The material and sensual rewards of modern society are meager compensation indeed when one loses the ability for profound fulfillment of biological sexuality.

Policies that undermine the maintenance of sexual differences undermine mutual needs and attractions for one another, which undermines the family, which undermines the individual's ability to love and be self-sufficient, and necessitates socialism. This puts the individual in the position of having no choice but to rely on society. As daycare becomes the norm, mothers will inexorably lose their ability to care for their own children. From generation to generation, this inability cannot help but grow—a cumulative erosion of motherly skills—until the average woman giving birth will have ever less of a conception of how to care for and nurture the infant that has grown inside her.

Feminists know that the weaker and less prevalent the family becomes, the greater will be the role of other factors in influencing our behavior. In this society it has been, and continues to be, the feminist philosophy that fills this void more than any other factor. None of the tools feminists use—including the government—can replace the family, they can only indoctrinate. Though it is the government that

makes the laws, the government is not an entity in its own right. It
responds to pressures from outside—the will of the people, the influence of the media, special interests, etc. Whatever may influence the
government, it cannot replace a mother, a father, a family and tradition; it cannot teach us love, understanding, compassion, values, or
morals. Without the roots that have historically been provided by the
family, we can be blown in any direction the winds of the currently
dominant philosophy may carry us—no matter how ill those winds
might bode. If government is the agent of that dominant philosophy
(as it is now the agent of feminism), there will be specific individuals
within the government who will claim to know what is best for all of
the rest of us and who will be expert at acting as if they operate in the
"best interests" of all the nameless, faceless multitudes who make up
American society. But, whether they have their jobs because they were
elected, or were merely appointed by those who were elected, they
won't necessarily be qualified by education or experience to actually
know what is in the best interests of the people, and will, therefore,
end up acting in the best interests of the sponsoring philosophy.

Not only do today's feminists believe that the government can replace the nuclear family, they are attempting to make it happen. In
their efforts to create a society of "independent women," feminists
promote policies that move us ever closer to an androgynous, technocratic state, devoid of families—but also devoid of the emotions
necessary for normal human interaction. In his book, *The Inevitability
of Patriarchy*, Steven Goldberg offers this evaluation of such a state:

> The only arguments leading to the conclusion that a society could
> separate aggression and attainment that I can even imagine rest on an
> assumption of the possibility of man's behaving in what some might
> think of as a totally rational way. This view would see man's rational
> mind, his cerebral cortex, as capable of overriding the filter system,
> the hypothalamus, that invests all thought with emotion. It is true that
> man has some capabilities in this area that other species do not (no
> one has ever heard of a chicken who was celibate for moral reasons),
> but to expect that a large number of the members of any society will
> ever be able to override emotions would seem to me pure utopianism.
> Even ignoring the possibility that the emotion-producing qualities of
> the hormones affect the cortex directly and the fact that apes as well
> as man have cerebral cortices, one might question whether we would
> *want* to give primacy to rational man. It is true that if we could do

away with the emotions there would be little or no need for many of the institutions of sexual differentiation and the institutions that satisfy, channel, and control lust, caring and love. But without such emotions and the institutions they engender, what would serve the purpose now served by the will to live? things would be easier, utopia would be possible, and life would be very boring.

With the coming of androgyny, patriarchy disappears; mutual need for one another disappears; mutual attraction for one another disappears; long-term relationships disappear; the family disappears, and socialism rises to replace it (not only as provider but more importantly as teacher); technocracy reigns; human nature is socialized away, and we become robots. But when technocracy falters (as it most certainly will) in its attempts to fill all our needs, turmoil and social breakdown occur, leading to barbarism. When this happens, human nature will again assert itself and, perhaps ironically, patriarchy will return!

Man's drive to dominate is so relentless that he will dominate within monogamous society or promiscuous society or any other type of society. If he does cede authority, it will be only temporarily, because (barring we become robots) society will either degenerate, entropize, or be conquered. One of these will eventually occur, at which point men will again dominate.

CHAPTER SIXTEEN

The Solution

Our society needs a plan; our children need something to hold onto, to look back on, to look forward to, a place to learn what love is and how to love. If the family is not present, society (government) will be depended upon to fill a role that it cannot adequately fill.

We cannot allow the nuclear family to be undermined, because it cannot be replaced. This society will degenerate to barbarism, if not to complete primitivism. It can accurately be said that this is already the case in some fairly large sections of our major metropolitan areas, where nuclear families have been most adversely affected.

In the world feminists envision for us, single parents will increasingly be forced to fill the role of two parents, a situation which would be observed by any child and would certainly have lasting effects. Even in today's world, parental influence among children has been greatly diminished, stolen by the media and the education system; without the family, parental influence will become even more reduced. If this becomes the case, why even have children?

Mothers won't be needed in the society we are creating.

Wives won't be needed in the society we are creating.

Children won't enjoy childhood, or bring enjoyment, in the society we are creating.

We are creating—in line with the wishes of feminists—a society in which people are becoming so pragmatic that the urge to bear children has already ceased making sense to many.

Social decay can already be seen in our society, as our families have been impacted. It can be seen in our overflowing prisons, our rehabilitation wards, our drug and alcohol problems, and the incredible increase in violent crime (including rape). It is obvious in the behavior of our increasingly neglected and uneducated children, in the fact that we can't produce enough psychiatrists to meet the demand, and in the preponderance of lonely people. The increased suicide rate, the incredible abortion rate (one out of four pregnancies in the U.S. are aborted), the rise in illegitimacy, the growing number of custody battles, the lack of respect and love for parents, the lack of morals, selfishness, and narcissism, all symbolize the social decay that is overtaking our nation.

We are literally creating a society in which the adult individual has no need to be part of a nuclear family. In fact, we are creating a society where being a member of a nuclear family is increasingly unattractive to an ever-greater number of people.

Of the degeneration of American society, the previously quoted Dr. Voth says:

> How we care for infants and children is a central, crucial and, I believe, the most important element in the future of America and of the earth itself.
>
> How we care for infants, the children and the youth of this earth will, in my judgment, determine whether or not we avoid an irreversible race toward disaster. Our planet must be inhabited by a sufficient number of people who have the ability and the inner psychological resources to strive for and achieve excellence, as well as to find joy through ways of living which do not require endless gratification of narcissism, selfishness, and egocentricity. These are the people who are able to give of themselves and find joy in doing so, rather than take for themselves, and who are perceptive and responsible enough to tackle the horrendous problems facing man. These are the people who make any organization flourish, be it a family, a small business, a corporation or a society. The reason is very simple. They put more in than they take out.

Apparently feminists (and others) fail to realize, or else choose to ignore, the fact that the nuclear family, and individuals from it, have always "paid society back" for the social benefits they receive. Alternative lifestyles do not provide the climate conducive to developing individuals capable of doing the same.

We are an extremely troubled nation, on a course leading toward a violent social and economic revolution, with an increasingly fertile climate for it. We are an angry nation. Our nation and its people are being fragmented, rapidly polarizing toward two different and incompatible ends—the formation of two opposing cultures that cannot co-exist. The 1994 election and post-election commentary and statistics show the number and divisiveness of the different voting blocks.

Though many hypotheses have been put forth throughout this book, the primary hypothesis, above all others, is that the "feminist movement" (and the changes resulting from it in women, even those who don't claim to be feminists) can be appropriately described as the number one source of ailments facing this society and the individuals within it today. Feminism is *not* the solution, it is the problem.[1]

In the 1992 Presidential campaign, three candidates—and the mass media—implied again and again that the government was the source of all that ails us. Each candidate claimed he was the one who could make the changes that would "fix it." Unfortunately, though the government is certainly responsible for some of our problems, we can't blame it for all of our problems; and unless we recognize that fact, we won't begin to solve them. It is not the government that has intentionally encouraged us to abandon our traditional moral standards, it is feminism. As was the case in 1964, when women were included in the civil rights legislation, the government has been—to an overwhelming degree—influenced by feminist philosophy, a trend that continues today.

The extent of this influence is easily seen in the way feminists speak about government actions. Recently, after Congress passed legislation

---

[1] The government is not at the core of our problems; the media, the economy, racial divisions aren't, either. The work ethic, divorce, promiscuity, illegitimacy, abortion, broken families, lack of morals, the failure to follow any type of religious principles, none of these are the core problem. Though it is popular for people of both sexes to blame the other sex, neither sex is completely to blame, by itself. Though each is undoubtedly contributing its own compounding problems in its own way, none of the problems above can justifiably be classified as *the* problem, as feminism can. It is the influence of feminism that has—*by far*—more to do with causing and exacerbating problems in our society than any of them, or any other "concern" that can be classified. Negative behaviors associated with men, regardless of how much more easily identifiable or dramatic they are than those associated with women, are largely (and predictably) the result of changes in women's behaviors, caused by feminist philosophy and all it encourages. Some would claim that the problems associated with all these things can be put under an umbrella, and be said to be the result of general liberal philosophy dominant in recent years, but even that is inaccurate because feminist philosophy has dominated, and continues to dominate, liberal social and political philosophy.

engineered by feminists, radical feminist Andrea Dworkin felt comfortable explaining the feminist success, by saying: "Senators don't understand the meaning of the legislation they pass" anyway. (Feminist influence is exemplified by sexual harassment laws, affirmative action laws, abortion laws, etc.)

As the candidates said, we do need change; but not only the principally economic and political types of which they spoke. The status quo is not good enough when it comes to our people-based social problems, either. The question isn't whether we will or won't make changes, the question is the direction in which those changes will take us. We can either continue following the feminist agenda and philosophies, or we can begin taking a look at reality. We need a change not just in the way people think about feminists, feminism, and the principal ideologies of feminism, but in how we speak out and take action in response to the efforts feminists relentlessly put forth in promoting their agenda. This is more important than ever before, now that we have a devout feminist for our President, and an extremely influential and strident feminist as his wife.

Feminism is the key factor that has contributed to, and continues to contribute to, the breakdown of this (or any) society's most important socializing institution: the nuclear family. As has been said, "Anything that weakens the family, also weakens society." The phrase "family values" has small meaning, compared to the "value of families."

Is this an overestimate of the influence of feminists, and the feminist movement? No. It has been shown that this society has been falling in line with the feminist ideology wishbook for 30 years.

Because of the number of topics covered, the following brief synopsis is offered to again point out (and to enable the reader to keep in mind) the main points of the material presented.

The words of Representative Beverly Byron, before the House Armed Forces Committee, typify the conscious, premeditated quality of the actions of modern feminists. In this case, those words regard feminist efforts to promote their cause of having female military personnel assigned in *all* combat roles. According to Byron, lifting the exemption of female pilots from combat flights is "what America perceives as the next step; totally consistent with the *reasonable, acceptable, incremental process* that I have found *so successful over the years*" (emphases added). The recent history of feminism is that of a *contrived* movement.

Feminists have also had—and continue to have—an agenda and a modus operandi. The modus operandi consists of four main tactics. The first—which has been the foundation for the movement and subsequent rationalizations—is the Big Lie: that life was hell for women in post-W.W.II America, and that non-feminist women had no hope of living meaningful lives or of achieving fulfillment. Not only were those *not* the conditions of women during that era, but women were better off, as were men, children, and society as a whole; this was, in large part, due to the fact that women filled meaningful and essential roles during those years.

The second main tactic of feminists is, and has been, to condemn men, while portraying women as their victims, so as to build distrust and enmity toward men, among women. This was done to motivate women, raise their hackles, and unite them against men in support of the principles of feminism, while instilling guilt and self-doubt in men. The combined result was the creation of the "politically correct" environment. In the presence of extremely ill-tempered women, men—who had come to feel varying degrees of unnecessary guilt—became loathe to debate issues concerning feminism. These first two tactics motivated women, and silenced dissent and alternative viewpoints from both men and women.

The third main tactic was to essentially "capture" our unprecedentedly powerful mass media system. This gave feminists the ability to overwhelm and control other sources of influence, and to voice their own viewpoints to a degree that could be called indoctrinating.

The fourth main tactic was to capture (also "essentially") academia —especially the social sciences. Academia became, perhaps, the ultimate example of how thoroughly political correctness could silence dissent, and, more importantly, it began to generate biased study after biased study, lending support and credibility to feminist ideology.

Using these first four tactics—and other minor tactics, such as cornering the market on the use of euphemisms—feminists created for themselves a rigged debate, which they could control almost completely, and their influence grew and spread.

Only because of the climate they had created were they able to put forth and promote their ideology for so long—an ideology founded on lies, supported by lies, and steeped in illogic. The keys to this illogic are their viewpoint that the sexes are not significantly different, and the consequent, and inevitable, question: "Why shouldn't we be able to do what men do?" A perfect example of this illogic occurred with the very first feminist this author ever debated, who insisted, "The only difference between men and women is that women can make babies and men can't."

Authors Anne Moir and David Jessel documenting many of our differences in their book, *Brain Sex*, expressed observable reality when they wrote:

> Men are different from women. They are equal only in their common membership of the same species, humankind. To maintain that they are the same in aptitude, skill or behaviour is to build a society based on a biological and scientific lie.
>
> The truth is that for virtually our entire tenancy of the planet, we have been a sexist species. Our biology assigned separate functions to the male and female of *Homo sapiens*. Our evolution strengthened and refined those differences. Our civilisation reflected them. Our religion and our education reinforced them.

The continual efforts of feminists to refute (except when it is exclusively to their advantage not to) the fact that significant differences do exist is the biggest reason feminism will never amount to anything more than behavioral gibberish. Its logic, or lack thereof, won't stand the test of time.

Regarding matriarchies, it was pointed out that despite the claims of some feminists, and their allies, there has never been one. Patriarchy is the natural mode of existence of human beings.

Part Two of the book focuses on what feminism really entails, and the perils inherent in it. What it is really about—above all else—is gaining female power over men. It is for this reason (as well as others) that they promote parental, economic and sexual androgyny. Androgyny, in turn, creates a long list of discomforts for children and individual adults of both sexes, but, more importantly, it harms, even ruins relationships between the sexes, in turn devastating families—all of which contributes to behavioral gibberish and ultimately jeopardizes society. An androgynous society will inevitably lead to one of two states. Either we will become a boring, loveless society of automatons, blindly following the dictates of technocratic masters, or degeneration and entropy will occur, leading to a state of societal barbarism.

The degeneration of this society can easily be seen to correlate with the true beginning of the modern feminist movement (1963) and its rise in power. Feminism is unquestionably the dominant influence regarding unprecedented negative female behavior.

The 50 percent divorce rate, the teen pregnancy rate, a 28 percent illegitimacy rate—which is still climbing—the growing number of fatherless children (victims of divorce and illegitimacy), 30 million abortions since 1973 (now 1.6 million per year, or one out of every four pregnancies), the rampant spread of all types of venereal diseases (AIDS, herpes, and a host of others), all can be described as repercussions that are to varying degrees directly (or at least indirectly) related to the feminist movement. Each of these repercussions, in turn, spawns its own. To underestimate the power of the movement, or to ignore it, is to put our future in great danger.

The movement, which virtually owns our educational and mass media systems, cannot be permitted to continue manipulating its followers, our society, and our leaders as it presently does without fear of repudiation, because our entire society is rapidly degenerating toward social ruin as a result of following the movement's manifesto.

To predict that the implementation of the movement's vision of society will bring about some sort of utopia is neither rational nor intelligent. Such a vision must not be allowed to become reality. Should feminism's agenda become reality, we will in a sense cease being Americans, because we will cease to be free. We will, in truth, be reared and programmed by feminist-indoctrinated mass media and educational personnel—ruled by a matriarchal, socialistic government of technocrats attempting to be pragmatic, in the misguided, dishonest feminist tradition.

The movement cannot aptly be described as a supporter of any righteous cause, period. The clever leadership is willfully pushing us in a direction that will completely destroy any remnants we have of a healthy society, and destroy as well the institutions necessary to maintain and rebuild one. The movement, at this time, can best be described as undermining and destructive.

The goals, policies, and philosophies of the feminist movement all serve to undermine the viability and existence of the nuclear family—without a prevalent number of strong nuclear families, we are lost.

The leaders of the women's movement and their backers are no friends of women; they are no friends of humankind. Does anyone ask what their qualifications are? How do they get selected to represent so many women and promote so many issues of such great importance? Do American women even know these women, who claim to be speaking for them? These are people who have great influence on their future. Do American women even know the extent to which they are being misinformed and misled? It is time to be informed!

Mary Jo Bane, assistant professor of education at Wellesley College and director of the Center for Research on Women, has said: "In order to raise children with equality, we must take them away from families and communally raise them."

Margaret Sanger, founder of Planned Parenthood, has said: "The most merciful thing a large family can do for one of its infant members is to kill it."

Esther Langston, professor of social work at the University of Nevada at Las Vegas, has said:

> What we are saying is that abortion becomes one of the choices, and the (woman) has the right to choose whatever it is that is best that they need as necessary and best for them in the situation for which they find themselves, be it abortion, to keep, to adopt, to sell, to leave in a dumpster, to put on your porch, whatever; it's the person's right to choose.

Beverly Harrison, professor of Christian ethics at Union Theological Seminary, has said: "Infanticide is not a great wrong. I do not want to be construed as condemning women who, under certain circumstances, quietly put their infants to death."

Mary S. Calderone, M.D., head of the Sex Information and Education Council of the United States (SIECUS) and former president and medical director of Planned Parenthood Federation of America, has said: "We have yet to beat our drums for birth control in the way we beat them for polio vaccine, we are still unable to put babies in the class of dangerous epidemics, even though this is the exact truth."

Simone de Beauvoir, existentialist philosopher and author of *The*

Second Sex, has said, "No woman should be authorized to stay at home and raise her children. Women should not have the choice, precisely because if there is such a choice, too many women will make that one."

The National Organization for Women (N.O.W.) has officially proclaimed: "The simple fact is that every woman must be willing to be identified as a lesbian to be fully feminist."

Are these the voices of the people American women have chosen for their leaders and representatives? Aren't these the real extremists, rather than those traditional Americans who feminists manage to paint as extremists?

Because of the politically correct climate of the past 20 years, the discussion of past and future repercussions of the feminist agenda has not been even close to adequate. This is one reason so many feminist ideologies are now so widely accepted; they simply have not been adequately debated or studied—to the detriment of our society.

Do men need to unite to fight feminism? Yes, they do. Should reasonable, thinking women, who value their femininity, unite with men? Yes, they should.

It is past time to dispossess the movement from its perpetual, almost sacrosanct status. Indeed, it is time to discredit much of what the movement now stands for, and to limit its influence. Most female feminists don't seem to comprehend that men do not have to accept or tolerate feminism, or its agenda. If a significant percentage of men would put their foot down as a unified group, the blight known as feminism would end. This is, in fact, what this book advocates.

This is not an attempt to steal freedom from women. On the contrary, under the guise of increasing individual freedoms (particularly those of women), it is feminists who are trying to steal basic freedoms from all of us, including women. They are trying to steal it by depriving us of having influence over our own children, by advocating lifestyles and social systems that destroy the existence of our families —or that strip them of value, so that they exist in name only. They are forcing upon us and our children the teaching of feminist ideologies through the media and academia—in daycare, in public schools, and even in private schools—basically subverting any influence a man or woman may hope to have on his or her offspring. It is in this way that they deprive us all of the most basic of rights.

Feminists are forcing on this society lifestyles that destroy families and make it necessary for the government (which is each and every one of us, as individuals) to become socialistic in order to care for *their* needs in place of the family and in place of personal responsibility. It is in this way that they enslave us all.

The recommendations this book makes are not attempts to steal freedom from women, but offer instead evidence of the need to compel women to fulfill essential roles and responsibilities unique to them within society. We cannot allow women to completely abandon *these* roles, because society cannot survive without their being fulfilled. We cannot allow women to completely abandon *these* roles, because children have needs and have the right to have *these* roles filled by the women nature intended for them. We cannot allow women to completely abandon *these* roles, because men, as a whole, have an inherent right to expect there will be an adequate number of available women among whom they may hope to find partners for life (whether or not they successfully do). We cannot allow women to abandon *these* roles, because children and men need them fulfilled, or the cost resulting from this neglect will doom society.

It is a contention of this book that women are needed to fill a myriad of essential, uniquely female roles beyond the production of offspring. Such roles must be filled by women over the whole of society, just as they must within individual relationships with children and men. If not enough of these essential roles are filled by women, then men, children, and even women themselves, will all be negatively affected by the lack. This is presently occurring, and growing worse. It is a contention of this book that society must be structured in such ways that women are compelled to fulfill these roles. It is a contention of this book that the seemingly never-ending harangue against men will never compel them to adequately fulfill their own natural roles (one of which includes compelling women to fulfill their own). It is a contention of this book that we must realize that feminism and present female behaviors are the causes of many of the degenerative aspects of male behavior. It is a contention of this book that a valid moral case can be made to justify men's "compelling" women to fulfill traditional female roles. It is certainly true that women are not here only to serve the needs of children and men. However, the unacceptable alternative to unique duties and expectations of women, as a whole, is that there should be no uniquely feminine duties or expectations of women in any society. We have reached the point where society is now telling women what no society has ever told men: "Do whatever you want, and no one will pass judgment." The verdict is in; women have been given unprecedented rights resulting in the freedom to neglect important responsibilities—and they have. Predictably, the costs have been high. The solutions offered in this book constitute a very short, simple list, proven by nature and history, when compared with the long—and ever-growing—list of untested feminist proposals.

In the 1964 civil rights legislation hearings before Congress, Supreme Court Justices Warren E. Burger and William Brennan outlined what would be required of prospective civil rights legislation in order that it pass a Constitutional litmus test. The Justices (using shallow, though righteous-sounding, logic) were negligent, failing to consider historical, universal sex-differentiated roles and rules, and the instinctive behavioral differences between sexes that brought them about.

In his support for the new legislation, Justice Warren E. Burger said, "What is required by Congress is the removal of artificial, arbitrary, and unnecessary barriers to employment when the barriers operate invidiously to discriminate on the basis of racial or other impermissible classification. . . ."

His use of the word artificial may be construed to mean unnatural, "lacking in spontaneity," or "contrived"—terms used in Webster's Dictionary to define unnatural. How can the various forms of discrimination against women in the area of employment be defined as "unnatural" when such "discrimination" has, in fact, existed in some form or other in every society that has ever existed (wherever there hasn't been a legal barrier built to prevent it)? How can such discrimination be defined as "contrived" or "lacking spontaneity" when it has arisen universally? Are we to assume that the men of all cultures (from the smallest of primitive tribes to the greatest of nations) got together at some historical point in time and labored to devise a plan usable for all the world?

His use of the word "arbitrary," in this instance, is equally flawed. There are two definitions of the word arbitrary. The one relevant here is, "based on or determined by individual preference or convenience rather than by necessity or the intrinsic nature of something." First, employment discrimination based on sex is, as discussed (by virtue of its being a universality), intrinsically natural. Second, it can certainly be argued that discrimination of this type is necessary. No society has thrived without such discrimination. Dramatic increases in most of our present social ills coincide with the granting of this right, and this is not a coincidence.

Justice Burger claims that sex-based "discriminatory barriers operate invidiously," or are invidious. Invidious is defined in Webster's as "tending to cause discontent, animosity, or envy." The record of the past 30 years shows that denying men the natural right to hire discriminately has caused enough discontent, animosity, and envy among the people of this society that the naturally discriminative employment practices that were in existence in the 1950s can truly be described as promoters of harmony by comparison.

Lastly, he uses the word "impermissible." The fact of the matter is that, based on all forms of historical precedence and logic, it is the prohibition of sex-based discrimination that should be classed as an "unnatural," "artificial," "arbitrary," "unnecessary," "contrived," and "impermissible" action "lacking in spontaneity."

Justice William Brennan wrote that, "a gender-based generalization cannot suffice to justify the denigration of the efforts of women who do work and whose earnings contribute significantly to their families' support. . . ." (The word "denigrate" means to deny the importance or validity of. . . .) Discriminating in favor of men in the workplace is not the same as denigrating women. Women have been, in fact, exalted in recognition of the importance of their feminine roles, while simultaneously being discriminated against to prevent their interference with male roles. Men have *always* known women had roles that were as essential as their own, while intuitively recognizing the need to develop their own (the men's) roles. Men have an instinctive need to achieve in ways and areas that are separate from the spheres of women. (We would be well-advised to remember that the male's need to achieve can be recognized in all societies.) All evidence would point to men having always instinctively realized what perilous creatures women will become if they are given too much employment opportunity, and the neglect and other indignities men, themselves, will suffer.

Is this a gender-based generalization? Perhaps, but it is essential, nonetheless. The core reasons men have always discriminated against women in areas of employment are little related to the types of jobs men have thought women capable of filling. Men's inherent tendency to discriminate against women is far from being based on something as shallow, or conscious as making an unnecessary "gender-based generalization."

The Justices ruled in an attempt to be altruistic, but without adequate study and contemplation of the natural order of things or of the possible repercussions from ignoring nature.

Simply believing in equal rights for women makes one a feminist. It makes one a feminist because this belief brings with it the demand that we deny to everyone the right to hire discriminately—an unfairness on its face, which brings individual discomfort—but, more importantly, denying men the right to hire discriminately guarantees that all that is feminism is sure to follow.

If we were to change the equal rights law as it regards women, men would begin to discriminate naturally. It would just naturally begin to happen. As a result, women would have to refocus their goals; mothers and fathers would have to rethink their goals for their daughters; elementary schools would have to recognize that trying to socialize boys and girls in the same way doesn't make sense because the work world of adults, and all that it brings about, will always be sexist. This book contains no precise proposals for forcing such things. It is more a matter of removing that one law, and then letting nature take its course. It may sound as if the author of this book wishes to become dictatorial, but that is not the case. The proposals put forth here—tried, tested, and in tune with universal norms—are such that they will actually lead to greater personal freedom for everyone. More freedom for parents, families, and individuals; freedom from government and its technocrats, from academics, the media, and from feminists—whoever our leaders may be in the future.

It may be hard to imagine the Equal Rights Amendment excluding equal employment opportunity for women. But what is even harder to imagine is equal employment opportunities being available but not widely utilized. Any society allowing equal employment opportunity for women will have feminists, and will suffer the repercussions of feminism. Eventually women will be encouraged (even goaded) to compete with men, which recent history shows has already been done.[2]

No lasting society from the past ever granted women all-encompassing rights equal to those of men. This is particularly true of equal employment rights. Equal employment rights for women should be rescinded. The continuation of such rights will ensure the ruin of this society, or any other.

---

[2] One way in which feminists do this is to tell women that anything less than success and achievement—on male terms—is sadly lacking. This, of course, damages women's self-esteem if they fail to compete with men, which is why so many women today feel they must abandon their nature and achieve on a par with men—even if it means ignoring the needs of their children and husbands. Observation shows that women are developing the same needs to achieve and the same problems with self-esteem that have always been associated with men.

CHAPTER SEVENTEEN

Men's Rights

It has always been difficult to argue persuasively against feminists because of their effective reliance on the words "equal" and "rights," and other words that carry extreme moral implications. No short, singular argument—righteous or not—can begin to stand up to those two words.

A "right" is that which allows someone (on the basis of morality, law, or nature) to do something or have something, to be left alone and not interfered with. The abuse of a right occurs when a person or group takes advantage of a right in such a way that the action they take, or their failure to fulfill an obligation, is of an indefensibly harmful nature to another individual, to a group of individuals, or to society as a whole. A bad "right" is any right passed into law that guarantees such harm will occur. Though rules can be drawn, the interpretation of what is unrighteous or indefensible is, to a large degree, subjective and debatable—which is what this book is about. This book contends that many actions taken by today's feminists are indefensible and should not be allowed. Rights that have been granted that even indirectly encourage or guarantee abundant levels of indefensible behavior, harmful to society or to other individuals, should not remain in existence. John Engleman has written that "Intolerance and repression are socially useful when socially destructive behavior is repressed."

Many recently granted rights (including so-called "equal rights for women") were ill-advised to begin with, and are now being abused to the detriment of other individuals and society. In many instances, they either directly deprive others of their rights, or are directly or indirectly detrimental to others and society, in a variety of ways.

A right can be granted by one individual or group to another, or a right can be fought for and won. A right is only truly "granted" if it is, in fact, voluntarily bestowed upon the grantee, rather than gained through the use of some type of threat, pressure, or force that cannot be denied. If a right is obtained or maintained through the use of some type of power or force, then that is an instance in which "might made right." (This need not necessarily be deemed "unrighteous." Note this, because it becomes a key point.) The words "equal" and "fair" are not *always* synonymous with "righteous."[1]

If and when a right is "granted" (by the definition given here), it has in all probability been granted by the party with power or authority over the grantee. When this is the case, it has, almost ipso facto, been granted for humanistic or altruistic reasons. This has been the case with all the rights ever granted to women.[2]

The real questions remain to be asked: When should a right be granted or rescinded? What standards should an argument (or appeal) for the granting of a right reach before the right is granted? When should "might make right"? Not very long ago in America, we adhered to the philosophy described by the old saying, "Your rights stop at the end of my nose"—in other words, when you do or say something that has a direct, negative impact on me. Given the way

---

[1] For example, millions of people in less hospitable climates, or in repressive or overcrowded countries, would give almost anything to live in America. The fact that this country keeps them out—refusing to allow unlimited immigration, as do virtually all countries—is an example of might making right. For in reality, playing the devil's advocate by using the type of logic feminists frequently use, what has given us the right to protect this land, this portion of the earth, for our own use? The "right of might" is the answer. Most people of both sexes would agree that there is nothing unrighteous or immoral about using our might to protect this right, thereby denying others of what they (using feminist logic) could claim as a right, also. Most people, including feminists, would say that our keeping them out is simply a matter of a people (American citizens) exerting their territorial imperative. This is an example of one of an endless number of feminist contradictions. Though feminists virtually always portray male advocates of the "might makes right" principle as demonic, and will never acknowledge a just cause for its use, they don't object to it when this method of gaining or retaining a right can be used to their advantage. (Whether or not a decision on an issue of rights is fair or righteous to men and children is of little or no consequence to today's feminists. They have become rights gluttons.)

[2] Only an ongoing lack of consensus among men, about the appropriate extent of women's rights, has allowed and enabled any compromises made on female terms to become reality. This regrettable, ongoing lack of consensus among men is, indeed, the only reason compromises have been, and are being, successfully forced by feminists.

rights are being granted today, it seems that this philosophy has lost its significance.

Consider this example: A man and woman co-create a child (a fetus). The woman has the right to abort the child, regardless of the man's wishes. The woman has the right to bear the child, regardless of the man's wishes. She can demand physical custody of the child, and child support, regardless (for all practical intents and purposes) of his wishes. Legally, her "nose" has become very long, based solely on the fact that the child in question happens to be inside her body. The child is granted no rights (no "nose" at all) despite its being equally alive. The man has no rights (no "nose" at all) despite the fact that the child is equally part of him—genetically speaking, he has contributed exactly the same amount to the child's creation as she has.

Should abortion as a right be based on the logic Justice Sandra Day O'Connor used as a rationale in her opinion on Pennsylvania's abortion regulations? "It is a promise of the Constitution," she wrote, "that there is a realm of personal liberty which the government may not enter." If a woman's right to abortion—solely because it is her body—is righteous reasoning, then why shouldn't drug users have the same right to use drugs? (It is, after all, their own bodies they abuse.) If it is argued that what the drug abuser does to his body leads him or his kind to become detrimental to society—which is definitely debatable—then why hasn't the issue of abortion rights been subject to the same argument? It should be.[3]

Before a right is granted, it should be required to pass a series of litmus tests considering its possible impact on all of society. It is time to demand that the granting of rights be far more completely debated, and many of the recent slew of rights, which were granted simply because they sounded so righteous on the surface, be severely questioned and rescinded, if need be, for the common good. Each proposed right should be fully debated and the determination be made that it will not infringe upon another individual's rights ("nose")—directly or indirectly—in such a way that it is of greater negative significance to

---

[3] Another feminist argument is that abortion can't be made illegal because it is unenforceable. (In almost the same breath they claim that discrimination based on sex can be made illegal and that this *is* enforceable.) We can't stop women from aborting their children, but we can stop men from hiring men?

that person or group than the deprivation of the right would continue to impose on the prospective grantee.[4]

We must recognize that at least one law of Newtonian physics applies equally to the social changes (whether we consciously observe them or not) that are created with every right granted: "For every action, there is an equal and opposite reaction." It is inevitable that results from any change in rights will be mixed—some positive, some negative. Every conceivable consequence resulting from the granting of a right, regardless of superficial appearance, needs to be searched out and evaluated more closely than was done with those rights granted in 1964 using basic, but shallow, logic. This needs to be done in the most conscientious way to determine what the inevitable chain of repercussions will encompass and where it will eventually lead. Nor does each and every possible repercussion need to directly relate to the granting of the right. But if it is a connecting link in the chain of possible consequences, that must be determined in advance. In essence, the potential impact of the granting of, or recision[5] of, any right, should be studied long and hard—along the lines of environmental impact studies—before a decision is made.

If there appears to be a correlative list of potentially negative repercussions due to the granting of a specific right, an investigation is warranted. (In the case we are discussing, it has been shown that there exists a long list of negative repercussions resulting from the granting of equal employment opportunities to women.) The question is, Do the advantages to individuals and society outweigh the disadvantages?[6] If not, then the next question would be, Do the disadvantages

---

[4] Equally important, it should be determined that it will not—and cannot, beyond all reasonable doubt—directly or indirectly imperil the safety, security, or future of the city, state, or country that will be granting the right. If it does, then it is actually infringing upon the rights of whatever populace is involved, and putting it at risk.

[5] The same type of litmus test should apply when discussing whether or not to rescind a right as the one that should be used to grant a right.

[6] It would be wise to remember that immediate personal benefits gained by any grantee are, or would be, of little worth or consolation should society flounder or disintegrate.

Individual negative repercussions—or even a list of them—resulting from the granting of the right may well pale in comparison to the apparent, but superficial, benefits the right would give to the grantee, or to society. This fact, however, should not be allowed to determine our course of action, for it is the tallied-up, compounded weight

result from someone's short-term failure (primarily men's, of course) to adapt to the new rules?[7]

Rights should certainly not be granted that are in direct or severe conflict with our finitely flexible human nature, without the most careful consideration of their necessity. We can only socialize ourselves —twist human nature—so far. Any rights argument should include discussion of how the granting of a right might contradict accepted, universal socialization practices. This is key because the existence of universal practices, ipso facto, denotes a natural, biologically based reason for them. Universality is not coincidental, nor a result of communication between societies. Behaviors and social institutions that exist universally are not the result of conscious planning. They are the result of biological imperatives.[8]

It is on the basis of all these arguments that the recent slew of so-called "rights" (granted or coerced out of us) is questioned here— particularly the civil rights legislation granting equal employment for women, adopted in 1964. At this time, it is necessary to clarify one thing on the issues of men and women, equal rights, and race. Men are men. We might have our differences (racial, religious, cultural, or

---

of all relevant, realistically insoluble negative consequences and repercussions upon any group, or upon society as a whole, that should be the primary concern in the rights decision-making process.

[7] In other words, granting that feminism is an inevitable result of the granting of equal employment rights to women, can society adapt to feminism and prosper in the long run? The answer to all of these questions is no. How long must we change and experiment with every new feminist concept, before we make a decision as to whether or not we will continue to listen to feminist dogma? And, at the least, when will we start closely examining where feminism has brought us, and where it will take us if we allow it to progress?

[8] Historical universality must be acknowledged and taken into account. Simplistically speaking, for much of our history as a species, the physically strongest male was the dominant leader of his tribe, clan, or family. Over the course of time, universally, societies deemed it beneficial to nullify this advantage by removing the right of the strongest male to physically exert his will over the rest of society. Most people would agree this has been productive, and a righteous reason for depriving the strongest males of the option to use their physical strength.

On the other hand, all successful societies have remained patriarchal. We might ask why this has been the case. And, we *should* ask what effects we would suffer by attempting to subvert this universal rule. After careful consideration, can this natural law be deemed so unnecessary that we can simply nullify it with no negative consequences, as we did when we deprived the strongest males of their right to dominate by force?

otherwise) but, in comparison to those between the sexes, the "real, inherent" differences in us are small—even minuscule. Any presently significant differences between men are not fixed at birth and they need not be perpetual. Above all else, men of all races, religions, and cultures should try to work together. In the end, discrimination among men for no reason other than those just mentioned is harmful, and counter-productive to creating a harmonious, multi-racial society.

Contrary to feminist thought, the first thing we must do is recognize the number and magnitude of the differences between the sexes. These differences include needs, capabilities, and behaviors—differences that make different roles and responsibilities essential. Like all others before it, our society must conform itself in response to these biological facts (unless we are all to become robots).

The laws that have been created on the basis of the claim that the sexes are not different are the laws most likely to need change. Any laws that prohibit or discourage men and women from filling natural roles must be rescinded—regardless of whether or not such recision might sound immoral at first. The only way to ensure that women will fulfill their essential roles and responsibilities to children, to men, and in society, is to deprive them of excessive encouragement and opportunities to abandon those roles.

We live in a society in which the word "right" is being abused. We live in a society where women no longer request rights, but are ever-increasingly demanding rights. We live in a society in which women's rights supporters no longer argue for rights based on the morality of the "right" (abortion, for instance), or the fairness of the "right" (divorce-court settlements, for instance), or the overall benefits the "gaining" of the "right" will provide for society (the plight of so many children, for instance). Feminists have moved beyond "requesting" the right to abortion; they now "demand" the right to abortion. They've moved beyond demanding "abortion rights"; they now demand the "right" to *government-funded* abortions. They demand the "right" to withhold from their husbands (or whoever the father is) knowledge of the fact they are pregnant and to have an abortion, without his knowledge; they demand the "right" to have an abortion regardless of their husband's (or whoever else's) feelings on the matter, if he does know. They demand the "right" to withhold the name of the biological father from the child, if they so choose. They demand the "right" to withhold pregnancy information from parents, regardless of the age of a pregnant minor; they demand the "right" to abortion, regardless of the age of the pregnant minor, and regardless of the parents' feelings. They demand the "right" to withhold news of a birth, if the biological father was unaware of the pregnancy. They demand the "right" to give birth to a child, abandon the husband (or biological father), and then demand child support from the ex-husband or father; they demand the "right" to be supported by welfare, should they choose not to work. They demand the "right" to some type of socialized or employer-paid daycare, if they do choose to work; they demand the "right" to either socialized or employer-paid medical services.

In the eyes of feminists, the real question over rights isn't whether or not the granting of any given right is righteous; the real question is just how much the female half, and certain other so-called "minority groups," can demand from the male half, the Caucasian portion, or the heterosexual majority of society.

Abortion is one of the rights that have been abused simply because it became a "right."[9] There are many excellent reasons to deny "abortion rights." One reason is moral. There is something amoral about a society wherein the females abort one out of every four of their pregnancies (1.6 million per year), particularly in view of the rationales given for this method of birth control and the number and variety of options available to reduce its necessity. It is abnormal, in humans and throughout the animal kingdom for a mother to kill her young.

---

[9] Welfare is another of the rights that have been abused simply because it became a "right." George Gilder discusses welfare in his book, *Sexual Suicide*:

> We must abandon the idea of completely eliminating poverty by distributing money to the poor, in accordance with formulas artfully designed to repress costs and enhance work incentives. There is no way it can be done. Welfare reform cannot eliminate poverty because as it approaches an "adequate" level, it necessarily subverts the male role as provider and promotes family disintegration. Family breakdown in turn prohibits emergence from dependency. With the male gone, the woman gets the money, begets the children, and becomes a financially unmarriageable burden on the state. If welfare is high enough, she may be technically unpoor. But her family is an instrument for the perpetuation of poverty, and she no longer seriously attempts the socialization of males. She can not afford to.

The right to unconditional, no-fault abortion must be rescinded because it has helped to lead us into a situation in which men—even the lifetime mates of women—have no say, no "*choice*," or, to use another favorite word of feminists, no "rights" in the matter. Ours has become a country in which women are now actually in a position to "demand" that society pay for the abortions of individuals!

The virtually unlimited right to abortions must be rescinded because of the unnatural ways in which its availability affects our sexual behaviors. When you break the rules of nature, there will inevitably be negative repercussions. In regard to this, we have already discussed a long list.

Widespread abortion contributes to making virtually null and void the sexual constitution on which we evolved. If you don't believe in feminism, but support abortion rights, you are helping to support feminism and—in a circuitous way—all it stands for: promiscuity, breakdown of family, socialism, etc.

If you don't support abortion rights, but support most other aspects of feminism, you are definitely—if inadvertently—supporting abortion. By supporting the principles of feminism (and thereby supporting a movement that inherently increases the rate of out-of-wedlock pregnancies), you are creating a perceived need for abortions, and supporting a coalition that guarantees the continued existence of this form of birth control.

It is time to quit talking about abortion—as author Anna Quindlen does—as if it were "just a medical procedure." It is time to quit talking about it as though it is an "unqualified right" of women, simply because it's their own body. It is time to quit saying, "think of the poor pregnant woman . . . and the poor unwanted child." Abortion laws, as they presently exist, and the morals and behaviors impacted by abortion laws—as they presently exist—are playing a huge role in the degeneration of society. There are only a few situations in which abortion might be justified as *legal*, if still immoral. One is in the event of forcible rape, in which situation the mother-to-be had no "choice" in becoming pregnant. Another is in the case of incest, concerning parties related by blood. A third is when the mother's health is seriously jeopardized. When contemplating the population problem, a case might be made that abortion is justifiable as necessary for survival of the species—as is the situation in certain places throughout the world. But the population problem in America is far from that point. (Notably, when feminists insist that abortion is essential, and appeal to overpopulation concerns, their real motivation is power. They equate abortion rights with personal freedom—freedom of responsibilities toward men.) Secondly, it is absolutely impossible to consider that disallowing the father any say is rooted in justice—how could it possibly be a *right?* The father's being part of the equation would naturally increase the mother's use of judgment about the procreation process.

One of the subjects never discussed by feminists is men's rights. Do men have any rights? If so, what are they?

A list of the rights feminists wish to take from men would include wives, and mothers (for themselves and for their own children); an equal voice in procreation; the right to raise their own children under their own roofs; the right to teach their own children their own morals rather than having them taught by daycare centers and schools; the right to any authority in shaping the success or failure of their own families; the right to live without the burden of supporting other people's children so as to underwrite selfish and irresponsible lifestyles; and the right to live without having to cope with the social burdens of feminist-promoted alternative lifestyles. Their list would also include men's right to work with other men, and the right to bond among themselves. In other words, feminists wish to deprive men of the right to maintain a normal, healthy society.

The issue of male-bonding is worth exploring at this point. This is a term that has only recently come into frequent use. Unfortunately, thanks in large part to feminists, it is now used primarily to ridicule a phenomenon that is as natural and as ancient as human culture. Interestingly, though it involves and refers only to men, the term is used primarily by women. The reason feminists prefer its use as a term of ridicule is that male-bonding is something they fear, resent, and want to eradicate, if at all possible. When men bond with one another, women lose a significant amount of power over them.

Few people realize its importance or the scope of its meaning in men's lives. And even fewer are consciously aware of all it encompasses. The process known as male-bonding is a means of communication, the expression of feelings and affection in a complex language both spoken and unspoken, but uniquely male. Male-bonding establishes, and continually reinforces, dominance within groups (the hierarchy of authority), and assures cooperation, unity, safety, and harmony within those groups.

Male-bonding can occur whenever two or more men find themselves together (without the presence of women, or without their presence being recognized). Regardless of where or when it occurs, its occurrence is normally initiated on the subconscious level, rather than the conscious level. When male-bonding occurs, different forms of communication are used than on occasions where the company is gender-mixed. Much of this relates to aspects of maleness that only "real men" (as opposed to androgynized men, or women) can appreciate.

It can occur almost anywhere at anytime, with or without planning, in places as varied as the golf course or the basketball court, the boardroom or the construction site, the drinking establishment, or a kitchen (during a poker game). In some ways, it is happening all the time between "real men" who are anything less than adversaries, and sometimes even then. Women simply are not, and cannot be, a participatory part of this equation, unless recognized as interacting on a different plane.

When bonding occurs in working situations, particularly where the work is ongoing, it often provides the best of all possible working environments for men. At work, men are compelled to work hard among themselves for the sake of pride, to be considered part of the team, and to take part in the male camaraderie. These things simultaneously turn the job into a challenge (and often a competition), create motivation, and make the job closer to fun, by making it closer to a game.[10]

This isn't to say that competition must always exist for male-bonding to occur. But if there is a place for competition to creep

---

[10] On the construction crew, bragging and exaggerations of every sort fill the air, as standard operating procedure. On the construction crew, if his co-workers think Bob is a good person and a good carpenter, generally they won't get overly sentimental to let him know it. Instead (after he's done bragging about it), they'll just say something like, "Aaaah, you're not bad."

The corporate boardroom situation is very different. The struggle for success in that game may, in fact, be particularly intense. The men there may still show affection for one another, but it tends to be in the form of much more subtle shows of respect— eminently rewarding, nonetheless.

in, it probably will. Depending upon what it deems best, the management of a company can choose to encourage its men to focus their competitive energy outward, toward rival companies, or within the company itself, toward other employees. In either case, competition spawned by male-bonding can be utilized very productively.

Though trips for camping or hunting may epitomize people's conceptions of the practice of male-bonding. In reality, such a trip is just one situation in which male-bonding occurs. One of the rewards of male-bonding is subtle but simple: the awareness of participating in a unique form of communication.[11]

When women involve themselves in men's activities, the chemistry of everything changes; the means of communicating, the competition, the standards of measurement, the freedom of a man to acknowledge his place in the hierarchy of dominance, all are thrown out of kilter. For women, just being there with the men feels great. Win or lose, they're involved in the ultimate challenge: competing with men. For most men, the discomfort created by women's presence is difficult to verbalize. "Win or lose" (if the direct competition is against a woman) no longer has the same meaning as it would against another man. Most men will either be forced to take the competition less seriously, as a protective measure against the possibility of defeat, or to take the competition much more seriously—to the point of winning at all costs. A third alternative, and one that is increasingly seen in today's work environment, is that men will quit and thereby avoid competition completely, a circumstance which would damage any society.

Male-bonding occurs because it is a natural, rewarding, and significant part of life for men. It isn't that men can never enjoy the company of women at work, or on a camping trip, or wherever the two may mingle, it is just that there are times when men are driven to be by themselves. Men and women are different, and "real men" (that is, men who enjoy being men, but still enjoy women as mates) want

---

[11] Campground activities are often ritualistic in tone or intent, and are ways of welcoming boys into the ranks of men. (Anyone who has participated on a "snipe hunt" in the forest, or any other ritual designed to educate a "tenderfoot," can relate to this.) Such ritualistic behavior has been practiced in every society (in one way or another), for thousands of years. In more primitive societies, these rituals equate to stealing boys from their mothers, or at least from their mother's influence.

to preserve their different behaviors. Why? Because life wouldn't be any fun, otherwise. "Real men" love "real women," and if women become too involved in the pursuits of men, it ruins them as women. It also ruins a great source of pride and fun for men. Men around the world have both instinctively and through experience, come to these same conclusions.

Discrimination on the part of men exists not simply because of some conscious intent to oppress women, but because most men will not willingly take any action that will result in a loss of status, that will end in a reduction of their sense of being part of a team effort, that will require them to compete directly with a woman, or that will necessitate their reducing the status of another man, in favor of increasing the status of a woman. The "glass ceiling" that women complain of definitely exists in corporate America. It also exists everywhere in the world. And it will continue to exist as long as men have any opportunity to exercise choice in who gets promoted to sit next to them at the Board of Directors' meeting, or with whom they must share credit for their successes in business or industry.

In every previously all-male occupation that women have invaded, the status of that occupation has, ipso facto, been lowered for men. On the other hand, any previously all-male occupation where a woman can compete with a man, ipso facto, represents an increase in her status. Men have the right to maintain the status of their roles in families, and in society.

Also, men who have no children or who support their own children have the right to be free of exorbitant taxes that the government uses to support children and contribute to further breakdown of the family, and all the additional costs such breakdown creates.

Men have the right to be free of taxes on their labor that will contribute to the growth of illegitimacy and the consequent number of sons and daughters deprived of relationships with their fathers.[12] They have the right to avoid joining the growing number of fathers deprived of relationships with their children, and to avoid forcing other men to join that group.

---

[12] Men (and women) have the right not to be forced to pay taxes for government-funded child care.

Men have the right to demand good mothering for their children, and the children of others in society.[13]

Men have the right to their own roles and to allow themselves not to be manipulated into playing a perfectly equal and identical role in parenting as women. (According to feminists, if men do not play an identical role, then women aren't being treated equally, because they must bear an increased responsibility in the area of parenting, and suffer the subsequent decrease of opportunity in others.) Identical roles are the feminist dream, but are neither natural or normal.

Men have the right—for myriad reasons—not to face the expectation that they will live in equiarchic relationships.

Men have the right to an equal (or greater) voice in matters directly or indirectly concerning birth control, birth, and the rearing of their own children and the children of this society. Wake up, men! We are literally talking about the complete right to control the procreation of this species! Men are literally losing any say in how our children are being brought up—directly deprived of their individual voices by divorce courts and situations of illegitimacy, or indirectly—through the expectation of equiarchy and the influence of feminist-dominated media and educational systems.

Why wouldn't we expect that there would be a large number of angry, perturbed men in our midst during an era in which men have allowed the needs, emotions, and actions of men (measurable or not) to be ignored, patronized, or bludgeoned, as they are today, by women and by society as a whole? Simultaneously, men are being deprived of certain natural rights and being subjected to undue burdens—thanks to misguided, albeit male-dominated courts, and the unrelenting, unanswered, contrived, conniving efforts of feminists.

---

[13] Tax-supported child care is also extremely unfair to couples with children who choose to survive on only one income. By caring for their own children at home and surviving on only one income, these couples are already making an income sacrifice. Tax-supported child care would require an increase in their taxes to pay for the care of the children of their two-income neighbors, and others. That increase in taxes virtually guarantees that the woman must give up her right to devote her time to the proper care of her own children, in favor of getting a job to offset the increased taxes. She is thus coerced into conforming her family to the two-income standard, and denying her husband and children the benefit of her presence in the home.

Rights, rights, rights. . . . It is the men of this society who need to be emancipated. It is men who have no procreative rights. It is men who have their children taken from them at the whim of the courts. It is men who will be paying ever-increasing taxes to fund programs designed by and for women, to aid women in stealing their children, gaining power, and promoting all that feminism is. It is men who have the least opportunity to work with individuals of their choice.[14]

Granting women the right to protection from any type of sex-based discrimination in all fields of work, regardless of the situation (i.e. denying men the right to hire discriminately based on gender), fails all the criteria given earlier for rights litmus tests.[15]

Excepting the history of the past 30 years, the granting of such rights is without historical precedence. As discussed, this goes a long way toward proving it is in conflict with our nature to grant such rights, particularly when we recognize that the right of men to discriminate in the area of work has always been utilized in one form or another, in all societies.

The granting of equal rights to women deprives male employers and male employees of having the respective natural right to hire men, and to work side-by-side with men, when and if they choose to do so.[16] No society has maintained its existence if the male has ceded his right to discriminate in hiring and working among his fellow men. The word "discriminate" is not a synonym for evil behavior or evil prejudice.

This law is responsible for starting a series of chain reactions that is

---

[14] Unlike women, who strove to work side-by-side with men for the sake of pride more than for any other reason, men will never strive for the opportunity to work in female-dominated fields for the sake of pride; only money will motivate them to do so.

[15] Before going further, it should be noted that the phrase "equal employment rights for women," as it is understood today, is in fact a misnomer. Equal employment rights for women should refer to women having the right to start their own IBMs, their own Ford Motor Companies, and to hire persons of their own choice with regard to sex. For clarification, "equal employment rights" are discussed here as they are defined today.

[16] Equal employment laws deprive women of the same rights; however, for many reasons, women inherently have less desire to hire discriminately amongst themselves.

jeopardizing our society by making feminism inevitable. When feminism flourishes, women in significant numbers will, ipso facto, fail to adhere to their biologically determined roles and responsibilities, thereby depriving children and men of *their* natural rights (the satisfaction of certain natural needs unique to them). This is detrimental to society as a whole.[17]

The fact that men have resisted letting women enter all arenas of the workplace has, of course, been well-documented. Again and again we are asked, "How could there possibly be any good reasons for allowing men to pay and hire discriminately, based on sex?" Or we are simply told that there are *no* good reasons. Feminists of almost every stripe—male and female—now believe it to be completely unfair and wrong, concluding that there are absolutely no reasons workplace discrimination based on sex should be tolerated anywhere, at any time. So effectively has this belief been forced into the public consciousness that it can be classified as the place where feminism has gained its highest level of acceptance, both in unanimity and strength of belief. Many or most people now believe that discriminating in the area of employment is not only immoral, but also counter-productive to the good of society. This is unfortunate because, though on the surface it may appear that there are no good arguments for discriminatory hiring, there are sound reasons for it—only we must look far deeper into the process and expect to find the answers in no single factor. For fear of exposure, feminists have labored tirelessly to prevent the

---

[17] It is interesting to note that as men either strike out in anger, or drop out in frustration due to this neglect, feminists attempt to convince us that women have nothing to do with men's anger and frustration.

If we are going to be as pragmatic as feminists pretend to wish us to be, we might well ask: "What right, as a whole, do normal men have to expect a reasonable level of sexual satisfaction? If all of the women in the world said no more sex, would men have a right to demand it?" Under such circumstances, few would doubt that men would have a biological right to demand it. And whether or not they would have the "right" to demand it, there can be little doubt that men would take it, by force if necessary. This, however, does not mean that men are either good or bad; it only indicates that men are driven to follow, and will follow, their natural biological functions. What should men have to contend with from women, and what roles must they perform to get sex? Sex is never truly free, particularly on the scale of an entire society. This is important because, looking at the bottom line from men's viewpoint, excluding all the extras derived from the socialization process, sex is women's primary (if not only) bargaining chip.

issue from being studied and, even more so, from being discussed in public.

Why should a man live the type of a life that is now deemed righteous by feminists? In other words, why should men continue submitting to feminist wishes? For that matter, why should men even bother to listen to the feminist argument, even if it could be successfully argued that it is a "righteous" one? Why should men be anything other than selfish and narcissistic? Why should the universally dominant and far stronger male sex accept equiarchy or—even more incredible —matriarchy? In the feminist world, no attractive man ever needs to be monogamous. The only reason that many men are listening and accepting right now is because they have become conforming as sheep; other men are, in fact, rejecting feminist arguments.

Today, men are frequently criticized for, or accused of, keeping a distance between themselves and their children. Rarely is any attempt made to recognize that there may be a natural logic to this pattern, where it occurs. In fact, there may be several reasons for it. A man may instinctively realize that if he becomes too close, too much like a friend to his children (especially during certain critical stages of their development), he may lose authority or their "respect," and thus will make parenting more difficult.[18] A child can have many friends, but only one father.

A father might want to keep a distance so that when he does show attention and affection, it is of particular importance, bringing a special joy to his child. Taking the kids out to the movies once in a while may be a great thrill for them; taking them out every night could easily become routine and be taken for granted.

Perhaps he realizes the kids will get used to his frequently playing with them, or how quickly they will adapt to it and come to expect and rely on it. If a father works all day long, perhaps a long day with a commute, he may want to relax after dinner, and to contentedly enjoy

---

[18] This distance could, in some ways, be compared to that which exists in the employer-employee relationship. Employers have long realized that in order to maintain effective authority, as a general rule, it is best not to become too familiar with employees, for obvious reasons. This does not mean that a father cannot express the fact that he loves his children, it just means that men have probably been instinctively inclined to develop father-child relationships, rather than friendships.

his children out of the corner of his eye, from behind the newspaper, with a bent ear.

All men are not meant to be as nurturing as feminists would have us, and especially not as motherly as some would like to make us. As a goal, it is unnatural and, should it be accomplished, it will carry with it inevitable negative repercussions, like all the other unnatural goals and accomplishments of the feminist movement.

Are there some men who should be closer and more nurturing to their children? Of course, but. . . .

As discussed, men have traditionally equated work with being both a reason for their existence and a primary means of self-measurement. Should it be this way? What would happen if men lost or abandoned their need and reliance upon self-esteem satisfaction? We would have to rely on our good nature to motivate us to do what is right and necessary to survive, to be happy and content. Men couldn't and wouldn't and haven't survived without the need for self-esteem. Human nature can not supply us with the necessary motivation. This is a key reason for the failings of socialism. Socialism fails everywhere because it fails to take human nature into account, feminism has the same problem.

It is important that men work in order to keep out of trouble, and men will invariably get into more trouble if they're not working than will women.

Assume, for the moment, that we were able to create a non-sexist society, one completely without sex-roles. Assume we were able to remove distinctly male pride and male honor. Assume we could eliminate all religions, as we know them, and the teachings of restraint that go with them. What would be the carrots, the motivations, or the "big sticks," that would keep men on the straight and narrow (not simply showing physical restraint, but also functioning as productive members of society)? What would be the rewards for working hard, the motivations that would keep them from becoming lazy?[19]

---

[19] If men slack at all, not only will other nations out-produce us, but there will soon be no one to pay for the programs that feminists demand of society, such as the upkeep of children. If a man is lying on the couch, feeling unmotivated and lazy, few individual women can just kick him off and tell him to get to work. The motivations that have always driven men to work are not accidents. If we throw out the old motivations that have universally driven men, we must find new ones. Requesting that men work, simply for altruistic reasons, will not motivate men for any length of time. Yet this is what

When the natural roles of both males and females are replaced, as is happening now, it has a direct impact on men's inclination to fill their roles and inevitably generates bitterness, as women seek to invalidate the need for men. The only way that men's bitter feelings toward independent, "liberated," feminist women will subside is for men to start looking upon women as if they were other men. This, of course, brings with it a host of new problems. As stated repeatedly, in every society men and women have had different roles and responsibilities, with the male's needs to protect, to provide, and to achieve being always recognizable.

Eventually, the granting of equal rights not so much allows, but serves in a coercive way to encourage, women to neglect their biologically based human responsibilities to men, children, and themselves, by actually filling the roles of men. As this is done they, ipso facto, deny men the opportunity to fill their own roles, thereby denying men the feeling of having a reason to exist. Obviously—if there is no remedy—this impacts men.

There comes a time when it is proper for might to make right—as with immigration laws.[20] The same is true with feminism—women cannot be allowed to abandon the roles and responsibilities nature intended for them. The men of this society must unify and force women to fulfill their roles and responsibilities. This will entail removing from existence certain "rights" that they now enjoy.

As a means of diminishing the promiscuous behavior of women, men should be freed from the liability for child support to women unless pregnancy occurs during legal marriage. Combined with changes in welfare and abortion laws, women would be forced to be far more sexually responsible, which is what is needed in today's society, a restriction of male sexual opportunities.

Moreover, women should absolutely be denied *any* opportunity to be inseminated by artificial means unless they are heterosexual, married women with physical problems that prevent normal reproductive function. Further, the full and willing consent of the husband should

---

feminism proposes, when seeking to take away men's position in marital relationships, in the family, their proud role of provider within families, and their proud role as achievers in society.

[20] We cannot allow unlimited immigration into the U.S. without putting our own future in jeopardy.

be required at all stages of the insemination process, as this will prevent single-parenthood and the denial of men's right to an equal voice
in the procreation of the species.[21]

Society can't create human beings (much less civilized men), nor
can women do the job alone . . . men are needed. The problem is as
Margaret Mead has stated, "Women can make babies, but only men
can make men"!

Rights. The word is used and abused. Your rights, or anyone else's,
stop at the end of my nose. Every individual in this country (female
or male) has a long nose. The protections of that long nose extend to
their offspring and their future, the welfare of their country, and the
environment they live in. For example, a person who practices and
advocates a lifestyle that makes the true family an improbability is
putting the future of everyone's offspring at risk by aiding in the de-
struction of an essential social institution—they are infringing upon
everyone else's rights. People who practice lifestyles that put their
own children at risk are also putting at risk the future of everyone
else's offspring, not to mention the parents of those offspring—and
they are infringing upon everyone else's rights!

Liberals preach "tolerance." Tolerance is something we all benefit by practicing—within limits—and people should be able to do as
they please up to the point that it begins to have serious, negative
effects on the world we all live in. Then we should fight to make
those people fall in line with what we believe is right for the next
generation's survival. Not only is the forceful protection of our social
structure our collective right, it is our collective responsibility.

---

[21] While such a proscription on artificial insemination might seem unduly harsh at
first glance, it is necessary to put a stop to a situation that is currently spiraling out of
control, and affecting each and every citizen. One example of that "spiral" was recently
reported in the *National Review*:

> . . . in San Francisco, homosexual activists were confronted with a problem re-
> quiring the wisdom of a demented Solomon. Thirteen years ago a gay man do-
> nated his sperm to a lesbian who, with her "companion," wished to have children.
> A little girl was born and the "parents" later decided they no longer wanted her
> to have any contact with her biological father. The man filed a paternity suit
> —and won standing as one of the girl's three parents. . . . As fissures like these
> develop and require mediation, the mediating party will more and more be . . .
> the government—leaving taxpayers in the position of the person who pays the
> salary of the referee at a pro wrestling match.

Every society in the world has been organized in a patriarchic structure. Today, feminists have convinced many that the universality of patriarchy is an example of mother nature having made a mistake, and that the real plan wasn't for us to be patriarchal. Consequently, they fight patriarchy and (by doing that) they fight nature—as they do by repudiating universal sex roles. When we accept equiarchy or matriarchy as being naturally preferable to patriarchy, our behavior is altered in ways that contradict nature.

It isn't realistic to expect the "majority" of average, normal couples to contentedly compromise on "all" issues, regardless of their importance or the polarity of the couple's respective viewpoints. On the contrary, it is a direct contradiction of human nature. This is why every government has one President, king, Prime Minister, or head of state, every business has one chairman of the board, every job has one foreman, every team a captain, every nursing staff a head nurse. Why do almost all small business partnerships fail in bitter disputes, *unless* one person possesses final authority *or* there are clear (hopefully written), distinct separations between the partners' roles, responsibilities, and rewards?

Equiarchy? The continual insistent promotion of the goal of equiarchy will neither protect nor enhance our future, nor is it an act of compassion. Backed by the now-holy word "equality," it, in truth, serves as a promoter of conflict and separation. Every social animal ever observed (including humans) organizes its groups in a hierarchical way. The great majority of all human sexual relationships in all societies have been male-dominant. What may be worse, though, than equiarchy's being a promoter of conflict is its tendency to bring about the matriarchic relationship.

Matriarchy? It means almost certain misery for both sexes. Simple observation shows that the female-dominated heterosexual relationship is generally one of complete unhappiness. It is generally a more grossly unfair, repressive relationship than its patriarchic equivalent. The misery is complete, as the odds of a dominated man being able to bring satisfaction and contentment to his wife are slim. (Sadly, children also suffer in these relationships.)

In her book, *The Creation of Patriarchy*, in which she does recognize that all societies have been patriarchic, Gerda Lerner closes with the following, "A feminist world-view will enable women and men to free their minds from patriarchal thought and practice and at last to build a world free of dominance and hierarchy, a world that is truly human."

Most of those who live in patriarchic relationships do not spend much time thinking about it. But since a "feminist world view" represents a dramatic and traumatic shift in power and responsibilities (i.e. toward matriarchy), it will result in anything *but* minds freed "from patriarchal thought," it will result in anything *but* "a world free of dominance and hierarchy." In reality, the only way such a thing could take place is for all of humanity to be dehumanized.

One argument against patriarchy is that it is unfair—it doesn't allow for absolute equality. Can the happiness and contentment of a person's life be measured only in terms of the authority they possess? Does this mean employers inherently live happier lives than those employed by them? Does this mean parents are inherently happier than their children? Does this mean that husbands—with final authority in the marital partnership—are inherently happier than their wives?

Must our lives be identical to one another to be equally rewarding? The answer to all these questions is no. It is possible that the differing privileges and responsibilities given to men and women can even things out. Men have been relinquishing authority since the early 1960s, allowing women (sometimes even encouraging them) to neglect their natural roles: mother, wife, and homemaker. The results have been catastrophic.

Is patriarchy unfair? No. Exerting authority over women is no less moral, no less fair, than our not allowing unlimited immigration. Our very survival is at stake. Women and mothers are needed to civilize men. If women fail to accomplish this task, as is already happening at an alarming rate, women will suffer the consequences along with everyone else.

The individual nuclear "family" mirrors the patriarchic structure of society. The majority of all families, in all societies, are male-dominant in structure, as Steven Goldberg says:

> Male dominance refers to the feeling acknowledged by the emotions of both men and women that the woman's will is somehow subordinate to the male's and that general authority . . . ultimately resides in the male. . . . As (is) the case with patriarchy, male dominance is

universal: no society has ever failed to conform its expectations of men and women, and the social roles relevant to these expectations of men and women, that it is the male who "takes the lead." Every society accepts the existence of these feelings, and conforms to their existence by socializing children accordingly, because every society must. . . .

The general male-female relationship should, as in the past, remain patriarchic. Granted, this authority—a male's right and responsibility—should, in some percentage of cases, be used in a less literal and autocratic sense than in the past. This means the granting of some areas of authority to women—most of which will preferably be agreed upon before marriage. Acknowledging and developing a relationship before marriage gives couples a greater opportunity to negotiate through somewhat more of a "two-person democratic process" than in the past. The decision-making process needs to be discussed, negotiated, and agreed upon before marriage.

In traditional marriages, authority was generally clear-cut, and even stated in the wedding vows. Recently, couples have tended to enter relationships with expectations that differ from one another's and then have attempted to clear up the subsequent misunderstandings and resulting fallout, after the fact—often with little success. In conjunction with the need to better develop a means of authority distribution through discussion prior to marriage, marital vows need to reflect the shared understanding between partners. If it should be agreed that the wedding vows need to be changed from what they once were, or presently are, one solution would be to change the woman's part in the ceremony to include a vow "to love and grant final authority."[22] The man would then vow not to abuse the authority granted to him. On the part of either the woman or the man, the neglect to abide by these promises would constitute a breaking of the vows.

The attempt at equiarchy encourages both partners to become subtle, "expert" arguers, debaters, and manipulators—except in those

---

[22] The type of relationship in which a state of final authority occurs is not necessarily an autocracy or dictatorship. Final authority need not have anything to do with who makes the *majority* of decisions. It need not even have anything to do with who makes the most *important* decisions. Obviously, there will be cases in which final authority does end up with the woman, but for the reasons related earlier, this is not the ideal, especially when the male's lack of authority is made publicly apparent or is used to belittle him, as is frequently the case when authority is possessed by women.

cases where it induces loud arguing conflicts. Instinctive leadership is lost. In such situations, neither partner can comfortably accede to the other's wishes for fear of being taken advantage of. Constant tension is the typical result of the struggle for power.

Additionally, it must be accepted that, to some degree, power does corrupt and that absolute power generally corrupts absolutely. Men have never had the power that women are theoretically capable of having, nor will they ever, because the drive to copulate is stronger in men than in women. This places a man more at the mercy of a woman's sexual availability than she is at his, and typically moderates his use of power over her. There is, however, less limitation for a woman when she has authority within the relationship. Two hundred years before Christ, the Roman philosopher Cato understood this fact and phrased it well: "Suffer shall all men if women ever become our equals, for once they are our equals, they are forevermore our superiors."

Men need to take the lead in the majority of relationships, not only for the reasons mentioned, but also for the sake of keeping relationships from being dominated by feminine logic. The additional threat, should women wrest authority in a significant number of relationships, is that it will eventually end up negatively impacting the patriarchic state of society (where matriarchy is even more of a threat, due to the greater scope of the issues involved and the greater need for logic in resolving these issues).

Today, the logic, righteousness, and naturalness of patriarchy is being argued against; its existence is being undermined. Male dominance is unarguably the natural state of being. To attempt to refute the righteousness of patriarchy is to refute the logic of nature. No other reasoning *should* be needed.

What do men have to do to make women happy?[23] What must women accomplish during their lives in order to meet their basic need to achieve—necessary for the development and maintenance of self-esteem—and to feel that they have a reason to exist? Though this

---

[23] Before we get to that, why should they be any happier than men? We should remember—whatever stage society is in, or ever will be in—that there has never been a utopia, and undoubtedly never will be.

will vary with individuals, and will depend upon societal expectations, the first thing women must do is meet the needs of children and men.

What women do *not* need to do is work and compete side-by-side with men, in all occupations, in order to develop a healthy self-esteem and obtain fulfillment from life.

A woman "centering" her life on the household, wifely duties, and child-rearing responsibilities, means exactly that—"centering." It means that those things are the center of her life, the most time-consuming part of life, especially during child-rearing years, but this does not prevent women from doing other things in life that bring additional and other types of rewards.

Will giving birth, successfully rearing children (and simultaneously bringing happiness and contentment to a man, while caring for their home) fulfill this need? In many or most cases, yes. Doing these things is performing a function beneficial to society, in an occupation that doesn't involve direct competition with men; it can fulfill this need. If the maternal role is devalued, it will not fulfill this need. If the role is valued—as it should be—it will. Unfortunately, too many women to-day are being told that they must measure their worth not only in the same ways a man does, but on the same playing field. Far too many women, for instance, think that giving birth is equal to motherhood —it really is only the beginning.

Women, even the most aggressive or masculine, need not compete with men. To compete with men in the same fields is unnatural and a losing cause, even when it is accomplished. The only way women will ever be able to compete with men is if they are socialized in the same ways as men, which is also unnatural (it has never been done before). The woman who competes with men throughout her life will have to make far too many sacrifices and will be surrendering more than she knows.

Also, the devaluation of the roles of wives and mothers must cease. If the same feminists who have concentrated so much on building hatred and mistrust between sexes had put as much effort into improving the lives of women within families, and improving families themselves, this country's families (men, women, and children) and society itself would be prospering. Instead, their message has been that the family is a dysfunctional social unit, and the housewife is nothing more than a cheap prostitute.

One woman wrote a letter to Ann Landers about her anger at being classified by other women as "just a housewife"; in it, she gave her job description:

> I am a wife, mother, friend, confidante, personal adviser, lover, referee, peacemaker, housekeeper, laundress, chauffeur, interior decorator, gardener, painter, wallpaper hanger, dog groomer, veterinarian, manicurist, barber, seamstress, appointment manager, financial planner, bookkeeper, money manager, personal secretary, teacher, disciplinarian, entertainer, psychoanalyst, nurse, diagnostician, public relations expert, dietitian and nutritionist, baker, chef, fashion coordinator and letter writer for both sides of the family. I am also a travel agent, speech therapist, plumber and automobile maintenance and repair expert. During the course of my day I am supposed to be cheerful, look radiant and jump in the sack on a moment's notice.
>
> Studies have shown it would cost more than $75,000 a year to replace me. I took time out of my busy day to write this letter, Ann, because there are still ignorant people who believe that a housewife is nothing more than a baby sitter who sits on her behind all day and watches soap operas.
>
> If I could afford to pay someone to do all of the things I do, I would be delighted to go back to working an eight-hour day with an hour for lunch and two 15 minute breaks.
>
> What do I get out of my job in the absence of a salary? Joy, happiness, hugs, kisses, smiles, love, self-respect and pride in knowing that I have done a full day's work to ensure the physical and emotional well-being of those I love.
>
> Now if you want to classify me as just a housewife, go ahead.

The career woman who refuses the many, wide-ranging responsibilities that the woman above has accepted is misguided and selfish. What feminists are achieving is not sufficient to outweigh the harm that results to society from what they're *not* achieving.

We do not need to force girls to be feminine, starting at birth. Girls do, however, need to be brought up different from boys, appreciated for the special and unique people they are, so that they can grow up looking forward to being mothers and homemakers, during the crucial years of child development, and can be content performing jobs that do not conflict or compete with men's. The easiest way for this to happen is to stop encouraging or forcing everyone to try to socialize girls as if they were boys. Nature will take care of the rest.

One of the most successful career women in history, Nobel Prize winner and author of many best sellers, Pearl S. Buck, has several interesting observations on this particular subject. In her book, *To My Daughters with Love*, she writes:

> Do I, who am a professional writer, believe that home-making is the most important work in the world for a woman? Yes I do, and not only for others but for herself. As a writer, I know that it is essential for a woman to be a homemaker, and this is true whatever else she is.
>
> Man and woman, we have our separate but cooperating functions to fulfill for our own completion, as well as for the human beings we serve because we are responsible for them.
>
> Woman, the house wife and homemaker, creates more than she knows. While she sweeps and cleans and makes the beds, while she cooks and washes and puts away, she is creating human beings. She is shaping dispositions and building character and making harmony. The greatest need in the world today is for people of sweet disposition, good character and tranquil, harmonious nature.
>
> The influence of woman, the homemaker, reaches indeed far beyond the walls of her house. Her reach is beyond her own comprehension. She creates the center where the world begins, the world and all its peoples. It is from her that they spring. As every human being, man and woman, emerges from her womb—and none can be born otherwise—so they emerge from the home she makes to receive them when they are born. True, man is her mate and co-builder, but for some reason, perhaps divine, it is she who is the more responsible for the creation of life in all its forms.
>
> I believe a disorderly, lazy, selfish, incompetent homemaker is a bad woman. She has the most important job in the world, the most exciting opportunity, and if she does not perform it, she is not to be forgiven. If she is ignorant, then such ignorance is a crime because of the damage it does to the group of human beings, for whom she is responsible.
>
> Seldom indeed do men and women rise above the atmosphere of their childhood homes. They may become rich and powerful, they may build houses very different from the one they first knew, but they carry within themselves the atmosphere of the first home. If that home was a place of order and beauty, however simple, then they are tranquil and able to cope with life's problems. If there was neither order nor beauty in the home, the lack follows them all their lives. They may not know what is the matter with them or why they are eternally restless and seeking, but they know they live in uncertainty and inner confusion.

In a world going faster and faster, do we really need women to increase the pace and confusion by emulating men—by abandoning their homes for the street and work? Do we need them to diminish the serenity of the home not only by the lessening of their presence, but also by their changed demeanor when they are present.

Some feminists currently make the argument that feminism is an environmental cause. According to them, women need more education and need to work outside the home, because the birthrate among educated working women is lower than among uneducated, unemployed women. The lower the birthrate, so the argument goes, the less human population there is to damage the environment.

Like many feminist arguments, this is so simplistic as to be almost laughable. While there may be some benefit to the goal of lowering the birthrate, there is no reason to believe that feminism will significantly benefit the environment. For the sake of argument, suppose that a woman has one child rather than three. If she is truly a feminist, she will most likely remain unmarried, which means that rather than sharing her home with the child's father, she and the child will have separate quarters. Since the father must also have housing, there will then be twice the number of housing units needed for the three as there would if they constituted a nuclear family. Similarly, she will have her own vehicle and, if she works in a production environment, will contribute that much more pollution to the environment. If she works in a non-production environment (a service industry, for example), she will add to pollution anyway, if only by utilizing that much more energy in the form of electricity or other fuel. If she has an income, she will also be that much more a consumer, and will need extra clothing, extra consumer-electronics goods, and so on. If women are truly concerned about the environment, the best course of action for them is to become homebodies who instill environmental concern in the children of their small families, while keeping the birthrate down. Men are capable of producing enough material goods to supply both sexes, and do enough damage to the environment without women's help.

Women aren't doing their jobs. This is the greatest reason for the increase in the number of men who aren't doing theirs. It is time for feminists to quit creating the false impression that men are inherently bad, and cannot be relied upon. There are millions of good men in this society. But, without good mothers, their numbers will decline. Without encouragement and social pressure to fill their natural roles, their numbers will decline. Without good wives, their numbers will decline. Men aren't born good or bad. They have basic instincts that govern emotions, and behavior, but to be good or bad isn't included in these. If men are socialized in a civilizing environment, they will generally be civilized—if not, they will not. What is required to civilize men? Good mothers, good women, good fathers, and good families. These things require sex-differentiated roles.

What is necessary for these things to take place? Women must be put in their place! Even Betty Friedan, the woman whose 1963 book (*The Feminine Mystique*) was the impetus for the modern feminist movement, has changed her mind regarding the feelings and needs of women. At the beginning of *The Feminine Mystique* she makes a statement to the effect that each American housewife realizes she is living a life which is thoroughly meaningless. Twenty-eight years later, Friedan is quoted in the June 17, 1991 issue of *U.S. News and World Report* saying, "It's time now to change the rhetoric and admit that many women want nothing more than to stay home with their children." Shouldn't American women have the right to stay home with their children? In the feminist world, this becomes impossible because women's having power over men takes precedence over motherhood or family. In the feminist world, every woman will be needed to exert authority over adult males, to maintain the feminist power structure.

How do we prevent this? First, we must reject feminist efforts to censor both private and public discussion of any aspect of feminism. Truth must be heard. Second, we must contemplate the monstrous repercussions that are attributable to the denial of man's right to work and hire amongst his fellow man if he so chooses. We must reject and revolt against any law abridging this right. Realizing the lack of judicial foresight in this area serves as the ultimate testimonial to the fact we must do something about the way in which the judicial system operates in this country today. Robert Bork addressed this issue in *National Review:*

> In his first Inaugural Address, Abraham Lincoln asserted: The candid citizen must confess that if the policy of the Government upon vital questions affecting the whole people is to be irrevocably fixed

by decisions of the Supreme Court . . . the people will have ceased to be their own rulers, having to that extent practically resigned their Government into the hands of that eminent tribunal.

This is what we have done. Bork goes on to explain: "Lincoln was thinking of *Dred Scott*, the infamous decision that created a constitutional right . . . to own slaves." Bork goes on to point out that Lincoln's observation is even more pertinent today because of the increase in the number of decisions being made by the court and the fact that they are affecting more people more completely. "The only practical way of reining in the Supreme Court" Bork says "is a constitutional amendment making its rulings subject to democratic review. As matters now stand, the Court's assumption of complete governing power is intolerable, and yet, absent a constitutional amendment, we have no way of refusing to tolerate it." Having adopted the ideology of feminism, intolerable is what the Court's decisions have become.

As discussed previously, women must ultimately make the decisions that will lead them to accept, enjoy, and even cherish those roles that have made families, cultures, and nations prosper, those roles that nature intended for them. But men's part in encouraging (or forcing, if need be) women to make those decisions is significant. First, we must all recognize what "manhood" is, and appreciate its value. Author David Gilmore writes extensively of this value in his book, *Manhood in the Making*:

Its critical threshold represents the point at which the boy produces more than he takes. Manhood is the social barrier that societies must erect against entropy, human enemies, the forces of nature, time, and all the human weaknesses that endanger group life.

In the end, manhood necessitates the retention of some degree of authority over women—not only for the good of all individuals within society—but for the survival of society, and indeed, true humanity itself. When we realize where arguing has gotten us, we may also realize that the best argument against a feminist might not be an argument at all but a simple statement. Shut up. Something American women have already effectively done en masse to American men, if American males can still be called men.